PASS
THE
NUTS

Also by Dan Coughlin:

Crazy, With the Papers to Prove It

Dan Coughlin

PASS THE NUTS

More Stories About the Most Unusual,
Eccentric and Outlandish People I've Known
in Four Decades as a Sports Journalist

GRAY & COMPANY, PUBLISHERS

CLEVELAND

Gray & Company, Publishers
www.grayco.com

ISBN: 978-1-59851-073-7

Printed in the United States of America
10 9 8 7 6 5 4 3 2 1

This book is dedicated to the three most influential sports columnists of my era: Hal Lebovitz, Chuck Heaton and Bob August. Hal was with the *Cleveland News* and *The Plain Dealer*. Chuck spent his entire career with *The Plain Dealer*. Bob wrote for the *Cleveland Press* and the *Lake County News-Herald*.

They had much in common. All were born in Cleveland. They went to public high schools here—Hal to Glenville, Chuck to Lakewood and Bob to Collinwood. They went to college in northeastern Ohio—Hal to Western Reserve, Chuck to John Carroll and Bob to Wooster, where he met his wife. They were gentlemen, they were compassionate, they understood their responsibility.

They were all 89 years old when they died.

Bob was the last. He passed away in September 2011. His funeral service was in Wooster on Oct. 2, 2011. I always considered Bob the best sports columnist in the country in the 1960s, '70s and '80s. I traveled a lot in those days and I read everybody. Bob was simply the best writer. He never used literary gimmicks or tricks. He didn't need them. He was elegant. We all envied him but none of us could emulate him.

He also was a cherished companion. On Sunday nights after Browns games, I often flew home with Bob on the last plane. Nobody wanted to take a nap when Bob August was sitting next to you. He never talked about his World War II service. He was a naval officer and commanded a landing craft at Normandy on D-Day and later he served in the Pacific Theatre. I suspect he had some horrific experiences. He was entitled to swagger but instead he had a limp.

He was so humble; he probably did not realize how good he was. If so, he was the only one.

For good reason, they called the sports pages the fun and games department. At *The Plain Dealer*, I sometimes made predictions about the outcome of a high school game. When Shaw High School beat Lakewood, 39-0 in 1967 (with a wager on the line), I had to "eat my words." *(Author's collection)*

Contents

Introduction

When my first book, *Crazy, With the Papers to Prove It*, went off to the printer, I still had untold adventures and unexplored characters and I was impatient to tell their stories. Countless people said, "If you don't write about Harry Leitch, I won't read your next book." They said the same about Browns Hall of Fame guard Gene Hickerson, who had Elvis Presley's home phone number memorized. Dave Plagman, the old sports handicapper, actually mailed me a column I wrote about him almost 20 years ago and said, "I'm a chapter." Richie Scheinblum said he's more than a chapter, he's an entire book. Les Levine said, "I'm not a chapter." I said, "Yes, you are."

Within these pages are people I have known for decades. It is time I told you their stories. Many, sadly, have passed on to that great bibliography in the sky, such as George Steinbrenner, Harry Caray and Punxsutawney Phil.

Speaking of my first book, let me tell you how that went. In 2010 when I signed a contract with Gray & Company, they told me about all their services for authors.

"We have a publicist who will set up all your appearances and interviews," said David Gray.

"I won't need that," I said. "I know everybody in the media. Heck, I've worked here for 45 years."

"We'll take a professional picture of you for the cover," David said.

"I don't need that," I said. "My wife has a camera. We can go out in the driveway when the sun is out and she'll take a nice picture."

"We'll see," said David, slightly reminiscent of Philip Seymour Hoffman as a CIA agent in the movie, *Charlie Wilson's War*.

So, we went to Danny Vega's studio and took a professional picture in color and in focus. It entailed about a hundred shots and a change of clothes halfway through the shoot.

When it was time to take the picture for the new book's cover, I said, "We've got a lot of pictures left over from the first book. Why not use one of them?"

David Gray gave me that Philip Seymour Hoffman look. And so we took another photo, this time at the Great Lakes Brewing Co., sitting at the bar with a beer and a bowl of peanuts. Thanks to Pat Conway, one of the founders of the brewery, who knows how to make a guy feel comfortable. They sat me down at the bar and put a Dortmunder Gold in my hand. "Smile," said Danny Vega. They couldn't wipe the smile off my face.

As for the wickedly short title, *Pass the Nuts*, it is the result of a broad committee. I first solicited naming rights to several pals who came up with a long list. Many of them played off the title of my first book, whimsically heavy on the insanity/therapy theme. Joe Smith, John Sheridan, Wally Mieskoski and even my son, John, threw out entries. They were so close. They were almost there. With these offerings in hand, the Gray & Company naming committee—David Gray, Rob Lucas, Chris Andrikanich and Jane Lassar—gathered around a pot of coffee with their freshly sharpened No. 2 pencils and they did not even get up to stretch until they agreed on *Pass the Nuts*.

Over the past year, *Crazy, With the Papers to Prove It* was one of the best sellers in Northeast Ohio, not bad for a neighborhood book. I'm the first to acknowledge that Stephen King and Dan Brown sell millions. Good for them. Back in my heyday at *The Plain Dealer* in the 1960s, '70s and '80s we sold half a million papers on Sundays, so when I had a Page One story on a Sunday, a million people probably read my stuff. That's my target. Notice that picture on the cover. I'm toasting each and every one of you who got me started on my road to a million.

Mike Cleary:
Fired by Steinbrenner

Mike Cleary was the first person ever fired by George Steinbrenner and it was the best thing that ever happened to him. It was good for two reasons. First, he never had to work for Steinbrenner again. Second, everything else that ever happened to him was an upgrade.

Cleary was the general manager of the Cleveland Pipers, Steinbrenner's pro basketball team in the American Basketball League, a short-lived renegade league a notch below the NBA.

The ABL lasted only a season and a half, from 1961 to partway through 1963. It folded in the middle of its second season because it was nothing more than a "spite" league. Abe Saperstein, who owned the Harlem Globetrotters, felt he had been double crossed by the NBA. He claimed that he was promised the NBA expansion team in Los Angeles, but when the Lakers moved there from Minneapolis in 1960 that promise went unfulfilled. Angry and vengeful, Saperstein cobbled together enough investors to launch an eight-team league to compete against the NBA. Saperstein was a crafty promoter, but his emotions blinded his business sense. This was a war he would not win.

Teams were thrown together quickly. Steinbrenner bought Ed Sweeny's Cleveland Pipers of the semi-pro National Industrial Basketball League, which included such amateur basketball legends as the Akron Goodyear Wingfoots, the Peoria Cats (sponsored by the Caterpillar Co.), Bartlesville, Oklahoma, Oilers and Denver Truckers. They were called the Pipers because Sweeny owned a plumbing company.

He had the foundation for a decent pro team and his coach, John McLendon, was no neophyte. He was a renowned college coach. Despite its minor status, the ABL sometimes stood up and went toe-to-toe with the older, established league. That was the case when Steinbrenner signed Dick Barnett away from the Syracuse Nationals of the NBA. Barnett was an established NBA player, the type who enhanced the image of the Pipers and the entire ABL.

Barnett was attracted to Cleveland because he was reunited with McLendon, who had coached him in college. They had won three straight National Association of Inter-Collegiate Athletics (NAIA) national championships together at Tennessee A&I (later known as Tennessee State).

"It was an afternoon news release," said Cleary. "In those days we rotated releases between morning and afternoon papers. That was the way things were done. All the teams did it and the papers respected the arrangement. Nobody jumped the gun. The Barnett story was the afternoon papers' turn. Bob August wrote the story for the *Press*, which was going to start it outside on Page One. They were going to treat it as a major story, which it was.

"That night Gib Shanley saw it on the wire. It might have been his first night in town. He came from Toledo. He didn't notice the release date on the story so he used it on his 11 o'clock show.

"Right after Shanley's show, Chuck Heaton from *The Plain Dealer* called. He said that since the story had been on television, he had to run it in his morning paper. He wrote two paragraphs.

"Because the story was in the morning *Plain Dealer*, the *Press* cut it to one paragraph in the afternoon. We went from a Page One story to two paragraphs in the morning and one paragraph in the afternoon," said Cleary.

Steinbrenner was livid. He called Cleary into his office and fired him on the spot. He gave him five minutes to exit his office.

Cleary should have called Shanley and thanked him.

This is what it was like working for Steinbrenner and, by extension, Steinbrenner's father.

The Pipers' office was in the Rockefeller Building on Superior Ave. at West Sixth St. Also in the building were Steinbrenner's American Shipbuilding headquarters and the headquarters of Kinsman Transit, the massive steamship company owned by Steinbrenner's father, Henry. You would think it was a neat little family arrangement and you would be wrong.

"George asked me to stop by his office," said Cleary. "George's father poked his head in the door and asked me, 'What are you doing here? Wait outside. He's mine until five o'clock.' Another time George was on the phone. His father said, 'Is that a personal call?' And he reached down and disconnected the call.

"There was an old lady who worked for George's father. I asked her how long she had worked there. She said half a century or something. I said George's father was quite demanding. She said I should have known George's grandfather."

So there was Cleary, out of work. Not long before that he had declined an offer from Ken Krueger to become general manager of his Kansas City Steers franchise in the ABL.

"I called him back to tell him things in Cleveland had changed and did he still need a general manager," Cleary said. "I called information in Kansas City. 'Missouri or Kansas?' the operator asked. I didn't know there were two of them. 'The big one,' I said."

The job was still available so Cleary packed up his wife and children and moved to Kansas City, Missouri. Soon afterward, the Cleveland Pipers arrived for a two-game series.

"We always played a two-game series," Cleary said. "There would always be a fight in the first game to build up the crowd for the second game. The visiting team got 25 percent of the gate. After the second game, I handed Pipers' coach John McLendon an envelope with his share of the gate. I told him not to be in the room when George opened it."

The envelope contained a check for 27 dollars and change, several hundred dollars less than Steinbrenner expected. Cleary also enclosed this note to Steinbrenner.

"Dear George, Inadvertently when I left, you forgot to give me my last two weeks' pay. Knowing how magnanimous you are by nature, I was sure you would want to give me two weeks' severance pay, also."

Because Cleary knew the flight the Pipers took from Kansas City to Cleveland, he knew that McLendon would hand the envelope to Steinbrenner at about 5:15 p.m.

"Right on schedule, at 4:15 Kansas City time, George called. 'You got me this time, you son of a bitch. Now we're even,' he said. We've been friends ever since," said Cleary.

* * *

At the end of the season, the NBA team owners agreed to take Cleveland into the league as an expansion team, but there was an entry fee involved and Steinbrenner could not raise the money.

"George's father would not give it to him," said Cleary. "He gave him money for shipbuilding, but not for basketball."

Unable to get into the NBA, Steinbrenner folded the Cleveland Pipers. He was out of the basketball business.

One can only speculate how the sports world would have changed if Steinbrenner's Pipers had gotten into the NBA. It is possible that Steinbrenner, while occupied with pro basketball, never would have bought the New York Yankees.

Nick Mileti's life would have changed. He never would have founded the Cavaliers because Cleveland already would have had an NBA team.

The ABL entered its second season with six teams, including Kansas City, but Saperstein pulled the plug on Dec. 31, 1962. The ABL lost one million dollars during the 1961-62 season and was on schedule to lose another million in its second year.

* * *

With the ABL out of business, so was Cleary. He went to work for the NAIA. After a short time he moved to the NCAA, which was headquartered in the Kansas City suburb of Shawnee Mission, Kansas.

"That was 1964. The NCAA had 11 employees—six men, five

women. Today they have 160 employees in the enforcement division alone," said Cleary.

In 1965 he became the executive director of a new association for college athletic directors association. At their first convention in Chicago, 300 athletic directors attended. At Cleary's last convention, in 2011, attendance was 3,000 athletic directors. Cleary retired at the age of 78. He had been in his position for 46 years.

When Cleary founded the organization, the headquarters were in Minneapolis because the Wheaties Sports Federation provided him a free office and a secretary and paid half his salary. In 1969, he moved the office to Center Ridge Road in Rocky River and eventually took it to Detroit Road in Westlake.

He always had a simple explanation for working until he was almost 80.

"If you don't go to work, you can't go to lunch," he always said.

Cleary's old friend Dino Lucarelli put his life in perspective.

"When Mike Cleary dies and goes to heaven, it will only be a lateral move," said Lucarelli.

* * *

Steinbrenner was a complex individual. He really was one of the most generous people in Cleveland history. When John Nagy was recreation commissioner in Cleveland, he would occasionally ask Steinbrenner to help young Olympic hopefuls finance their training and their travels to Olympic trials and later to the Olympics themselves. Most of them were track athletes. George never hesitated to whip out his checkbook. The list is long and Steinbrenner never sought publicity. He paid the private high school and college tuition for a friend's son. He provided a wheelchair lift and a handicapped ramp for another family. There are countless examples of his charity.

For many years he quietly subsidized the Cleveland National Air Show, as well.

Steinbrenner was like a finely cut diamond. These silent acts of kindness were one facet. At other times he was the master of the grandstand play.

For example, I was in New York to cover Muhammad Ali's fight with Ken Norton in Yankee Stadium on Sept. 28, 1976. My old friend George Lamb met me in New York. Lamb was a degenerate sports fan with a special weakness for world famous events, which Ali vs. Norton certainly was. It was the last heavyweight championship fight held outdoors in an American ballpark. There was a time many years ago when it was common to stage major fights under the lights outdoors in ballparks. That was long before pay per view and Las Vegas.

The night before the fight George Lamb and I were drinking in P. J. Clarke's bar on Third Avenue. Several other reporters and columnists in town for the fight wandered in. P. J. Clarke's was a popular spot for visiting sportswriters. It was overpriced, of course, but not like some other joints and it was pure New York. The place was well lit and everybody was clean and dressed decently. I introduced George Lamb around. He bought a round of drinks and actually got change for a fifty. It was crowded, all the stools were taken, but there was plenty of standing room.

About that time George Steinbrenner strolled triumphantly into P. J. Clarke's. Heads turned and eyes followed him as he walked confidently the entire length of the bar until he reached us. Steinbrenner was feeling good. This was his fourth year as owner of the Yankees and they had just clinched the American League's Eastern Division championship, the first of his regime. The Yankees went on to beat Kansas City in the playoffs but lost the World Series in four straight to Cincinnati. We didn't know that yet, however. At the moment, Steinbrenner was the toast of New York. He had restored the Yankees to glory.

I made the introductions again. George asked if anyone needed tickets to the fight. He had nothing to do with the fight, which was promoted by Bob Arum, but he had access to all the tickets he wanted. After all, Arum needed Steinbrenner's cooperation to use Yankee Stadium during the baseball season. They had a nice hand-in-glove accommodation.

"No thanks, George. We've got our press credentials," everybody said.

Steinbrenner bought a round of drinks and he left.

The next morning George Lamb and I took a stroll around Manhattan. It was unusually warm for late September, perfect for an outdoor fight in Yankee Stadium. When I got back to my room, there was a telephone message. I called the hotel operator and she relayed the message: "Call Mr. George Steinbrenner at this number." It was his office number at Yankee Stadium. I dialed it and his secretary answered. I told her who I was.

"Mr. Steinbrenner wants to know if you need a ticket to the fight tonight," she said.

I told her I was all set. Tell him thanks for me.

He knew darn well I did not need a ticket to the fight. He knew I was there to cover it and I had a ringside ticket. What he did not know was my hotel. Nobody knew my hotel, including *The Plain Dealer* sports department. I happened to be staying in the New York Sheraton because the Indians stayed there when they were in New York and I got the club rate, but nobody knew that. He made a secretary call every Manhattan hotel until she found me, all that to reinforce an impression that he was a swell guy. It worked. I remember it 35 years later and I'm still telling people he was a swell guy.

"That's how he operated," Mike Cleary told me not long ago. "All those years he owned the Yankees, he also had season tickets here in Cleveland for the Indians games. At eleven o'clock in the morning of home games, he had his secretary call a list of people offering them tickets to the game that night. Never before eleven o'clock. By then it was usually too late for people to make plans for the game, but they remembered he made the offer. Later, when the Yankees came to town everybody called him asking for tickets. He could always say, 'I'm sorry, they're gone. By the way, I offered you the tickets on this date and that date and you didn't want them.'"

His generosity knew no boundaries.

Two of his favorite Cleveland bartenders were Nino Rinicella and Eddie Hallal from the Theatrical Grill. When the Yankees got in the World Series the first time, he invited them to New York for the opening game. He flew them to New York and paid all their expenses. Before the game he had them on the field and introduced them to the players. The introductions were not necessary, however. When Yankee manager Billy Martin spotted them, he trotted over.

"Hi, Nino," Martin said.

"Hi, Billy," said Nino.

When the Yankees were in Cleveland they spent more time in the Theatrical than Steinbrenner did.

Steinbrenner was on the receiving end of such kindness once. Wellington Mara, who owned the New York football Giants, gave George tickets to a private loge for a game at Giants Stadium in New Jersey, but when George and several friends arrived, he realized he forgot the tickets.

He went to the "Will Call" window and explained his predicament.

"No problem, Mr. Steinbrenner," said the man behind the window.

He called a superior who appeared quickly. The man knew exactly where they were supposed to go. He stopped what he was doing and personally escorted George and his group to their loge.

"What a great employee," marveled one of Steinbrenner's guests. "Don't you wish every employee was that nice?"

"If he worked for me," said George, "I'd fire him."

Harry Leitch:
Life Was a Party

I always said that covering sports in Cleveland was like going to the circus and Harry Leitch was a big reason. He was the ring-master.

"He was the least boring man I ever knew," his wife Jane said with genuine admiration just before she divorced him.

Several versions of their divorce proceedings circulated in 1972, of which Dino Lucarelli's is fairly close to the truth. So is Mike Cleary's version.

"Mr. Leitch, please describe your typical day," said the judge.

"Well, your honor, I get up about ten o'clock and meet a few clients for drinks at noon at the Blue Fox. Then I meet a few more clients for lunch at the Silver Quill. After that I go back to the Blue Fox and meet more clients for drinks. Then I go home and take a nap and at seven o'clock I meet some clients for dinner at the Blue Fox. I go home about midnight and go to bed. The next day I do the same thing."

"And for this you make $150,000," said the judge, seeking confirmation.

"Yes, your honor," said Harry.

"Are you hiring?" the judge asked.

I have always enjoyed that version, but I went to Jane for a first-hand account of the event. After all, she was there.

"It wasn't a judge, it was a magistrate," said Jane. "Harry wasn't there. I told the magistrate that Harry left the house every morning. We had a nine-bedroom house. He always got up in the morning, no matter how late he was out, even if he got in at 2 a.m.

He would make his first call every day and somebody would hand him an order. He was a heck of a salesman. He would take a customer to lunch and then he would take a customer to dinner and on Sundays he was the spotter for the Browns' radio announcers. And the magistrate said, 'For this he makes $150,000?' I said, 'Yes.' I could tell the magistrate wanted to be Harry. He didn't want to be *like* Harry, he wanted to *be* Harry. 'You're married to a legend,' he said. 'You try being married to a legend,' I said. 'Divorce granted,' he said."

Jane and Harry had a hell of a 22 years. Let me tell you how it all began.

Jane Sutphin was fresh out of Flora Stone Mather, the women's college of Western Reserve University, and was lucky enough to find work. What made her lucky is that she worked for her father, Al Sutphin, who was loaded. This was fortunate because Al was married to an Irish-Catholic woman and they had half a dozen children. Al was the sole owner of Braden-Sutphin Ink, the Cleveland Barons hockey team, the Cleveland Rebels basketball team and the Cleveland Arena. This was the late 1940s and Cleveland sports were ruled by three moguls—Bill Veeck, who owned the Indians; Mickey McBride, who owned the Browns; and Sutphin, who owned everything else.

Sutphin put his daughter Jane on the payroll to sell season tickets for the Rebels basketball team, which had done poorly at the gate. The Rebels were an original member of the Basketball Association of America in its inaugural season of 1946-1947. You know it now as the NBA. This is a reminder that Cleveland was in the NBA 24 years before the Cavaliers came along. Jane picks up the story.

"He told me to call on all the Catholic business owners to sell them season tickets for the basketball team. I was up to the U's. I called on United Screw and Bolt. 'Is Mr. Kramer in?' I asked. 'Which one?' the receptionist asked. 'The sales manager,' I said. Out came Eugene Kramer, the handsomest man I have ever seen in my life, tall, beautiful suit, gracious manners. I told him that he could get two season tickets for the price of one. He was about to say, 'I'll take six tickets,' when this little, short man comes out and interrupts. It was Harry. He was a salesman there. He said he wanted season tickets for hockey. I told him they were sold out. He said he wanted tickets to the fights. They were sold out. I said I was only selling basketball tickets. In the meantime, this gorgeous Mr. Kramer says, 'I'll think about it,' and goes back in his office. This jerk cost me six tickets. Then he started calling me for lunch. I said no. He asked me out to dinner. I said no. He kept calling me. He pestered me so much I agreed to go to lunch. It was the only way to get rid of him."

Jane had misgivings about their lunch date and tried to call Harry and cancel it. She searched the phone book for the name Leitch but there were several versions and she couldn't locate him, so off to lunch they went. And so began the courtship of Jane Sutphin.

"He wouldn't leave me alone. The only way I could get rid of him was to marry him," said Jane.

The day after their wedding Harry went out to meet some friends and didn't come home for four days. The magistrate made a note of that.

Years later Jane remarked to Mary Bixler, wife of the Browns assistant coach Paul Bixler, that it was not unusual for Harry to stay out all night.

"Paul has never not come home," said Mary Bixler.

"He was never out with Harry, was he?" said Jane.

Harry once left in the morning to play golf. He came home four days later.

"What happened?" asked Jane.

"I made the cut," said Harry.

In the meantime, nobody bought season tickets for the basketball team and Al Sutphin folded it after one season. The Arena was still a hopping place even without pro basketball. It had high school and college basketball, six-day bike races, roller derby, big time pro boxing, the Golden Gloves boxing tournament, pro rassling, two separate ice shows, the K of C Track Meet, high school hockey and, of course, Cleveland's beloved Barons hockey team. Marrying Jane was like marrying the Arena. Harry knew what he was doing.

"Actually," said Jane, "he wanted to be Al Sutphin's son-in-law. He even started introducing himself as Al Sutphin's son-in-law."

Al Sutphin had six children. Harry and Jane had six children. Al was non-religious and married a Catholic. Harry was non-religious and married a Catholic. Al was a sports degenerate. So was Harry.

Harry wasn't a bad baseball player in the 1930s when he graduated from St. Ignatius High School and played for the Plover Cafe in the Lakewood Class A League at Madison Park. In fact, he had a tryout with the Boston Braves in 1940. Harry was a skinny 140-pound middle infielder, barely 5-and-a-half feet tall.

"Come back when you've got some meat on those bones," Braves manager Casey Stengel said when he sent him home.

Harry took Stengel's advice. By the time I knew him, Harry was still 5-and-a-half feet tall and he was 5-and-a-half feet wide.

Harry left United Screw and Bolt after 11 years and started his own manufacturers' rep company. He picked up some lines, selling nuts, bolts, springs and the like and sold like a fiend. Buyers couldn't wait to see Harry walk through the door. He drove a big red Cadillac because his father-in-law drove a big red Cadillac. Through his father-in-law he met the biggest men in Cleveland sports. He became friendly with Browns coach Paul Brown and his wife, Katy, while on vacation at the Sutphin family farm in Fort Myers, Fla. The cream of Cleveland's sports celebrities gathered there every winter. In the 1950s Harry became the spotter for Browns radio announcers Bill McColgan and Jim Graner. He continued when Gib Shanley replaced McColgan in 1961. Harry was the spotter for 26 years, often getting the names and numbers correct.

"He wasn't much of a spotter, but he was good for morale," Shanley said.

The Browns became his life. He once left Jane and other members of her family in the middle of the 1968 Olympics in Mexico City because the Browns had lost two games in a row. He bought a sombrero and flew home to get them straightened out.

His son Billy marvels at another aspect of his father's aura.

"He was a close friend of Paul Brown, but can you believe, Paul Brown was gone one minute and the next minute Art Modell was Harry's best friend? Harry was right back on the team plane," said Billy Leitch.

On Mondays he would regale his customers with exciting stories about the Browns' road trips.

"You'd better double that order of nuts and bolts," his customers would say.

For many years Harry hosted lavish parties at what is now known as the Renaissance Hotel on Public Square. Sadly, that hotel, an anchor of downtown Cleveland, has had so many different names hardly anybody can keep them straight. It was called the Sheraton at times. It has had a different name every 20 years. Maybe we should call it Harry's Hotel.

"Finally, I said I can't take another football season with Harry," Jane said during our refresher interview for this book. "Here's how desperate I was. I called the travel agent who arranged our trip to the Mexico Olympics and asked him to get me out of the country. He sent me to Africa for two weeks. I got 10 different shots. I called home from Nairobi and Tim said, 'Didn't you hear about the party at the Sheraton? All the players were there. There was a snowball fight. It went on until five or six in the morning.' Harry made a video. He had everybody wave at Jane."

Harry also went to World Series games in New York and he went to Cooperstown for the Hall of Fame inductions of his baseball pals. The year Early Wynn went in the Hall of Fame (1972), Harry called Jane from Cooperstown and said, "Get the spare bedroom ready. I'm bringing somebody home."

He brought Casey Stengel and his wife, Edna, home with him for a night. Incredibly, Casey remembered Harry from his tryout in 1940. Of the hundreds, maybe thousands, of brief acquaintances over the years, Casey Stengel remembered Harry.

"I see you put some meat on those bones," said Casey.

Jane picks up the story.

"Casey and Edna sat on the couch in our living room telling stories. All the time Casey talked, he had his elbow on Edna's thigh. After three hours Edna asked if she could see their bedroom. She was exhausted. She tried to stand up and she fell down. Her leg was paralyzed. We rushed her to the emergency room. We thought she had a stroke."

Harry was a committed gin rummy player. Games sometimes lasted for days. Gib Shanley once complained that you played until Harry won. On a pre-season trip to the West Coast where the Browns played exhibition games against both the Rams and the 49ers, Harry conducted a gin game in his room that lasted for seven days, interrupted only by a football game.

"How much was your bar bill?" asked Browns public relations man Nate Wallack.

"I don't know," said Harry. "My ice bill was $300."

I was lured into a gin game with him on a team flight to the West Coast. At half a cent a point I thought that was harmless. By the time we were flying over Chicago he had taken $35 from me.

Jane made the mistake of going with him to a nut and bolt convention in New York. Jane said she wanted to leave early for the airport. She did not want to be rushed, which was Harry's usual way of traveling. He handed her a plane ticket. When she got to the gate at LaGuardia Airport, she learned that her flight left from JFK Airport. He never mentioned that. After another wild cab ride to JFK and an all-out sprint to the gate, she found the entire flight crew waiting for her.

"Mrs. Leitch," the pilot said, "would you please control your husband?"

They welcomed her aboard, where she found Harry causing a loud commotion. He had a glorious New York snoot full and he wasn't happy about anything.

"Sit down and shut up," said Jane.

"I'm not sitting with you," he declared loudly, and plopped down in the seat in front of them, next to a Hispanic couple, who began jabbering frantically in Spanish.

Because they missed their spot in line and were waiting behind several other planes, the pilot attempted to appease the angry passengers by inviting them to visit the cockpit. Harry was the first to jump up and head for the cockpit, whereupon it was discovered he had been sitting on the Hispanic couple's two-year-old baby.

You may get the impression that Harry was self-indulgent. Late in life, before he went to the assisted living home, Harry moved to California. He bought a spread in Rancho Bernardo, near San Diego, and he brought along his daughter, Katie, to run the place. Before long another daughter, Margaret, went out to keep them both company. Harry then decided they should go camping. In the middle of their first night, Harry woke them both to drive him to the bathroom that was 100 feet from their tent. Obviously, Harry was losing it. The girls said, "The heck with this." They came home and so did he. It was Jane's job to find a nursing home that would take him. Harry was becoming difficult.

"He would say to the old ladies, 'You're old and you're useless.' They made him eat with people with no short-term memories. By the time dinner was over they didn't remember his insults," Jane said.

When Harry died in 1993, somebody said it was the loudest wake in history. Art Modell, Lou Groza, Bob Gain and other former Browns players, front office workers and widows all gathered to tell Harry Leitch stories and celebrate a life that had been spent celebrating.

Harry's brother, Bob, made a cogent observation.

"If we had a bar on the other side of the room," he said, "Harry would sit up."

Jack Lengyel:
He Tormented Everyone

When Jack Lengyel was named athletic director of the United States Naval Academy in 1988, I rejoiced. I knew Lengyel. He was one hell of a commander. Athletic director today, Secretary of the Navy tomorrow and the day after that, he brings the entire Soviet bloc and the Arab conspiracy to its knees. He had that effect on people. Then the entire fleet sails for Tahiti and goes on a three-day pass. That was the agenda as I saw it. Luckily for the Soviets and the Arabs, he took the pension before he took action against the enemies of the Republic.

I first knew him when he was the young head football coach at the College of Wooster in Ohio. He got the job in 1966 at age 29 and everybody around him started to get gray hair. He had been an assistant coach at Cornell where he mercilessly tormented legendary hockey coach Ned Harkness. Ned won two NCAA championships and five Ivy League titles at Cornell and later he coached the Detroit Red Wings and also became their general manager. Ned was an earnest coach and a good guy. Lengyel feasted on guys like that. He had no respect for rank and tenure.

There was the occasion, for example, when Harkness was re-galing two prospects in his office about the glory of playing hockey for Cornell. He leaned back in his chair with his feet on his desk and fixed his gaze directly into the eyes of the two recruits.

In the hallway outside the hockey coach's office, however, Lengyel held a fire hose aimed at the bottom of the hockey coach's door and Cornell track coach Jeep Davis, an enthusiastic partner in crime, had his hand on the faucet which he turned on full blast. The recruits, awed and nervous by the spellbinding mono-logue, sat frozen in their chairs, afraid to mention the rising water gathering around their ankles and heading upward toward their knees. Lengyel's only regret was that he could not see the expression on Harkness' face when he replaced his feet on the floor and ruined his best pair of Florsheims.

Lengyel was relentless. Through the cooperation of the Cornell Agricultural Department, Lengyel secured 200 pounds of nature's favorite fertilizer, which he deposited in the front trunk of Harkness's Volkswagen to ripen in the summer sun.

You can push a man only so far and Harkness finally reached the breaking point. He retaliated. He and Davis arranged for Lengyel's car to be stolen and hidden in the middle of the basketball floor at Barton Hall Fieldhouse. Unfortunately, the theft did not go well. They snatched the wrong car, one belonging to a campus visitor.

Harkness tried again. Lengyel was playing squash when he was called to the phone. The athletic director wanted to see him right now, his secretary said. Jack took a quick shower. He was still perspiring when he got out of the shower and couldn't get dry in the humid locker room. He dressed quickly. Perspiration was still gushing from his pores. He rushed to the office of Cornell athletic director Bob Kane, a distinguished man who later became head of the United States Olympic Committee.

"Please sit down," the secretary said. "Mr. Kane will see you in a minute."

The buzzer on her phone went off. The secretary picked it up. "Yes, he's here," she said.

"What did you do?" the secretary said, turning to Lengyel. "I've never seen him so mad."

Lengyel sat there perspiring for 30 anguished minutes. What did he do? He recalled his activities going back several months.

"He'll see you now," the secretary said.

Lengyel entered the office and the man was reading the newspaper with his feet on the desk. He put down the newspaper and the man at the desk as Ned Harkness. The athletic director was out of town.

Retaliation comes with immediate gratification, but often invites terrible retribution.

"I'm a two-for-one guy," Lengyel often said. "You gore me with one horn, I give you two horns."

Harkness and Davis ignored the warning. They began collecting newspapers. Instead of throwing away old newspapers, they stored them in a closet and when they had enough they stuffed them in Lengyel's car like a bunch of fraternity boys stuffing phone booths. No living person could squeeze inside that car. When they were finished they smiled triumphantly. This was an Ivy League university. Some of the brightest scholars in America were enrolled there. And this was their faculty.

In the meantime, Jeep Davis, one of America's most revered Olympic track stars, persuaded the touring Soviet Union track team to run a dual meet against Cornell. Jeep made sleeping arrangements for them in a loft on the third floor of a dormitory. Cots were set up in the loft, which usually was empty. In the middle of the night Jeep was awakened by a phone call. A man with a thick accent was on the phone and he was very agitated. Jeep was able to determine that it was the Soviet coach and he had a problem. His team could not sleep because of pigeons that were defecating over them. Jeep could not understand every word, but he did catch phrases such as "international incident." Jeep dashed back to campus and discovered the Soviet track team peacefully sleeping. Not a pigeon was in sight.

While Jeep and the other coaches did the heavy lifting, Lengyel simply picked up the phone and made it up as he went along. He had a gift.

* * *

When Lengyel moved to the College of Wooster as head football coach, Harkness mistakenly believed he was safe from all this mischief. The sad fact is that no one is safe when Lengyel has your phone number.

When Cornell beat Harvard to win the Ivy League championship, Ned and his family hosted a victory party at his home. The hockey championship is a big deal in the Ivy League. Remember Oliver in *Love Story*?

Everyone was having a wonderful time. They were drinking and patting Ned on the back and congratulating him for another great coaching job. Keep in mind, however, that his goalie was Ken Dryden, so don't think he pulled it off with a bunch of kids straight out of Junior Hockey.

The phone rang.

"Hello," said Mrs. Harkness.

"Can I speak to Ned?" the voice said.

Ned came to the phone. It was another well-wisher, no doubt. The phone had been ringing all night.

"This is Bill Jones down the street," the man said. "Do you have a black lab?"

"Yes, I do," said Ned.

"He bit my boy," said Mr. Jones.

"He never bit anybody in his life," said Ned.

"Well, he did tonight," said Mr. Jones. "Do you have insurance?"

"Of course," said Ned, who felt like a defenseman skating backward and trying to kill a power play.

"I'm sure it will never come to that. But let me ask you this. Would you just come over and see my boy? Talk to him. He'll feel much better," said Mr. Jones.

"Tell me how to get there," said Ned.

For a man who lived down the street, Mr. Jones gave complicated instructions. Right, left, right, left. Half a mile. Two-thirds of a mile. White house with blue shutters. He wasn't exactly down the street. Not even a trained Labrador retriever hunting dog could find his way home following those directions. Harkness and a couple of friends left his guests and jumped into Ned's car. He was no longer driving the stinky Volkswagen. He had a full-size sedan. The directions made no sense, but they kept driving. Minutes passed. Half an hour passed. They found a white house with blue shutters. They pulled in the driveway and got out of the car. As they walked up to the front door, Ned suddenly stopped.

"Everybody get back in the car," Ned said. He realized he had been scammed and only one man would do that to him. He recognized that voice. Lengyel was Mr. Jones.

*   *   *

When Lengyel got to Wooster in 1966, it was a homecoming. He grew up in Akron and went to the University of Akron, just a few miles to the north. In addition to his old friends, he made many new friends, including the local Chevrolet dealer, George Lamb. These two guys were kindred spirits. They enjoyed going to lunch with a group and one by one everybody would excuse himself to go to the men's room and not come back. The last man was stuck with the bill.

Bill Love, an auto dealer from Orrville, was the last man sitting after having lunch with Lengyel and Lamb in Akron one particular day. Lengyel and Lamb went north to Cleveland and Love, without a trace of rancor after paying the lunch tab, headed south to Orrville. Lengyel and Lamb knew Love's routine. He always stopped in the bar of a Holiday Inn on his way home from Akron. Just before entering the old Stadium in Cleveland, Lengyel made a phone call to the bar of the Holiday Inn.

"This is the police," said Lengyel, assuming his laconic police voice. "We're following a flasher and we think he's in your bar right now. Is a man with an eye patch there?"

"No, but there's a man with glasses and one of the lenses is dark," said the bartender. "That's Mr. Love. He's a regular customer."

"He's a regular pervert," said Officer Lengyel.

The bartender gasped. Everyone at the Holiday Inn lounge knew Bill Love, who had recently undergone eye surgery.

"Keep him there. We're out of our jurisdiction but the local authorities will be there shortly. Keep feeding him drinks if you have to," said Lengyel.

Then they went to the ballgame. The next day Lamb called Bill Love.

"Damndest thing," said Love. "They kept buying me drinks all night. First time they ever bought me a drink."

Lamb and Lengyel were a one-two punch. They stopped in a nice restaurant owned by a friend. Lamb gave the bartender a shoebox to watch while they were having dinner.

"Don't look in the box," said Lamb. "Be careful with it. The top is not sealed."

Curiosity got the best of the bartender and he peeked in the box. Out flew canaries. The box was full of canaries. Customers spent the rest of the night swatting away canaries.

"What happened to my canaries?" George asked the bartender

"I don't know. They must have got out by themselves," said the bartender.

* * *

Bob Fishburn owned a company in Wayne County that made customized trucks, including trucks for ESPN for game broadcasts. These were expensive trucks with miles of complicated cables and wiring. Fishburn's home phone rang about 11 o'clock one night.

"Mr. Fishburn, this is the driver of the NBC truck at the Stanley Cup playoffs. We're 14 inches from the building and we can't get the truck out of 11th gear. We're going on the air in 30 minutes. What are you going to do about it?"

"What? What?" a confused Fishburn kept saying.

Lengyel was compulsive. Sometimes he even turned on his own accomplice. He called the George Lamb Chevrolet dealership in Wooster, knowing that George was out of town. The conversation went like this.

"Is Mr. Lamb there?" Lengyel said.

"No, sir. He's out of town," said the receptionist.

"Let me talk to your general manager," said Lengyel.

Click. Click.

"This is the general manager."

"I'm from the petting zoo. Mr. Lamb wants to put the petting zoo in his showroom. You've got to get all the cars out of the show room."

"He never told us about a petting zoo."

"He said it's for some kind of family promotion. Listen, I'm a little behind schedule. I'll be there in less than two hours with the animals. Can you be sure to get the cars out?"

When Lamb returned early that evening, he discovered that his showroom had been cleaned out. All the shiny new cars were outside in the rain.

*   *   *

Jack's Wooster football teams did very well but in 1971 he made a shocking move that changed his life forever. This fun-loving man who began every day with a smile and ended it with a laugh took the head coaching job at Marshall University in Huntington, West Virginia, the school that had been devastated by the worst airplane crash in sports history the year before. On the dark, rainy night of Nov. 14, 1970, Marshall was returning from a game at East Carolina in Greenville, North Carolina, on Southern Airways Charter Flight 932 when the plane crashed short of the runway. All 75 on board perished. The dead numbered 37 players, eight coaches, 25 boosters including businessmen and politicians, four crew members and an employee of the charter company. The wheels of the twin jet engine DC-9 clipped the treetops and it never reached one of the trickiest airports in the country, where the runway was carved into the side of a hill.

"I thought I was rebuilding a football team," Lengyel said years later. "It was more than that. It took a wide swath out of the community."

Some thought Marshall should drop football out of respect for the dead. Others thought Marshall should rebuild the football team out of respect for the dead. Dr. Don Dedmond, Marshall's interim president, acted quickly. He made the decision to continue the football program to honor the 75 who had lost their lives.

The choice was made to go on living and Lengyel set about finding players. The NCAA issued a special ruling that Marshall could use freshmen and transfers also would be eligible.

"We were a freshman-JV team with a few transfers and some kids who just wanted to play to help the team. We opened with Morehead State and we lost the game, 29-6. We did not do a good job with kickoffs or extra points, so after the game I put an ad in the school newspaper for a kicker. This was the time of hippies. A soccer player tried out. He was a good kicker. I told him to get a haircut and shave and you've got a scholarship."

When Marshall played its first home game against Xavier, Father Bob Scott, the priest who had presided over the burial of many of the players, blessed the team as it ran onto the field and Marshall scored a touchdown on the last play to beat Xavier, 15-13.

"That was a miracle," Lengyel said. "But when we beat Bowling Green, 12-10, in our sixth game, in my opinion it was one of the greatest upsets of all time. We were underdogs by 30 or 40 points. Bowling Green was unbeaten. Coach Don Nehlen had a great running back, Paul Miles. To give you an idea, Miami had beaten us, 66-6, and Bowling Green had beaten Miami, 33-7."

Lengyel stayed four years at Marshall, 1971-74. He left to enter private business in Louisville, Kentucky, despite the pleadings of the university president, the mayor of Huntington and countless alumni, citizens and fans. I never understood why he quit coaching until I saw the movie, *We Are Marshall*, starring Matthew Mc-Conaughey as Lengyel. The movie came out in December 2006, the year I announced that we were going to start a new family tradition on Christmas Eve. My wife, four kids and I had dinner at my favorite restaurant and then saw an inspirational movie. I said we would see a movie about a friend of mine, Jack Lengyel. The tradition lasted one year. It was one of the most depressing movies we've ever seen. I then understood why Lengyel felt he had done his duty after four years. The unrelenting gloom and despair were oppressive.

After a couple of years he returned to college as an athletic director at Louisville, Fresno State, Missouri and the United States Naval Academy. He was at Navy from 1988 to 2001 when he retired but didn't exactly stop working. At the age of 76 he is the St. Jude of college athletics, the patron saint of lost causes. He is usually brought in as interim athletic director for months at a time to fix programs that need help.

"I'm like the sheriff. I shoot first and ask questions later," he says. "I revise departments and put people on probation."

There will always be work for him because college sports have never been more broken. It appears that rebuilding Marshall was a test. It prepared him for the rest of his life.

Some old habits are tough to break, however. While several old friends were out at dinner, Lengyel said in an off-hand way to a man I'll call George, "By the way, George, did you remember to call your wife and tell her we'd be out late tonight?"

George assured him that he had made the call.

"I called his wife, too," Lengyel whispered in my ear. "I told her I wasn't getting into town until tomorrow. Let's see how he gets out of this one."

Can you imagine how he would have had the Arabs chasing their tails? Oh, the havoc he could have caused.

Gene Hickerson:
Elvis Took His Calls

It was a few years too late when Gene Hickerson was elected to the Pro Football Hall of Fame in 2007. They could just as well have inducted a tomato plant. Gene had just turned 70 and his mind was ravaged by dementia. At his induction ceremony he could not speak. In fact, he didn't even get out of his wheelchair. There wasn't a dry eye in Canton's Fawcett Stadium when Jim Brown, Bobby Mitchell and Leroy Kelly, Hickerson's three Hall of Fame running backs, pushed him in his wheelchair onto the stage. Massive men with paws the size of polar bears' dabbed at their eyes. Gene was the offensive guard who usually had cleared the path for Brown, Mitchell and Kelly into the end zone. Gene's old teammate and close friend Bobby Franklin, consumed by emotion, made the presentation speech for Gene, words he had practiced four times a day for six months.

Hickerson and Brown both were drafted in December of 1956. Brown was the first pick and Hickerson was taken in the seventh round. The NFL moved up its draft from spring until before Christmas, before the 1956 season had actually ended, because of the war between the NFL and the Canadian Football League. The Canadians were blatantly looting players from the NFL and competing for draft choices. Hickerson was only a junior at Mississippi and couldn't play until the 1958 season, which explains why he was picked so low. That was a favorite ploy of Browns coach and general manager Paul Brown. He would identify "can't miss" underclassmen and draft them as "future" picks. He could use a low-round draft pick to get a future Hall of Famer. The Browns

were usually so deep with talent that they could afford to wait a
year for a draft choice. Most other teams did not have that luxury.
They needed their draft picks right away.

Gene almost never played football. Not until his senior year in
high school did he pull on the shoulder pads and only because his
younger brother, Willie, persuaded him to try out for the Trenton
High School team near Memphis, Tennessee. When Gene trotted
onto the practice field for the first time, the coach's eyes lit up like
the headlamp on the Chattanooga Choo Choo. His teammates
stood back in awe. At 235 pounds, Gene was the fastest kid on
the team. No thought was given to putting Gene in a three-point
stance on the line. Gene was the tailback and he led the team in
rushing and scoring. He trampled opponents almost at will.

How the University of Tennessee missed Gene is easily explained. Gene was born and raised in Trenton, Tennessee. The
Volunteers rarely lost a player of Gene's caliber, but the Trenton
postmaster was an Ole Miss man. He called Ole Miss coach John
Vaught and extolled the prowess of Hickerson. College coaches
get those calls all the time and usually ignore them. When nothing happened after two weeks, the postmaster called again. Still
no action. Two more weeks passed and the postmaster called a
third time. The name Hickerson was becoming familiar in the
Ole Miss football office.

That winter, the Ole Miss recruiting coordinator took a bird-
hunting trip to Trenton and while there he called Hickerson's
home and got directions to his house. When the coach pulled
into the driveway, Gene stepped onto the front porch to greet him
and the recruiting coordinator's jaw dropped. He offered Gene a
scholarship on the spot. He had never seen him play football.

At Ole Miss, coach Vaught turned Gene into a tackle, but in
practice he made him run sprints with the backs. Before long everybody knew about him. In 1958 Gene was a starter in the traditional exhibition game between the reigning NFL champions
and the College All-Stars that opened every season. The College
All-Stars easily spanked the NFL champion Detroit Lions that
year. Gene then began a 15-year career as a gloriously decorated

guard with the Cleveland Browns, 13 seasons at right guard and the last two at left guard. He made all-league five times and made six Pro Bowl appearances. In 15 seasons, Hickerson had a role in sending five different Browns running backs to the Pro Bowl—Jim Brown, Bobby Mitchell, Leroy Kelly, Ernie Green and Greg Pruitt.

"He was a great player, but he was contrary. He'd argue with a sign post," said Bobby Franklin, who played with Gene at Ole Miss and the Browns. With the Browns, Bobby played all four defensive backfield positions and was Lou Groza's holder on field goals and extra points.

"Gene always had to do it his way," Franklin continued. "He never trained. He never ran. He never lifted weights. When Nick Skorich became the head coach, he made everybody run laps. Gene refused to run laps. He wouldn't do it and there was nothing Skorich could do about it. In pre-game warm-ups, Gene would always lean against the goal post and watch Frank Ryan throw passes to the wide receivers. Gene said to Paul Warfield, 'I can run better routes than that.' Paul said, 'Let's see.' Gene got down in a three-point stance and ran right into the dugout."

* * *

Hickerson was a bundle of contradictions. For example, he was a friend of Elvis Presley but loved classical music. He was a frequent patron of the Cleveland Orchestra at Severance Hall and he knew the famous conductor George Szell personally. He sneered at popular music, despite his personal relationship with Elvis, who also came from Memphis. Because of Gene, Elvis became a huge Browns fan. Every Monday, Gene would pick up an extra copy of the previous day's game film and ship it to Elvis, who studied the film like a scout. One night in a bar I scoffed when Gene told me about his friendship with Elvis.

"You go over to that phone and call this number and see who answers," Gene said.

He wrote a number on a cocktail napkin. We were in a bar, for Pete's sake, and the phone was a pay phone. I did not have a pocket full of quarters. I stuck the number in my pocket and threw it away later.

Jim Mueller, who was broadcasting Browns games on the radio with Gib Shanley, also reacted skeptically late one night to Hickerson's boast that he knew Elvis.

"Call this number," Gene said to Mueller.

Mueller did not need a pocket full of quarters. He was sitting in the living room of Hickerson's apartment on the Lakewood Gold Coast. He picked up Hickerson's house phone and Gene recited the number.

"Ask for Elvis," said Hickerson.

"Can I speak to Elvis Presley?" Mueller said when a voice answered the phone.

"Who is calling?"

"I'm a friend of Gene Hickerson," said Mueller.

"Just one minute."

Momentarily, Mueller heard Elvis Presley's voice on the other end of the line. After that nobody doubted Hickerson.

Over the years I spent many hours in the company of Hickerson. When you were with Gene, you kept your money in your pocket because he bought every round. But in 1970 he stopped talking to me in the locker room after games and never spoke to me there again. He objected to something I wrote in my clubhouse interview story. I didn't misquote him. I captured his words perfectly. What he didn't like was my interpretation which began, "Hickerson seems to be saying . . ."

After the next game I went up to him in the locker room and he said, "I'm not talking to you anymore."

He didn't. But in the bar that night we talked for hours. Gene could be rigid. His embargo applied only to the locker room.

*   *   *

From his first training camp, Doug Dieken was one of Hickerson's most loyal friends. Hickerson was the wise old veteran; Dieken a rookie.

Gene Hickerson was wheeled onto the stage at his Pro Football Hall of Fame induction by three Hall of Fame teammates: (from left) Leroy Kelly, Bobby Mitchell and Jim Brown. Gene led the blocking for all three.
(Canton Repository)

"My rookie year Gene said, 'Hey, rookie. Come on down to the Hanna Pub. It's my birthday.' Bo Cornell and I went. He wouldn't let us pay for a thing. The next week, same thing. He said it was his birthday. He just wanted to go drinking with us," said Dieken.

At the end of his career, Hickerson moved to left guard next to Dieken, the left tackle.

"We had a play where the guard was supposed to block the first guy coming across and the tackle was supposed to take the second guy. Gene never touched his man. The guy came right through and clobbered me. I got up and said, 'Gene, guard first, tackle second.' 'No,' said Gene. 'Guard first choice.' "

In practice during the 1970 season, Bill Yanchar, a rookie defensive tackle from Purdue, head slapped Hickerson.

"Don't do that," said Gene.

On the next play Yanchar head slapped him again. Gene said nothing. He simply kicked him in the shin as hard as he could. Yanchar limped to the sidelines.

* * *

Gene was poor growing up near Memphis. No doubt it was this upbringing that drove him to success in business. For many years he was a manufacturer's rep for Anchor Tool and Die in the steel business. He sold to the auto industry. He even worked during the football season. Every Monday, which was usually the players' day off, Gene called on customers. He once told me that he never cashed his Browns paychecks. I think he meant that he just socked them away in an account somewhere and he lived on the income from his steel company. He did well.

Dino Lucarelli recalled that every year Hickerson bought a loge at the Stadium, which he used to entertain his customers. Gene would come to Dino's office at the Stadium and hand him a personal check for the entire amount. I have never heard of an athlete actually buying tickets, much less buying a loge.

Jack Bush, the general manager for J & L Steel, told Gene that he needed soaking pit covers for his mill so Gene and Dieken started a company to make them. The name of the company was D & H, Inc.

"Why do you call it D & H instead of H & D?" someone asked Hickerson.

"Because when you go bankrupt they always go after the first name," Gene explained.

Dieken said the company lasted a year and a half.

"We actually sold a few soaking pit covers," Dieken said.

* * *

Gene was married briefly in college and had a son. The marriage did not work out and Gene vowed never to marry again, a vow he upheld. Years later a daughter surfaced and he treated her generously. He always lived alone, first in the Commodore Hotel in the University Circle neighborhood, then on the Lakewood Gold Coast and finally in a big brick house in Avon across from a golf course, a house far bigger than he needed. He had three families, however. His teammates were his first family. For many years he put on lavish holiday meals at Dieken's house in Bay Village for the bachelors on the team—the strays, as he called them. Gene liked to eat and he liked to cook. In the 1990s he and a partner opened a high-class restaurant in Playhouse Square. Gene closed it when his partner died.

Bob Hickerson (Gene's son), his wife, Eileen, and their children were Gene's second family. They live in Berea. Eileen is the sister of the Browns' former media relations director Kevin Byrne, currently a vice president with the Baltimore Ravens.

His third family was Mimi and Jim Hall and their children. They also lived close by in Avon. Mimi was Gene's old girlfriend. They moved on but they did not grow apart. Mimi and Jim got married and had children, but there always was a place at their table for Gene. That's where I found Gene on the Saturday before the 2007 Super Bowl when Gene learned he had been elected to the Hall of Fame. It was at their kitchen table that I attempted to record on camera his response to the news. One sentence, one 10-second sound bite was all we needed for Fox 8 and the Fox network. Mimi and I even wrote out the sentence and placed it before him. He tried courageously a dozen times but he could not do it as Mimi watched in agony. Gene was in the throes of that terrible disease.

Nobody heard his voice again but his career spoke volumes.

Dick Schafrath:
Can't Turn Down a Challenge

Dick Schafrath wanted to meet for lunch after his doctor's appointment with a shoulder specialist in May 2011.

"How did it go at the doctor's office?" I asked.

"Not good," said Schafrath.

Twelve seasons at left tackle for the Browns had left him wracked with arthritis in his shoulders and back and there was no hope for improvement. He was 74 years old. He was in constant pain and he refused to take painkillers.

That was the least of his health problems over the years. He battled cancer and won. He had a heart attack and doctors told him he wouldn't live beyond 1990. He had a pacemaker implanted in his chest. Now his long-range goal, he said, was to set the state longevity record for a living person. Since he plans to have a lot of time on his hands, he started taking piano lessons and learned to tap dance.

He also had a short-term goal, which was the reason for our meeting. Having survived a series of insane physical challenges over the years, he was preparing to undertake another one.

"I want to ride a horse across Ohio like the Pony Express did," said Schafrath. "I want to follow the trail Lincoln took when he crossed Ohio."

"And why do you want to do that?"

"I want to deliver a letter from one side of Ohio to the other faster than the Post Office," said Schafrath.

Essentially, he wanted to race the post office just for the hell of it.

Schafrath said he already had lined up four horses. He planned to alternate them. He figured it would take about 30 hours of non-stop riding.

"What is my role in this?" I asked.

"You may know some organization or cause that I could ride for," he said.

"Maybe an auto dealer will sponsor your ride," I said. "After all, it worked out so well back in 1971."

Schafrath really is a glutton for punishment. In June 1971, Schafrath ran from Cleveland Stadium to Maurer Field, his high school football field in Wooster, on a dare from George Lamb, who owned the Chevrolet dealership in Wooster. Lamb said that if Schafrath completed the 62-mile run, most of it at night and all of it on busy public roads, he would give him the use of a car for a year.

Many people thought Lamb was a sucker to make such a wager. Schafrath's freshman football coach at Wooster High School, Vic McIntyre, remembered Schafrath's incredible capacity for running.

"He lived on a farm about five miles outside of town. He would put his younger brothers on the school bus each morning and he would run behind it," said McIntyre.

"And if the bus made enough stops, I would beat it to school," Schafrath claimed.

Schafrath won the bet and got the car but it ended his football career. The run took 14 hours. When he reached Maurer Field, medics were waiting and he was taken directly to the hospital with an IV needle stuck in his arm. He never recovered. When training camp began, Schafrath's legs were shot. Halfway through the season he surrendered his left tackle position to Doug Dieken.

In his book, *Heart of a Mule*, Schafrath blames Lamb, morning disc jockey Jim Runyon, downtown Cleveland restaurant owner Pat McIntyre and me for "egging" him on. He rightfully focused on Lamb. The rest of us were more or less bystanders. We had signed up for nothing more than a good time. We harbored no malice toward Schafrath.

"This run was an obsession for George Lamb," Schafrath wrote in his book. "His preparation was elaborate and precise. He had organized a steering committee months earlier that met weekly at Pat Joyce's Tavern. He had formed subcommittees with different responsibilities—sheriff and police escort, departure plans, arrival plans, media, medical and refreshments."

The run began at eight o'clock on Friday night from Cleveland Stadium. Schafrath's younger brother, Mike, ran with him.

Schafrath picks up the story in his book:

"There was a crowd of about one hundred onlookers gathered to cheer us off. Soon after, the George Lamb committee arrived dressed in full running gear, each carrying a cold can of beer."

Schafrath recalled that Lamb had hired Weasel Rosenberg, the bugler from Thistledown Racetrack, to start the run. Everyone cheered when Weasel sounded the call to the post and they all started running up West Third Street. Lamb's committee peeled off at St. Clair Ave. and about 20 of them adjourned to the bar of the Hawley House, a turn-of-the-century hotel that was patronized mostly by panhandlers and the homeless. All of Lamb's committee members were his drinking buddies, half a notch above panhandlers and the homeless.

Back to the book:

"Mike and I were following a van driven by my wife, loaded with emergency stuff, water, food, extra shoes, clothes, flashlights, bandages, etc. I told her we were going to cheat every once in a while. I planned to jump into the back seat every five miles and rest for a mile or so. But before our first five-mile marker, the van started to overheat. Oh yes, I forgot to mention that the van belonged to George Lamb. We did not see her again until forty miles down the road seven hours later! My cheating plan would not have worked anyway because Lamb had paid a deputy sheriff to follow me every inch of the road to Wooster.

"Local high school track runners would appear and run with us a few miles in nearly every town we passed through. We never slowed our pace.

"About forty-five miles and nine hours out, I started cramping and feeling a terrible pain in my neck, knees, ankles and feet. Bad, constant pain. The pain went from the top of my head to the bottoms of my feet. Everyone, including George, was now begging me to stop. He said he'd still give me the car. It was already a great effort. But, no, I was the Mule. I kept limping along.

"At 11 a.m., fourteen-and-a-half hours from when we started, Mike and I arrived at Wooster Maurer Field to a crowd of local cheerers. We waved and said thanks, but because of cramps and dehydration, I was put onto a stretcher by an emergency crew, slid into an ambulance and driven directly to the hospital. I had lost nearly thirty pounds. They fed me fluids intravenously for a couple of hours. As I rested, I had a big smile from ear to ear—I kept thinking, car, I hope you're ready to travel!"

Browns training camp opened four weeks later with a new head coach, Nick Skorich, and a new offensive line coach, Ray Prochaska. Skorich knew Schafrath well. He had been an assistant coach on the staff for seven years. But Skorich was impatient with the veterans. They stayed with Schafrath for half the season and then moved Dieken ahead of him. Schafrath's glorious football career was over. He was selected for seven Pro Bowls. He won a college national championship at Ohio State in 1957 and he was the starting left tackle on the Browns' 1964 championship team.

Nobody was more committed than Schafrath. Halfway through his career he looked for an edge. Performance enhancing drugs? Not a chance. Hypnosis? Yes. He went to a hypnotist to improve his concentration. The night before a game he could visualize every play and how he would block it. He introduced right tackle Monte Clark to hypnotism. They would sometimes have "booster" sessions with the hypnotist once or twice during the season.

He told me this while we were drinking one night in Pat Joyce's saloon downtown during the off-season. The next day I called him and said I wanted to write a story about his hypnosis.

"Please wait until I retire," Schafrath said. "Bill Nelsen will make life miserable for us if he finds out."

Nelsen was the quarterback and he had a playful personality, but sometimes it had a sharp, biting edge. With Nelsen leading the way, the razzing in the locker room would have been relentless.

When Schafrath retired several years later, I called him and asked about the hypnosis story. That was fine. We went over it again. I called Monte Clark and asked him if he wanted to participate. He was already retired and was an assistant coach with the Miami Dolphins.

"Please leave my name out," Clark said. "I want to be a head coach some day and club owners will think I'm some kind of a nut, going to a hypnotist."

I did not include Clark and he did become head coach of the Detroit Lions. It didn't last long. Nobody connected with the Detroit Lions in those days lasted long. I don't know if I did Clark a favor or not.

But now it was over. The halcyon days belonged to antiquity. There was a time, though, when everybody wanted Schafrath. When he was a senior at Wooster High School, the Cincinnati Reds tried to persuade him to sign a baseball contract. Ohio State football coach Woody Hayes sat in the kitchen of the Schafrath farmhouse with Schafrath's mother and father and romanced them. Blanton Collier, head coach at Kentucky at the time, sent an assistant coach to Wooster and told him not to return without Schafrath.

"The assistant coach checked into a hotel a few miles away and every day he would drive over to the farm and help my father with the chores. Finally my mother told him that if he was going to spend so much time there he should move into the house. We had a bedroom for him. And so he did. He stayed about a week," Schafrath told me many years ago.

"I felt obligated about that and told my mother I was going to call Blanton and tell him I was coming to Kentucky. She said I couldn't make that call until I called Woody and told him first. I couldn't do that, so I went to Ohio State."

He had not finished his studies when he was drafted by the Browns in 1960. He was selected in the second round, the 23rd pick in the entire draft. He never forgot his unfinished business at Ohio State, however. He had promised his mother that he would graduate from college, so he did. He got his degree on Aug. 27, 2006, at the age of 69. He earned a bachelor's degree in sports and leisure studies, a curriculum seemingly designed only for Dick Schafrath.

Dick said that Ohio State coach Jim Tressel put him on a football scholarship, but I don't think he meant that literally.

"I had tutors and four girls to type my papers on a computer," Dick said.

Let's put it this way. It was *like* being on scholarship.

In any event, I'm sure Dick's mother is happy.

I must say that he did very well without a degree. During his football days he worked in public relations with Joe Madigan, a well-known Cleveland PR man. He owned a canoe livery in Loudonville, Ohio. He entered Republican politics and was elected to the Ohio General Assembly as a state senator, an office he held for 14 years from 1986 to 2000. He could hold his head high. He was an honest politician. Asked about a controversial bill that had just been signed into law, he told a reporter from *The Plain Dealer*, "I'd say we just screwed the people in this state equally from both sides of the aisle."

He wrote a book.

He married four times and had seven children.

Here was one busy guy, but he always was drawn to the physical stuff. Besides the 62-mile run, he wrestled a bear and he paddled non-stop across Lake Erie in a canoe, after twice failing and almost going down in high waves.

The first attempt came with a disc jockey who was no help paddling. Sports announcer Casey Coleman was his partner on the second attempt.

"I'll never forget Casey sitting in the back of the canoe drinking a beer without a worry in the world while we sank three miles out. We had a rescue boat that saved us but we lost the canoe," Schafrath said.

After he underwent surgery for stomach and intestinal can-

Nobody was more committed than Dick Schafrath (front). His second attempt to paddle across Lake Erie ended when the canoe sank. He eventually made it on the third try. *(Cleveland Press Collection, Cleveland State University)*

cer, Schafrath made his third attempt at a Lake Erie crossing and that time he made it. The trip took an exhausting 17½ hours and Schafrath was taken to the hospital again.

Finally, having passed his 74th birthday, he wanted to make a mad dash across Ohio on a horse. Keep in mind that he almost died when he collapsed of heart failure in a parking lot back in 1986 and he's been on some form of life support ever since. His pacemaker fires so often he must have the battery replaced regularly.

I can think of only one way this saga will end. He will fall off his horse at the Indiana line, where George Lamb will be waiting for him with a cold beer.

Morrie Kono: 20-20 IQ

I don't know why, but there are more funny men in football than any other sport.

Maybe it's because there are more players on a football team than other sports. There are just more players from which to pick. Maybe it's because footballs have an odd shape and bounce funny.

Who's the funniest man in sports? Artie Donovan, the old pro football lineman.

Baseball has Bob Uecker, but Donovan is funnier.

Look at the Browns. Doug Dieken and George Ratterman were great practical jokers. The old coach Sam Rutigliano had a bottomless well of one-liners. Bob Golic actually went to Hollywood and became a comedic actor. Even Art Modell could do standup. Oddly, most fans don't know and don't even remember the funniest of them all—the Browns' equipment manager, Morrie Kono, who at five feet, six inches tall ran the locker room like a sultan for more than 30 years.

A beefy tackle once complained that his jersey was too small. "If it doesn't fit, stretch it," said Kono. Near the end of his reign, I wrote about King Kono and his locker room empire. Let's pick up the story that ran on Dec. 15, 1976, in *The Plain Dealer*.

In a world of behemoths, Kono remains a small gem. He is probably the only semi-retired equipment manager who is in demand as an after dinner speaker, frequently working as a tandem with Browns trainer Leo Murphy, an equally funny man.

A player once asked Kono for a shoestring.

"Which one, left or right?' demanded Kono.

The player looked down at his feet before answering.

Murphy picked up the next line. The player filled out a questionnaire. "What is your IQ?" was the question. The player wrote down, "20-20."

Kono tells of a player who was asked his shoe size. "Medium," said the player.

Kono was there when Paul Brown ordered every player on the team to drink a small bottle of a powerful laxative after practice at old League Park in the early 1950s.

"The whole team had been out drinking the night before and Paul heard about it. He wanted to clean out their systems," said Kono.

Kono was the first to recognize a bogus scouting report on the New York Giants.

"Paul Bixler asked George Ratterman to drop off his scouting report at the Stadium to have it typed," Kono recalled. "The next day at the team meeting they passed out mimeographed scouting reports that said things like, 'Can't pass while lying on back...wears face mask, has no teeth...if tackled, will not go all the way.'

"I knew right away who did it. Paul Bixler should have known better than to give the scouting report to Ratterman. George was a great quarterback, but he never played because we had Otto Graham. So he sat around all the time thinking up practical jokes.

"Ratterman sat next to Lou Groza on a plane once and all the time he told him how pigeons are the worst disease carriers in the world. Sunday morning when the players got dressed for the game, Groza found a dead pigeon in his helmet. Ratterman had been saving the pigeon for just the right time. It was probably decayed."

Kono spent his early years at the Jewish Orphan Home on Woodland Ave. He lived with his grandmother while attending Cunard Junior High and Central High School. He never married and he never learned to drive a car. During the Depression he held odd jobs. For two years he planted trees in the small Ohio town of Gallipolis for the Civilian Conservation Corps.

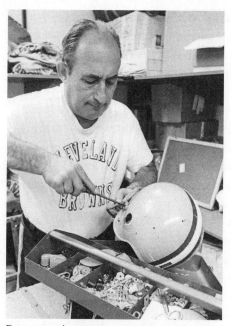

Browns equipment manager Morrie Kono
ran a tight ship. If it doesn't fit, "Stretch it,"
he said. *(Cleveland Press Collection, Cleveland
State University)*

Later he sold shoes for two years in Louisville, Kentucky. During World War II he was a supply sergeant in Indianapolis. After the war he worked for three months as a merchant seaman.

"My rank was ordinary seaman and I didn't want anything higher because I would have had to hang on the side of the boat and paint or climb up on the mast and paint. I never wanted to leave the deck. It was safer that way," Morrie said. He observed how the old salts did their laundry.

"They tied their laundry in a bundle and dragged it in the water behind the ship for an hour or so. I did that, but I lost all my clothes. I tied the wrong knot."

Most people think that Kono was the first equipment manager of the Browns, but he says that is not technically correct.

"I was the second equipment manager," he pointed out.

"The first one was a midget named Tommy Flynn. When he was unloading our first shipment of shoulder pads, he kept falling in the box and Wally Bock, our first trainer, had to keep helping him out. On the second day Bock called Paul Brown and told him he wasn't getting anything done. He spent all his time pulling Flynn out of boxes."

Because of his experience with shoes and Army uniforms, Kono was hired by Paul Brown as the second equipment manager. Kono got the job by default. "They made Flynn the mascot," said Morrie. "The players would put him up on the bar and he'd tap dance."

Flynn was an odd mascot. He certainly was no good humor man. His nephew, Ed Doubrava of Fairview Park, Ohio, told me that Flynn was the surliest, most mean-spirited midget he ever knew. Tommy did not last long with the Browns. Let's say he had a short career in pro football.

"Those were the days," Kono continued. "We had 33 players and usually four of them would be in the hospital. I'd have to hold the blocking dummy in practice. When I wasn't holding the blocking dummy, I was holding Don Colo's teeth. In the middle of a game he'd forget he was still wearing his teeth. I'd have to hold them. Chubby Grigg once said, 'Morrie, hold this for me.' I put out my hand. I thought he was handing me his teeth. He put his wad of chewing tobacco in my hand."

In the old days, said Kono, the players wanted to play football and have fun. Today they want to play football and make money. Kono figures he's one of the few guys left with a sense of humor and no money.

When Morrie died, he had a wealth of friends.

Creighton Miller:
Notre Dame's Free Spirit

When Creighton Miller came out of prep school in Delaware in the early 1940s, he was an acclaimed football player and he was expected to accept a football scholarship to Notre Dame. That was the family tradition. The name Miller was synonymous with Notre Dame football. His uncles and cousins all played there. His uncle, Don C. Miller, one of the Four Horsemen of Notre Dame, the most famous backfield in football history, became the United States District Attorney in Cleveland and later a Federal Bankruptcy Referee. Another uncle, Ray T. Miller, became Mayor of Cleveland. The list goes on.

But Creighton declined the scholarship. He would play football at Notre Dame, but not on scholarship. His father could easily afford to pay the tuition and there were many advantages to that. He could play on his terms, not on coach Frank Leahy's terms.

Creighton was the ultimate free spirit, a completely independent man. Before Frank Sinatra even thought about it, Creighton Miller did it his way. He had a particular distaste for spring football practice and Leahy could be a madman in the spring.

"Football is a fall sport," Creighton insisted. "In the spring I liked to play golf and go over to St. Mary's College and visit the girls. Frank got very annoyed with me and for a long time I wasn't very popular with him."

Creighton claimed that in four springs at Notre Dame he participated in not one day of spring football practice.

"Angelo Bertelli used to say that Leahy's spring practices made the Marine Corps training center at Parris Island look like a rest home, but, of course, I wouldn't know first hand," he said.

Had Creighton been an ordinary athlete, easily replaceable on Notre Dame's talent-rich squad, Leahy probably would have cut him loose. But Miller was gifted. He was the leading rusher and leading scorer on Notre Dame's 1943 national championship team. That year he was an All-American and finished fourth in the Heisman Trophy voting.

"Creighton had the quickest first step of anybody I ever saw," said George Connor, another Notre Dame All-American of that era. "He also had the quickest second and third steps."

In November 1943, Leahy, a chronic worrier, feared that prayer was Notre Dame's only hope against unbeaten Iowa Pre-Flight, a military team that was loaded with college stars and pros. During World War II, some of college football's best teams weren't college teams at all. They were military training bases. In 1943, four military bases finished in the AP wire service top 10. In addition, the Naval Academy was fourth and the Military Academy was 11th.

After Friday's practice, Leahy told the team to assemble early the next morning for a visit to Knute Rockne's grave. Everybody groaned. They knew the routine. They would wake up early and assemble at the stadium for a short bus trip to a cemetery near campus to pray the rosary at the grave of the legendary Notre Dame coach. It was late November and it was cold.

On an earlier trip to Rockne's grave, Creighton had wandered away from the group as Leahy led them in the Sorrowful Mysteries of the rosary. In between Hail Marys, Leahy realized his star halfback was missing.

"Miller! Miller, where are you?" Leahy called out.

"I'm over here saying a prayer at George Keogan's grave," Creighton yelled back.

Keogan, an old Notre Dame basketball coach who had died only a few months earlier, was buried a few plots away from Rockne.

"Never mind Coach Keogan," Leahy said. "We'll pray for him during basketball season."

On the morning of Nov. 20, 1943, Creighton prayed for nobody. He turned off his alarm clock and slept until it was time to report to the locker room for the normal pre-game ritual. Naturally, everybody else was already there, all prayed out.

"Leahy's mad as hell that you weren't at Rockne's grave. You better have a good excuse," Creighton's teammates warned him.

In Leahy's view, skipping the rosary at Rockne's grave marked Miller not only as insubordinate, but also as a heretic.

Creighton's mind worked almost as fast as his feet. He went directly to the coach and unfolded the story of an anguished night.

"I couldn't sleep all night," he began. "I heard the church clock strike midnight. Then I heard it strike one, two and three. I finally fell asleep about six o'clock this morning. When my alarm went off, I had to make a decision. I wanted to go to Rockne's grave, but I had to consider what's best for the team. I thought you would want me to get whatever rest I could get."

"Good lad," said Leahy.

By the way," said Creighton. "What did you do at Rockne's grave?"

"Oh, we just said a couple of Hail Marys," said Leahy.

Notre Dame squeezed past Iowa Pre-Flight that day, 14-13, behind a well-rested Creighton Miller.

An early tee time is one of the few things Creighton would set his alarm for on Saturday mornings. He often told the story of missing breakfast on the morning of Notre Dame's game against Northwestern in Evanston. Just before the kickoff his hunger pangs became unbearable. No one noticed when he slipped out of the locker room into a crowded concourse of Dyche Stadium to find a concession stand. On his return, however, locating the unmarked locker room door was more difficult than finding the end zone. He meandered aimlessly through the busy concourses of an unfamiliar stadium.

"There I was, wandering around in my football uniform eating a hot dog, when Father Cavanaugh came along," Creighton related.

Reverend John Cavanaugh, C.S.C., was the president of Notre Dame. The president of Northwestern accompanied him.

"See what I was telling you at lunch," Father Cavanaugh supposedly said to his Northwestern counterpart. "We're expected to win today and I don't know how. There's our star player and he can't even find his own locker room."

While Creighton was unorthodox, impish and high-spirited, he also was enigmatic and contrary. Unlike players today, whose touchdown celebrations resemble theatrical productions, Creighton decided to eliminate any show of emotion. The night before Notre Dame played Navy at Cleveland Stadium on Oct. 30, 1943, he confided to his road roommates, Angelo Bertelli and Johnny Lujack, that he would introduce an energy saving method of scoring if he crossed the goal line the next day.

In the darkness of their hotel room in the Hotel Carter on Prospect Ave. in downtown Cleveland, Creighton said that instead of running through the end zone and beyond, which was the custom in those days, he would step one yard into the end zone and stop. He would hand the ball or toss it to the nearest official.

With Notre Dame leading, 6-0, in the first quarter, Bertelli connected with Creighton on a pass in the right flat. Creighton trampled the first Navy tackler and then broke loose from three others and hurtled unimpeded toward the end zone while his relatives and friends in the crowd of 77,900 cheered wildly.

But suddenly and inexplicably he stopped on the 5-yard line, mistaking it for the goal line. Creighton turned his head and watched as a Navy defender lumbered toward him at ramming speed. The Stadium shuddered at the impact and the force knocked Creighton the remaining five yards across the goal line for the touchdown, sparing him Leahy's wrath and eternal ridicule.

*   *   *

Creighton was not the only creative genius in the Miller family and he was not necessarily the best storyteller.

"That would be my uncle Walter," Creighton pointed out.

Walter Miller was the "other" halfback from 1915 to 1919 in the backfields that featured George Gipp.

Shortly after graduation and while still living at home, his mother sent him to the store for a dozen eggs. He returned two years later after a sojourn around the world as a circus acrobat and was roundly scolded because he forgot the eggs.

Later travels took him south of the border, where he became engaged to the daughter of the president of Mexico, but they did not marry.

Walter Miller also was a wonderful storyteller. The head of the duPont family once offered to pay him $100,000 a year to stay around and entertain them with his outrageous yarns. In the 1920s, that was more than the president of the United States made. Walter Miller, however, was actually worth the money. But Walter declined and became a lawyer for the East Ohio Gas Company.

"Uncle Walter's greatest accomplishment was teaching his parakeet to sing the Notre Dame Victory March," Creighton claimed.

Until then Walter didn't even like birds. The parakeet belonged to his wife. Walter didn't marry until he was in his fifties and he believed that when he pledged love and loyalty to his wife, the package included any other living creatures that were important to her. Teaching the bird to sing the Notre Dame Victory March became his number one project. Perhaps his interest in animal acts dated back to his days in the circus.

"Teaching him the words was easy," Creighton said, repeating the accepted version of the family legend, "but he had a hard time teaching him the tune. The parakeet was tone deaf. Eventually, though, the parakeet would sit on my uncle's shoulder while he was shaving in the morning and sing the Victory March."

Fortunately for Walter, his wife didn't have a pony.

"They let him fly free around his apartment all the time. They even let him fly around the hallways in their building, which made their neighbors nervous. They didn't like the bird at all and for good reason. It's easier to teach a bird to sing the Notre Dame Victory March than to housebreak one.

"The neighbors knew that whenever my uncle and aunt went away for a weekend, they let the bird fly free around their apartment. They also knew one thing that drove the bird crazy. He hated the doorbell. The phone didn't bother him. But when the doorbell rang, he would fly around in concentric circles, chasing himself.

"One weekend the neighbors took turns ringing the doorbell until the bird went crazy and committed suicide by smashing his head repeatedly against the doorbell chimes. At least, that is what my aunt and uncle assumed. They found his body on the floor below the chimes."

Creighton sat back in his chair at table 14 of the Pewter Mug and lit up a cigar, indicating that the story was over.

"Not everybody buys the suicide story," Creighton added. "Uncle Walter's wife thought it was murder and she pinned the rap on the Avon lady."

*   *   *

As a lawyer he moved to Cleveland and specialized in maritime law, representing George Steinbrenner's American Shipbuilding Company. He also helped organize the National Football League players' union and was its first legal counsel. In 1976, he was inducted into the College Football Hall of Fame. He was an outstanding amateur golfer, winning the club championship at Shaker Country Club seven times. He drank only beer and he smoked cigars. He lived to the age of 80 and never married. Why would he? His Saturdays were reserved for football, golf and his cronies.

Creighton was in law school when Cleveland Browns founder and owner Mickey McBride asked him to help put together the team that would debut two years later in the All-American Football Conference. McBride's son, Artie, was a classmate of Creighton's at Notre Dame and urged his father to bring Creighton into the organization.

"Mickey McBride said he would pay me three hundred dollars a month to help him scout and sign players for the team that would start playing in 1946. I told him I couldn't possibly be worth three hundred dollars a month because I would be going to law school and helping coach the Yale football team," said Creighton.

"Maybe he liked my candor because he said, 'Then we'll make it a hundred bucks a week for fifty-two weeks—fifty-two hundred a year.' I took it. I was getting thirty-five hundred a year to coach the Yale backfield and they paid my tuition to law school, so the total offer matched the best offer from the New York Giants, which was ten thousand. That was pretty good for a kid just out of college in those days."

As the first employee of the Cleveland Browns, Miller made the initial overture to Paul Brown, who became the team's first head coach. Naturally, the name of Notre Dame coach Frank Leahy came up, probably suggested by Artie McBride, but Creighton knew that Leahy's marine drill sergeant style would not work with professional players, especially the service veterans just returning from World War II.

Creighton remained with the Browns as an assistant coach in 1946 and as the team's legal counsel until 1953 when McBride sold the team to a group of Cleveland businessmen who a few years later sold the team to Art Modell.

In 1956, Miller became the first legal counsel for the National Football League Players' Association, which infuriated Paul Brown. The first union meeting was held in Hall of Fame wide receiver Dante Lavelli's basement on Westover Ave. in Rocky River with his Browns teammates Abe Gibron and George Ratterman. Further meetings moved to Creighton's office downtown in the Hanna Building.

Some years later it was observed that Creighton had been

erased from the 1946 team picture that hung on the wall of Paul Brown's office in the Stadium. Brown ordered general manager Harold Sauerbrei to have a touch up artist paint out Creighton, which was easy to do because he was standing on the end of a row. However, it took some artistic skill to fill in the space by painting in the arm of equipment manager Morrie Kono, who was standing next to Creighton in the picture. The touch up artist was good, but not that good. Another copy of the same picture was displayed in the Cleveland Athletic Club, a picture that included Creighton standing on the end of the row with Morrie Kono and the coaches.

"I learned a big lesson from that," said Creighton. "Never stand on the end in a team picture. It's too easy for them to erase you."

Creighton was involved in football for many years after graduating from Notre Dame in 1943, but not as a player. He was drafted by the New York Giants, but eschewed pro football for Yale Law School.

Come to Miami, Bring a Gun

Never quit one job until you have another one. It's just common sense. Well, I violated that rule and I paid dearly. I paid for a house twice.

When Channel 8 launched its first morning news show in 1988, I was the first sports anchor. It was a one-hour show, from 6 a.m. to 7 a.m., with a basic format that mirrored the evening news show, a tried and true template. Denise Dufala and Ric Young were the news anchors, Andre Bernier was brought in as the weatherman and I was the sports guy. I had never done much anchoring. It was good training to develop confidence, poise and an easy delivery. I'm not saying I mastered all those things, but it was good practice. Why, however, did we do this at six o'clock in the morning?

"That was the year we were continually tired. It was torture," recalled Mark Schroeder, who produced my little sports segment and later replaced me as the morning sports anchor.

Mark arrived at the station by three o'clock each morning. I got there a few minutes later. There was a time in my life when I would come home at 3 a.m. Keep in mind that I spent most of my life until then working nights for a morning newspaper. When I wasn't at the paper, I was either at games or in bars. There are morning people and there are night people and I always was a night person. It's like golf and softball. Golf is a morning sport; softball is a night game.

"I remember some mornings when we would get off the air at seven o'clock and by 7:30 we'd start drinking at the Headliner bar," Schroeder said. "On St. Patrick's Day you were so loaded, you were directing traffic at East Ninth and St. Clair Avenue at five o'clock in the afternoon. The next morning Bob Kovach called your house about four o'clock and he was screaming into the phone, 'Dan, wake up!' The entire newsroom was watching. You seemed to answer but you kept falling back asleep. Maddy finally picked up the phone from the floor and she got you up somehow. You had one of your all-time funniest shows that morning."

I can deny none of that. I also cannot remember any of it.

Walt Geary, a retired Lakewood policeman, says he stopped me for a broken headlight every morning for a week. At three o'clock in the morning it's not easy to tell the difference between a guy driving to work and a drunk driving home from a bar.

On the other side of town it was the same for Schroeder.

"The Solon police were always stopping me," he said. "They thought anybody out at that hour was up to no good."

That's the way it is with night people who work mornings. Their lives are backwards. Jim Runyon, a popular morning man on old KYW radio (1100), got off the air at 10 o'clock and went directly to Pat Joyce's Tavern, which was only a block away, and started drinking.

"At eleven o'clock in the morning you loved him," said bartender Walter Kulon. "By one o'clock you hated him."

I was still writing two columns a week in the *Elyria Chronicle-Telegram* and *Medina Gazette* and I was trying to keep up with the Cavs and Indians. I was getting three or four hours of sleep and I was feeling sorry for myself. For most of my life I never set my alarm clock. I would sleep until I was no longer tired. Now the alarm ruled my life. I dreaded the sound of it every morning.

When the end of 1988 arrived I refused to sign a new contract.

"I'll do anything you want," I said to general manager Virgil Dominic. "I'll clean the bathrooms and shovel the snow. But, please, take me off the morning show."

"That's the only job we have for you," he said.

At home the kids were little and I was constantly cranky. This wasn't working. So I signed off the morning show. As Edward R. Murrow said, "Goodbye and good luck."

At the time, both Channels 3 and 5 were looking for daytime sports reporters and weekend anchors. I could solve either of their needs. Neither one returned my phone calls. So I took a temporary job as the publicist at Thistledown Racetrack for three months and then went to UPI, the wire service, as their Cleveland bureau sports reporter. These were not high-paying jobs.

In the meantime, I hooked up with two bright young lawyers, David Shall and Brad Weiss, who conceived a weekly TV sports panel show. It was called "Let's Talk Sports" and featured newspaper sports writers sitting around a table discussing and debating the issues of the day. We did that every day at the Headliner saloon. It would be nice to be paid for it. David and Brad were shopping the show around the state. The concept was to syndicate it in every TV market in the state. I needed that job. I worked closely with them. We drove from city to city, pitching it to television executives. We covered the state and one by one we signed up stations.

But we needed a lead sponsor. John Conway, whose company had exclusive rights to distribute Miller Lite in the Cleveland area, was interested. His vice president, Mike Brown, helped us try to land Miller Lite, but they never signed on. By midsummer, the show was not yet on the air, so I accepted an offer from the CBS-owned-and-operated TV station in Miami.

Steve Lefkowitz, an agent in New York, had taken me on. He had been shipping my tapes around the country and he hit the jackpot with WCIX (Channel 6) in Miami. It had been a sleepy little independent with a single 10 p.m. newscast and a bad signal before CBS bought it in late 1988. CBS changed everything. The Tiffany network added an hour of news at six and turned the 10 o'clock news into half an hour at 11 p.m. I was the new main sports anchor.

One of the people I worked with in Miami was news anchor John Hambrick, who had ruled Cleveland television in the 1970s as the Channel 5 news anchor. What a worker! Because of the Cuban influence almost everybody in Miami was bilingual. Ham-

brick learned Spanish and spoke it fluently. He anchored. He
went out on the streets and did stories. He was a great inspira-
tion.

After the 11 o'clock show on Friday nights, John and I would
sit around my sports area drinking beer that I kept in a small
refrigerator under my desk. He had left Cleveland for big-time
anchor positions in New York and Los Angeles before winding
up in Miami.

"I made a lot of money in this business but I only had one success," he said, referring to his glory years in Cleveland when he
dominated the ratings.

"Other than money, why did you leave?" I asked him.

"Because every day I would drive down Chester Ave. from
Shaker Heights and I never saw the sun," said the tall Texan. "It
got to me. It was depressing."

The sun had nothing to do with the Coughlin family moving
to Miami. Maddy did not want to go. The four kids did not want
to go. Nobody connected to us wanted us to leave. When we got
to Miami, everybody there wanted us to go back. The viewers
hated me. They were accustomed to smooth professionals. For
instance, another one of our news anchors was John Roberts,
who later went to the CBS network and was a leading candidate
to replace Dan Rather.

Another of our anchors was the beautiful Giselle Fernandez,
who went on become a star reporter and weekend anchor for
both CBS and NBC and to host "Access Hollywood."

Me, I was Cleveland clumsy. Miami had no idea what I was
about.

One of the papers mentioned that I went to Notre Dame and
that touched a nerve. Miami football fans hated Notre Dame and
everything associated with it. It wasn't a football rivalry, it was
a war and it was personal. When Miami visited Notre Dame in
1988, students walked around the South Bend campus wearing
tee shirts that read, "Catholics versus Convicts." Notre Dame officials attempted to suppress the tee shirt, but that was impossible.
It was too clever, it was too timely and it was a big seller.

Notre Dame played the Hurricanes in the Orange Bowl on Saturday of Thanksgiving weekend and my cousin Tommy Coughlin wanted four tickets. The game was sold out, but I told Tommy there shouldn't be a problem. After all, he had played for the Hurricanes. He was a three-year starter in the 1960s. Furthermore, the game was televised on CBS and I was working for CBS. We were business partners with the Hurricanes. It was early July when I arrived in Miami and my first get-acquainted visit was to the University of Miami sports information director.

"The only way you can buy tickets to the Notre Dame game is by buying season tickets," I was told.

Notre Dame was the only game on Miami's home schedule that generated any interest. The Orange Bowl, where the Hurricanes played their home games, accommodated almost 75,000 and crowds of 30,000 for the other games were common. I could understand putting a premium on Notre Dame tickets, but I didn't understand doing it to your business partner. I never got the tickets for Tommy.

The relationship between the two schools had deteriorated so badly by 1989 that their rivalry was suspended for 20 years for safety reasons. I had never witnessed such an emotionally charged college rivalry. I wrote a letter to Notre Dame's sports information director Roger Valdiserri warning him that eventually somebody would get shot and killed at a Notre Dame-Miami game in the Orange Bowl.

It seemed that almost everybody in Miami packed a gun. They carried them everywhere. Many people had two guns—one at home and one in their car. The photographers even stored bulletproof vests in their equipment lockers for covering race riots. One night after the 11 o'clock news show, we heard a gunshot in the parking lot behind the station. One of the engineers shot himself in the leg when the gun he kept in his pocket went off as he was getting into his car. It was only a flesh wound. That happened Friday. He was back to work on Monday.

Some co-workers expressed surprise that I did not own a gun—not even one. With three boys and a daughter at home—all under the age of ten—hiding a gun around the house was an invitation to disaster. I knew that from personal experience. When I was a kid, my grandmother, who lived with us, was a United States deputy marshal and she packed a pistol, a .22 caliber women's special. She never loaded it but she usually kept three loose bullets in her purse. Naturally, I found the gun. I could almost field strip it. I sneaked it out of the house to play cops and robbers or cowboys and Indians with my friends on the street. At last one of the other mothers called our house and said, "Your son, Dan, seems to be playing with a real gun. That can't be true, is it?"

When confronted, I thought I could reassure everyone." Yeah, but I never loaded it," I said.

That was the end of my pistol-packing days.

I wasn't going to repeat that experience in Miami. My kids would have loaded the damn thing.

I kept telling Maddy and the kids to look at Miami as an adventure. My old sports editor boss Hal Lebovitz liked to say that life was full of adventures. Pity the poor soul who never had an adventure. I didn't know how long we would be there, probably a year or two. We actually considered keeping our house in Lakewood and renting a house in Miami. Ultimately, we decided to sell our old house and buy a new one in Miami.

Every morning while we were in Miami, Maddy went to the eight o'clock Mass at Our Lady of the Lakes church and prayed to get us out of Miami. Dolphins coach Don Shula was at the same Mass every morning. Guess whose prayers were answered.

Shula never returned to the Super Bowl, but nine months after moving to Miami, we had the chance to return home. I landed the Indians' broadcasting job with Rick Manning on SportsChannel for the 1990 season. Management at WCIX-TV was happy to release me from my contract. They picked the wrong guy.

Things quickly fell into place back home. David Shall and Brad Weiss had "Let's Talk Sports" on the air in five Ohio cities. I slid in as the host. I had my two newspapers twice a week. In the fall, Channel 8 news director Phyllis Quail asked me to come back three days a week to help cover the Browns. When the Browns' season ended, I kept coming to work three days a week. It eventually became five days a week and later I signed another fulltime, three-year contract. Sometimes I filled in on the morning show, but not very often.

We were able to sell our house in Miami and we bought a new house in Rocky River. Our house payments were about the same as they had been before. Our original house in Lakewood with a 15-year mortgage would have been paid off in 1998. At that time I still had 23 years to go on our house in Rocky River. Essentially, I was paying for a house twice. It was an expensive adventure. But at least nobody got shot.

Cousin Tommy Coughlin: Hurricane Warnings

For a year after my first book came out, I was inundated with suggestions for characters in my next book. One name kept recurring. Well, this is my next book and the runaway winner is my cousin, Tommy Coughlin.

I feel like Homer when he sat down to write *The Odyssey*. Where do you begin?

Cousin Tommy made several fortunes and each time he hit the jackpot he ran it like a charitable foundation. Everybody benefited. He had several businesses, including two bars, the first in Rocky River where Pat Dailey performed for several years. Dailey even wrote a song about Tommy. It was called, "Get Your Ass to Cleveland," and it has this line: "Now, the first time that I came here, I was hungry, broke and tired. Then I worked for Tommy Coughlin and I left there stoned and wired."

Tommy's second bar, which was on West 117th Street in Cleveland, burned down within a year of opening. Tommy got the call in the middle of the night.

"It looks like a total loss," said the battalion chief. "It will be a big number on your insurance claim."

"What insurance?" said Tommy.

He made a career of bouncing back. His fortunes kept getting bigger and so did the giveaways. Coughlin Field at St. Edward High School is named after him.

*   *   *

He was one of the best athletes in the history of St. Ed's. In late February of 1962, Notre Dame invited him to South Bend, Ind., on a recruiting visit, which turned into the most bizarre recruiting trip ever at Notre Dame. The lives of everyone directly involved in Cousin Tommy's visit were adversely affected, beginning with Ken Maglicic, a freshman football player from St. Joseph High School in Cleveland. When Cousin Tommy's visit was scheduled, freshman coach Hugh Devore called Maglicic.

"You played against him in high school. Will you escort him around?" said Devore.

Maglicic gladly accepted because hosts were usually given a few dollars to entertain the recruit and some left over coins often found their way into the host's pocket.

Maglicic's roommate on the fourth floor of Cavanaugh Hall was Tony Carey, another freshman football player. Carey was from Chicago and he wanted to go home that weekend to see his high school, Mount Carmel, play in a tournament basketball game. Going home to Chicago after his last class on Saturday morning was no problem, but the game was on Friday night and that was a problem. In order to leave on Friday, Tony needed a letter from his parents granting him permission to miss his Saturday class and Tony knew they would not write such a letter. Tony was the youngest in a large, wealthy, Irish-Catholic family. His father was very strict. In many large families, by the time the youngest child comes along the parents are worn down and anything goes. Not so with the Carey family. They didn't cut corners or take short steps. Tony's father owned Hawthorne Racetrack and a brick factory and headed a law firm.

"I have an idea," Carey said to Maglicic. "Take that high school recruit and have him sleep in my bed Friday night. They'll never know I'm gone."

Maglicic agreed that it was a good idea. After his last class on Friday, Carey rode the South Shore Railroad to Chicago. He went to the game and slept at a friend's house. Saturday he went home as though he had just come in for a normal weekend visit.

Nothing about that weekend was normal.

Maglicic told coach Devore that he would keep the incoming recruit under his protective wing. Instead of putting him in a room at the Morris Inn, Maglicic said the recruit would sleep in his very room in Cavanaugh Hall, in the bed vacated by Carey. That was fine with Devore. He didn't know why Carey's bed was vacant. He didn't care where anybody slept. He was a football coach, not a concierge.

Cousin Tommy and Maglicic were not acquainted, but they were aware of each other. By the end of the night they had forged a firm friendship.

According to the policy at the time, Devore gave Maglicic a few dollars to take Cousin Tommy downtown for a movie and a milk shake at the Philadelphia, the ice cream parlor at the downtown bus stop. For decades Notre Dame guys would take St. Mary's girls to the Philadelphia for hot fudge sundaes. What could go wrong?

Maglicic rounded up some freshman football friends to help him entertain the recruit. Hot fudge was not on the menu. Off they went to Guisseppe's, a popular pizza joint.

"We'll buy him a quart of beer and he'll be fine the rest of the night. We'll pocket the rest of the money," Maglicic told his friends.

Maglicic drank his quart and got up to get another.

"Get me one, too," said Tommy, who had already finished and was waiting for Maglicic to catch up.

Years later, Maglicic attempted to recreate the events. Calculus class was easier.

"By the end of the evening he had about five quarts and so did I. We took the bus back to the Circle and signed in just before midnight. Tommy was supposed to sign Tony Carey's name. Tony always printed his name. I had shown Tommy a sample of Tony's printing. I signed my name. I didn't even look to see how Tommy signed in. I was just hoping he could print the name."

Apparently the sign-in process did not go well. In those days, each night at 10 o'clock all the dormitory doors were locked except one, where a security guard sat at a small wooden table with a sign-in sheet. At midnight the security guard locked the last door, gathered up the sign-in sheet and slipped it under the rector's door. On this Friday night the security guard knocked on the rector's door.

"We've got a problem here," the security guard said to Father Geuiss, the rector.

Half an hour later, Father Geuiss was pounding on Maglicic's door. Maglicic's head was spinning, but he got up and opened the door for the priest who stormed into the room in a rage. Father Geuiss looked around the room and surveyed the situation. He looked at Carey's bed and said, "Who's that? What's your name?"

"Tom Coughlin," said Cousin Tommy.

"Where you from?"

"St. Ed's."

"What are you doing here? That's St. Ed's," Geuiss said, pointing out the window toward St. Edward Hall, another residence hall a short walk from Cavanaugh.

"That's in Cleveland, Ohio," Cousin Tommy said.

"Don't get smart with me. Go back to St. Ed's."

"I can't go back to Cleveland in the middle of the night," said Cousin Tommy.

Father Geuiss was one confused priest, but he caught up quickly the next morning. He spent most of the morning on the phone. One call went to Chicago, to the Carey family. Another went to Father Collins, the prefect of discipline. A third went to head football coach Joe Kuharich, who told his number one assistant, Hugh Devore, to go over to Cavanaugh Hall and find out what the hell was going on there.

One assistant coach hustled Tommy out of there. He took him to breakfast and gave him a tour of the facilities. Devore and Maglicic huddled in the hallway outside the rector's office.

"What'd you tell him?" said Devore.

"I told him everything," said Maglicic.

"That was stupid, stupid, stupid, stupid, stupid, stupid, stupid," said Devore, who thought that was stupid.

"Let me tell you about this place," Devore continued. "The only place you plead guilty is in the confessional." Devore paused and then said, "and don't be so sure about that, either."

Maglicic waited in the hallway when Devore entered the rector's office to negotiate a peaceful settlement. Father Geuiss wasn't in a peaceful mood. He was still grumpy and a loud argument ensued. The shouting could be heard halfway down the hall.

Monday a formal hearing was held in the Administration Building, beneath the protection of Our Lady atop the Golden Dome.

Carey was suspended from school for the rest of the semester and sent home to Chicago.

Maglicic was restricted to campus for the rest of the semester. He was not even permitted to go to the Philadelphia for a vanilla milk shake.

Cousin Tommy was offered a full football scholarship to Notre Dame, which he accepted. There were some crazy people there, he acknowledged, but he liked Guisseppe's.

*   *   *

The next week Cousin Tommy got a call from the University of Miami in Coral Gables, Florida. They wanted to fly him down for a visit. His father was furious.

"You can't go. You told Notre Dame you were going there," said his father, Frank Coughlin who, like most Irishmen, was a big Notre Dame fan.

"I'd like to take the trip. I've never been on a plane and I've never been to Miami," said Cousin Tommy. There was no stopping him.

When Tommy got there, it was early March and the temperature was 70 degrees. People were on the beaches getting suntans. The weather was hot and the bars were cool. Tommy accepted Miami's scholarship offer.

"But the reason I went there was that they said I could play quarterback. Everybody else said I was an end. I always wanted to play quarterback. They didn't tell me that they already had a quarterback, George Mira, and he was All-America the previous season."

Cousin Tommy was a starting tight end for three years and sometimes he played defensive end. He was drafted in both pro leagues but he had played enough football. He hung up his cleats. There were other worlds to conquer.

Tommy says his father never forgave him for not going to Notre Dame. Like most Irish, he could carry a grudge. Nevertheless, he supported his son and traveled to many Miami games. When Miami played Georgia Tech in Atlanta, Frank Coughlin was there, leaning against the end zone fence loudly rooting for the Hurricanes.

Mira was calling the play in the huddle when he stopped and stared toward the end zone.

"Hey, Coughlin, isn't that your father down there?" said Mira.

Cousin Tommy turned his head just as Georgia State Troopers, one on each arm, escorted his father toward the exit.

* * *

The years passed and life was a never-ending party. Cousin Tommy had a magnetic personality. Everyone wanted to be around him.

"Didn't we have good times?" Cousin Tommy mused one day last summer. It looks like a question but it really was a statement.

For reasons that are lost in antiquity, sports agent Ed Keating lured Cousin Tommy to Keating's hometown of Atlantic City along with two of Cousin Tommy's friends, Tom Gallagher, a financial whiz from Chicago, and Tom Kelly, an author and humorist from Lakewood.

Keating took them to breakfast in one of his favorite neighborhood bars. Cousin Tommy and Gallagher sat at one table. Keating was at the bar talking to the bartender. Tom Kelly was off by himself in the corner reading the paper.

Gallagher, an old Indiana University lineman, held a seat on the Chicago Commodities Exchange. He was a big man who always did things in a big way. When he discovered that in Atlantic City you could buy tickets for almost every state lottery in the country, he bought 100 one-dollar tickets on the Illinois Lottery.

Gallagher had them in a stack more than two inches thick and he began to spread them on the table, as though to somehow sort them. Tickets were everywhere.

Cousin Tommy glanced down and caught the numbers on one of Gallagher's tickets. He wrote them down on a scrap of paper, got up, walked over to Tom Kelly and slipped him the numbers. He then rejoined Gallagher, who was still preoccupied with his tickets.

"Hey, Tom," Cousin Tommy called to Tom Kelly. "Are the lottery results in the paper?"

"I'll take a look," said Kelly. "Yeah, here they are."

"What are the winning numbers?" asked Cousin Tommy. "Read them off."

Kelly spontaneously added a perverse wrinkle to the drama. He read the New York Lottery winning numbers.

Gallagher glanced at each ticket, one at a time, tossing the non-winners on the floor. He asked Kelly to repeat the number several times. Nothing. Nothing. Nothing.

"Oh, wait a minute," said Kelly. "These are the New York Lottery numbers. You want the Illinois numbers, don't you?" said Kelly.

"Illinois. Yes. Yes. Illinois," Gallagher said impatiently. He got down on his hands and knees and began picking up all the tickets he had discarded.

This time Kelly read the numbers Cousin Tommy had given him. Gallagher repeated the exercise. He glanced at each ticket and flipped the non-winners on the floor. At last he stopped.

"What was the number again?" said Gallagher. His tone was particularly serious.

Kelly read it again.

"These are the Illinois numbers, right?" said Gallagher.

"Yeah, Illinois," said Kelly.

Gallagher looked at his lottery ticket. He looked back at Kelly.

"I won," said Gallagher.

To be certain, Kelly read the numbers again.

"I've got it. Those are my numbers," said Gallagher, who then began making phone calls to share his good fortune with his family, friends and co-workers. The jackpot was $5 million. Even for a big time commodities trader, that was a lot of money.

They all returned home that day. Keating, Tom Kelly and Cousin Tommy flew home to Cleveland. Tom Gallagher flew home to Chicago, where he looked up the number of the Illinois Lottery Commission and asked where he should go to get his money. They told him where to go.

Several months passed when Gallagher called Cousin Tommy and told him he was coming to Cleveland.

"Can you pick me up at the airport?" Gallagher asked. He gave Cousin Tommy his flight information.

The day arrived and Cousin Tommy was there. He drove around and around, as we had to do at Hopkins Airport in the days before the cell phone lot. Finally, thinking Gallagher was having problems at baggage claim, he parked in the pickup area and went inside to look for him. He wasn't gone long but when he returned, there was a ticket on his car.

"Well, what the hell?" Cousin Tommy thought to himself. "I already have a ticket. No reason to rush."

He began a more intensive search of Hopkins Airport for Tom Gallagher. Inspectors Columbo, Clouseau and Poirot wouldn't have found him. Gallagher never left Chicago. When Cousin Tommy reached him on the phone, all Gallagher said was, "Happy April Fool's."

When Cousin Tommy returned to his car, the tow truck was backing into position to hook him up.

Exactly a year later the situation was reversed. Gallagher drove out to O'Hare Airport to pick up Cousin Tommy. When Gallagher was finished chasing his tail at the world's busiest airport, he reached Tommy on the phone.

"Happy April Fool's Day," said Tommy.

Gallagher almost gave himself a concussion when he slapped himself on the side of the head.

"I must be the dumbest Irishman in Chicago," Gallagher said.

Brian Dowling:
A Living Legend

Brian Dowling is the biggest folk hero in Cleveland high school football history.

"How many people have been in the comic pages for 40 years?" he says with a chuckle, as though that explains everything.

Beetle Bailey, Charlie Brown and Dagwood come to mind, but not many others. Brian, however, is the only real person. Brian has been "BD" in the comic strip Doonesbury since Garry Trudeau began drawing it during their student days at Yale in the 1960s.

Brian also has been called the greatest high school football player from the Cleveland area. I haven't forgotten that four Heisman Trophy winners came from northeastern Ohio, namely Les Horvath (1944) from Rhodes, Vic Janowicz (1950) from Elyria, Desmond Howard (1991) from St. Joseph and Troy Smith (2007) from Glenville.

Some will insist that Robert Smith from Euclid was better than all of them. Pound for pound, O. J. McDuffie from Hawken School has his supporters. Navy quarterback Tom Forrestal from St. Ignatius was on the cover of *Life Magazine* when he made All-America in 1958. Tom Cousineau of St. Edward was the first player taken in the 1979 NFL draft. Harry Stuhldreher from Massillon was one of the Four Horsemen of Notre Dame.

A long list of Pro Football Hall of Famers from northeastern Ohio includes Big Bob Brown, East Tech; Larry Csonka, Stow; Lenny Dawson, Alliance; Dan Dierdorf, Canton Glenwood (now GlenOak); Benny Friedman, Glenville; Jack Lambert, Mantua Crestwood; Dante Lavelli, Hudson; Tom Mack, Cleveland Heights; Mike Michalske, Cleveland West Tech; Marion Motley,

Canton McKinley; Chuck Noll, Benedictine; Alan Page, Canton Central Catholic; and Don Shula, Painesville Harvey.

What I'm saying is that you should pick out a comfortable chair to discuss the greatest players who came from our neck of the woods because it will take all night.

At the National Football Foundation awards dinner in 2011, John Carroll University's young defensive coordinator Brian Cochran asked me about the greatest high school player I ever saw.

"Dowling," I said, and I itemized the reasons.

"No, I mean the modern era," he said.

For any era, the answer is still Dowling.

His charisma was responsible for drawing crowds of 37,673 and 41,183 for back-to-back Charity Games at the Stadium in 1963 and '64, the largest two-game totals since the 1940s. It was the last hurrah for that revered institution.

St. Ignatius and Benedictine met in the Charity Game for three years in a row from 1962-64. Ignatius had a record of 29-1 over those three years, the only loss coming in the 1963 Charity Game, a contest that lives in infamy and affected their rivalry forever.

Dowling was a junior when he succeeded the departed all-scholastic Ray Kubacki at quarterback in 1963. Kubacki went on to star at Harvard. In his first game as the starter, Dowling threw five touchdown passes, three to his cousin Mike Gaul and two to Jim Grace, in a 58-20 victory over a good Parma team before a standing-room throng of 12,000 at Byers Field. The Wildcats swept through nine opponents that season, averaging 35 points and 365 yards per game. Dowling threw for 1,100 yards and 16 touchdowns, 11 of them to his cousin. He also played safety and intercepted 11 enemy passes. He punted for a 35-yard average, although that was rarely necessary.

With St. Ignatius a heavy favorite in the Charity Game, Benedictine keyed on Dowling with unprecedented savagery. All-Ohio defensive end Jim Yacknow was especially vicious. Again and again, he smashed Dowling to the cold Stadium turf after he released a pass or after he handed off the ball. The referee kept his flag in his pocket, however.

"It wasn't illegal but it was unnecessary. It was borderline, especially after I handed off. It was obvious I didn't have the ball. That happened about four times," Dowling said earlier this year during our refresher interview for this chapter.

Yacknow left an impression on the St. Ignatius quarterback. Dowling suffered chipped bones in his spine and a bruised kidney in the first half, but he kept playing. On the last play of the first half, however, Dowling went down for the count. He couldn't get up. His collarbone was broken and he did not return in the second half. Benedictine walked off the field with a 30-16 victory and Dowling went directly to the hospital. He stayed for four days.

Yacknow, who caught a touchdown pass and blocked a punt in addition to the punishment he inflicted on Dowling, was named the game's Most Valuable Player. Ironically, he had nothing to do with the broken collarbone. Greg Betts reminded me that he made that tackle. Yacknow went to Notre Dame on a football scholarship but after two years signed a baseball contract with the Indians. He played in the minor leagues for a few years and then faded from sight.

The public was fascinated the following year when the Charity Game again matched St. Ignatius against Benedictine. A crowd of 41,183 turned out on a crisp, sunny Thanksgiving Day for Dowling's revenge. It was the biggest Charity Game crowd since 1948. Nobody from St. Ignatius turned the other cheek. The Sunday before the game I began my advance story in *The Plain Dealer* with a biblical quote: "'Vengeance is Mine; I will repay,' saith the Lord. Romans Chapter XII, Verse 19."

St. Ignatius was far superior in 1964. On the Wildcats' third play from scrimmage Dowling turned the corner and went 71 yards down the left sideline for their first touchdown, the first of seven.

"I always wanted to score on a long run. That was it. It was easy. I just ran down the sideline," Brian said not long ago.

Dowling ran for two touchdowns and passed for four. His last touchdown pass came with 57 seconds left and made the score, 48-6, the worst rout in Charity Game history. St. Ignatius coach

St. Ignatius quarterback Brian Dowling nurses a broken collarbone follow-ing the 1963 Charity Game against Benedictine. *(Cleveland Press Collection, Cleveland State University)*

John Wirtz wasn't satisfied. He wanted more. He called for an onside kick with a 42-point lead.

"We had practiced an onside kick all week," said Rick Rose, who was the Wildcats' placekicker and kickoff man. "I ran up to the ball slowly and it was actually Gary Andrachik who came up alongside me and kicked the ball. John Wirtz had read a book about kicking the top of the ball. It would take two bounces and bounce high in the air. That's exactly how it went. I was the one who recovered the ball."

Dowling trotted back onto the field with instructions to throw deep. He faded back to pass. He looked deep. It wasn't there so he scrambled under pressure and headed downfield. His path was clear. He had another touchdown just a few yards away when the referee blew his whistle. The play was dead. He ruled that Dowl-ing's forward progress was stopped in the backfield.

With half a minute left, Wirtz substituted for his starting quarterback. Wirtz made his point. Dowling played the entire game on offense and defense except for the last two plays. Seven St. Ignatius players went both ways, which was not unusual at the time. Today, hardly anybody plays both offense and defense on big time high school teams. At small schools, the best players almost always go both ways. They don't have depth. But not in the big time.

"No question he wanted revenge," Dowling said. "Wirtz could have pulled the starters but he didn't."

Up in the press box, Ohio State coach Woody Hayes observed the carnage and mentally salivated. Dowling stood six feet, three inches tall and had massive hands with big, bony fingers. Woody hungered to get him. In his career, Dowling threw 34 touchdown passes and intercepted 33 opposing passes, a state record that still stands. Everybody knew Woody's attitude about the forward pass, but he was starting to change. This quarterback could throw, but he could also run. Furthermore, if he never played quarterback, he could be an all-American safety. He also was a sensational basketball player, an all-scholastic guard. Dowling made 12 straight free throws in the fourth quarter against East High as the Wildcats won the city basketball championship before a crowd of 9,000 at the Cleveland Arena. Naturally, he was the MVP of the game. He also was an outstanding tournament tennis player. Everybody in his family played tennis.

Woody had to get him. Brian Dowling was to Ohio football what Middletown's Jerry Lucas was to basketball seven years earlier. Woody enlisted his many allies to help recruit Brian.

"One night the Cleveland Recreation Commissioner called our house. I answered the phone," said Brian. "He said the governor wanted to see me. He was going to stop by in an hour and he wanted to know if I would be home. I asked my mother, 'Who is the governor of Ohio?' She said, 'James Rhodes. Why do you ask?' 'Because he'll be here in an hour,' I said."

John Nagy was the Cleveland Recreation Commissioner and

James Rhodes was the governor. They came from different political parties but they were united in their loyalty to Ohio State. Rhodes pulled up in a limousine escorted by two Ohio State Highway Patrol cruisers and parked in front of the Dowling home on Harcourt Drive in Cleveland Heights. Rhodes could be a persuasive devil. He spent an hour in the Dowling family's living room, where he extolled the glory of playing for Woody Hayes at Ohio State. The entire Dowling family listened politely.

Jack Nicklaus called and invited Brian to play golf with him in Columbus. As I said, Brian was a tennis player, not a golfer.

When Woody Hayes made his visit, it lasted four hours. After two hours Brian was excused to do his homework. Woody and Brian's father, Emmett, talked for another two hours. At one point Emmett Dowling, who was a corporate CEO, told Woody that he could easily afford to pay his son's tuition if he chose Ohio State and suggested that Woody should use that scholarship for another lad.

"My dad did not want me to be under the thumb of a coach," said Brian.

"You run your business your way and I'll run mine my way," said Woody.

The recruiting season began as soon as Brian's football season ended and the basketball season began. He would get home from basketball practice and the first words he heard were, "Brian, get the phone. Call for you." Brian had a stack of letters from colleges. There were about 75 in the first wave. He showed them to his father. "Wow," said his father.

"My dad said we should reply to the schools we weren't interested in and tell them so they don't waste their time," said Brian. "My dad enjoyed writing those letters. He'd hand them to me and I'd sign them. I always thought I had pretty good handwriting, but I signed so many letters I didn't even recognize my name.

"I got a hundred offers. Ten or 20 recruiters sat in our living room. Some coaches came to dinner. Alex Agase of Northwestern was one. George Steinbrenner was recruiting for Purdue. He flew my dad and me to Purdue in a private plane. A recruiter from Notre Dame made an awkward reference to Yacknow. I visited Duke, Southern Cal and five eastern schools. At that time a good Ivy League team could compete with half the Division One teams in the country."

Purdue coach Jack Mollenkopf should have enjoyed an inside track. Brian's uncle, Gene Kramer, a Cleveland industrialist, was a Purdue recruiter and Mollenkopf's close friend. At the time it was acceptable for alumni to recruit. Not so today. Mollenkopf seized the moment at the wedding reception of one of the Kramer daughters. He quickly surveyed the crowd and spotted a tall, athletic-looking lad that he knew had to be Brian.

"I hope you're considering Purdue," Mollenkopf said after introducing himself. "Purdue is ideal for you. We throw the ball. Our offense is made for you."

"But coach, I'm already in college. I'm a senior at Notre Dame," said Brian's older cousin, Frank Gaul.

Mollenkopf was greedy. He already had Bob Griese.

"Here's what it came down to," said Brian. "I liked Michigan, Northwestern, Southern Cal and Yale. Michigan coach Bump Elliott was a really nice guy. Their entire backfield was from Ohio. John Pont had just left Yale for Indiana. Carmen Cozza was the new Yale coach. He was from Parma. John Pont said he still thought I should go to Yale, but if I didn't, he'd like me at Indiana. That was pretty classy."

He chose Yale, where he teamed up with tailback Calvin Hill, who later became a star running back with the Dallas Cowboys and the Browns. Years later, Brian read a book about the rivalry between Woody Hayes and Bo Schembechler. He then sent the book to Carmen Cozza with a note saying, "Boy, did I make the right decision."

His father died of cancer when Brian was in college and Cozza, although he was only in his thirties, became a surrogate father.

Calvin Hill wanted to play quarterback. He had been an all-state quarterback in high school. He had a great arm. Cozza claimed that Calvin was the only player he ever knew who could play all 22 positions. So Calvin played running back and Brian played quarterback. In 1968, there were two premier running backs in college football—Leroy Keyes of Purdue and O. J. Simpson of Southern Cal.

"I'd put Calvin up against both of them," Brian said.

There were several great throwing arms on that team.

"Carmen had been a minor league pitcher. He told me he could throw 90 miles an hour. I believed it watching him throw the football to our defensive backs," said Brian. "I was the quarterback and I had only the third-best arm on the team. Calvin threw a lot of halfback passes. He threw three touchdown passes. He threw one 60 yards to me."

Just as the St. Ignatius-Benedictine rivalry became legendary here, the Yale-Harvard rivalry was equally intense. It climaxed in 1968 in Cambridge, where both Harvard and Yale were unbeaten when they met in the 10th game. Their records were equal, but not the talent on the field.

"Harvard had only one player on their offense who could have started for us," said Brian. "That was Tommy Lee Jones, the actor. He was their all-Ivy League guard. We had Meryl Streep. Our fullback was going out with her."

Things were looking good for Yale with a minute left and the Bulldogs leading, 29-13. What followed was the most famous minute in the history of college football. Harvard scored and threw a pass for the two-point conversion. Harvard recovered an onside kick and went in for another touchdown and another two-point conversion. Harvard scored 16 points in the final 60 seconds to tie Yale, 29-29.

The Harvard student newspaper, the *Crimson*, headlined, "Harvard Wins, 29-29." That's how it felt. It felt like a win for Harvard and a loss for Yale.

"Both Calvin and I asked Carmen to put us in on defense in that final minute. We wanted to do anything rather than stand there and watch. Carmen said he couldn't do that to the guys who were in there. It would have shown a loss of faith in them," said Brian.

And so the football season ended. The fullback went back to Meryl Streep. Brian played fraternity basketball with his fraternity brother, George W. Bush, who later was involved in the ultimate tie for the presidency. Brian sent him a congratulatory note, two guys who knew how it felt to be tied.

Brian spent five seasons bouncing around the NFL, usually wearing a baseball cap and holding a clipboard.

"One coach told me I wasn't forceful enough. I told him my coach usually handed me the ball and I went out and won. In the pros you've got to self-promote. I never did that," he said.

When his pro football career ended he settled in the east, where his name opened doors and people took his calls. As he approached his mid-60s he met the love of his life, a charming lady who grew up in New Haven when he was playing there. It's nice to have a name. Hers is Marnie. She took his calls.

"By the way, remember those injuries I got in the '63 Charity Game? The bone chips in my back and the kidney and the broken collarbone kept me out of the Army in 1970," said Brian. "Maybe I should thank Jim Yacknow."

Break the Story First

In the 1960s, it was imperative that breaking news on the high school beat broke first in *The Plain Dealer*. Our sports editor Hal Lebovitz made that a priority. We hustled for everything, from coaching changes to college announcements by star players. I don't remember if we had Brian Dowling's announcement first when he declared for Yale. We probably did. I do know that two years later we broke the story when running back Larry Zelina of Benedictine decided on Ohio State.

Zelina was the high school player of the year in Greater Cleveland in 1966 when he led the area in scoring. I have a recurring memory of Larry exploding up the middle through a hole in the line and racing 40 yards untouched into the end zone. He did that a lot. He led the Bengals to two consecutive Charity Game victories, both over South High, and was the only player to be named Charity Game MVP twice. Along the way I had done a story on Larry in *The Plain Dealer Sunday Magazine* and had been at the Zelina home in the Harvard-Lee neighborhood. I had a good relationship with them and secured from Larry a promise that he would tell us first when he decided on college. All the usual suspects were after him. It was on a warm Monday night in early May of 1967 when he decided on Ohio State. Woody Hayes was sitting in their living room.

"But we can't tell anybody yet," Larry said.

"What?!" said Woody. "Why not?"

He wanted to put Zelina under protective custody with an official announcement.

"I promised Mr. Coughlin I would tell him first," said Larry.

Woody thought that was fine. A nice big story in *The Plain Dealer* would establish ownership.

"Let's get him on the phone right now," said Woody.

Larry dialed up *The Plain Dealer* sports department. Dick Zunt answered the phone.

"He's not here right now. He's covering the Euclid city council meeting," said Dick. "Can I help you?"

"I can only talk to Mr. Coughlin," said Larry.

Woody began to fidget. Surely, he wondered, what does a guy covering the Euclid city council have to do with me getting my player?

I will explain that to you right now.

John Sheridan, who covered high school wrestling for us, also was the editor of the *Euclid News Journal,* his hometown weekly newspaper. That was his full-time job. He did it all. He was the editor, police reporter, politics writer, feature writer, sports writer, he wrote editorials and he endorsed his friends in the local elections. He was busy covering the news and taking care of his friends. In the spring of 1967 he felt he needed a vacation. He wanted to take his corpulent body to the beaches of Fort Lauderdale. To make this possible, however, he had to find a replacement to put out the *Euclid News Journal.* Selfishly thinking only of himself, he put it to me this way, "If you don't put out the *Euclid News Journal* for me, I will not cover high school wrestling for you."

This was pure blackmail. John was only part time with *The Plain Dealer,* but he was the only person who knew anything about wrestling. I caved in without a fight. He had all the cards. For those two weeks I worked two jobs.

And so on that Monday night, Larry Zelina and his parents and Woody Hayes got out the white pages and looked for the number of Euclid City Hall. Don't ever expect that somebody will answer the phone in a municipal building at eight o'clock at night, but that night somebody did. A lady tapped me on the shoulder. "You have an important phone call," she whispered. "Follow me."

She led me to the city council office and handed me the phone. I interviewed Larry, got a comment from Woody and I was forever grateful to Larry for his loyalty. The city council story could wait until the next day. When council adjourned, I went back to *The Plain Dealer* and wrote the Zelina story for the first sports page. In 1968, Larry was a starting halfback on Ohio State's national championship team.

* * *

In January of 1965, Leo Walczuk called. It was about 10 o'clock at night. I answered the phone. I didn't know him but I knew *of* him. He was the father of basketball player Lee Walczuk, a junior who was averaging 30 points a game for Gilmour Academy.

"I'm going to transfer him to St. Edward tomorrow morning," Leo said.

Mr. Walczuk was famous for saying things like that. Ed Chay, my predecessor on the high school beat, said that a year earlier Leo had called at least twice saying that he would transfer his son to St. Ignatius one time and St. Joseph on another occasion. He never followed through. None of that ever happened. We could not take him seriously. He had cried wolf too often.

But I couldn't entirely dismiss him. The more he talked, the more serious he sounded.

I called St. Edward basketball coach Jim Connors at home on Robinwood Ave. in Lakewood. I reached him just before he went to bed. He knew nothing about such a development. He knew of Lee Walczuk. Everybody knew of Lee Walczuk. He was in the news all the time as he neared the 1,000-point mark in his career. He had started as a freshman at Gilmour, which had a nice team under Geoff Morton, a young coach of high esteem. Gilmour was winning about 80 percent of its games under Morton.

Connors, however, also had a nice team with a delicate balance. The Eagles had a 15-1 record. They had three players who averaged about 15 points each. They were senior John Wells, a 5-5 all-scholastic guard; junior Walter Violand, a 6-1 forward; and Ralph Pavicic, a big body 6-4 center. They were like a finely tuned watch. Each player had a distinctive role; each player knew his role and each player stayed within his role. Connors was not looking for mid-season transfers. Actually, it was well beyond mid-season. There were only two regular season games left and then the tournament.

I put nothing in the paper. A lot of fathers talk that way at night but wake up the next morning and think more clearly. For Lee to transfer to another private school and be eligible to play varsity basketball immediately, the family would have to actually move. They would have to pack up their many children and their possessions and move. Those were the rules of the Ohio High School Athletic Association. What Mr. Walczuk proposed seemed illogical. Gilmour was a top-of-the-line prep school with an outstanding basketball team. I know parents who would trade lifetime servitude to give their children that kind of opportunity.

Nevertheless, all night long I worried. He just might do it. And if he did, it would happen on *Press* time. School started at 8:33 a.m. If he's walking the hallways, some kid is gonna see him—hundreds of kids will see him—and all it takes is one kid with a dime to call the *Press* and say, "Guess what!" and they would have the story in their home edition. There was a pay phone a few steps away from the main office and another in the gym lobby.

The next morning at eight o'clock, Lee and his father were in the main office at St. Edward High School signing the papers and handing over a $150 check for Lee's tuition for the second semester, which was just beginning. And a kid did drop a dime. He called Hal Lebovitz at *The Plain Dealer*. Nobody called the *Press*. We had the scoop the next morning. To comply with the Ohio High School Athletic Association rules, the Walczuk family moved to an apartment on the Lakewood Gold Coast, within walking distance of St. Ed's.

At practice that afternoon, guard Dan McNamara nodded toward Walczuk and said, "He's the key." It was a magnanimous remark. Walczuk had just taken McNamara's starting job.

The reason Leo transferred his son was media exposure. Gilmour was not a member of the Ohio High School Athletic Association at that time, which meant it was not part of the state tournament. St. Ed's, on the other hand, expected to go deep into the playoffs. St. Ed's won its last two games of the regular season with Walczuk taking his thirty shots and everybody else standing around watching. St. Ed's was out of sync. The chemistry was wrong. Coach Jim Connors fretted. In the first tournament game, St. Edward, which had a 17-1 record, was upset by Lakewood, a team that had gone 8-10.

The next season was tense. St. Ed's needed two basketballs— one for Walczuk, another one for everybody else. Connors quit in December saying, "I've got a tiger by the tail," and football coach Joe Paul finished the season. Walczuk got a basketball scholarship to UCLA. His father packed up the family and moved there. Lee hardly ever played. Disillusioned with UCLA coach John Wooden and the preferential treatment accorded stars such as Lew Alcindor, Walczuk quit basketball and became an actor. He married a Polish beauty queen and had a number of children. Lee and his wife live in Hawaii where they have a business as wedding photographers.

Nothing turned out the way it was supposed to except for one thing. I got the story first.

Friday Night Fever

I began and ended my working career on the high school football beat and I could never imagine better bookends. Starting at *The Plain Dealer* in 1964, I covered big games every Friday night, mostly in Greater Cleveland. We had bureaus in Lorain, Akron and Canton and we were respectful not to step on anybody's toes there, so I stayed close to home.

Forty years later I was flying around in the Fox 8 helicopter, covering games from one end of our viewing area to the other, as far away as Ashland, Warren, Canton and Massillon, which became a regular destination. I had the feeling that everybody in Stark County watched Fox 8 and the ratings seemed to confirm that. Stark County was very important to us.

I landed at classic high school football stadiums that I never would have seen otherwise, such as Paul Brown Tiger Stadium in Massillon, the most famous of them all. After covering Paul Brown's funeral in Massillon in August 1991, I drove from the church downtown to the stadium for my standup, where I ran into NFL commissioner Pete Rozelle and Dallas Cowboys president Tex Schramm. They got out of a long, black limousine and wandered inside through the main gate, which was open. They walked onto the field near the north end zone and looked up at the bleachers on both sides. I asked them about their visit.

"We have heard so much about it, we had to see it," said Tex.

On Friday nights we would leave Burke Lakefront Airport and fly south at 1,000 feet. That's not very high. It's the height of three football fields. By the middle of October it would be dark and we could identify the lights of high school football stadiums below us in all directions. Ohio really is the heart of Friday night lights. Ohio is an old state and some of these stadiums date back to the

Cameraman Bob Wilkinson (left) and I prepare to board SkyFox for a Friday night run. Pilot Bobby Koenig is cleaning the windows so we can see the high school football fields as we buzz them. (*Akron Beacon Journal / Jocelyn Williams*)

1930s when solid concrete bleachers were built with roofs over the home stands. You can still find such structures in Massillon, North Canton Hoover, Alliance, Barberton, Elyria and Sandusky. At one time they were all state powers.

Don't think I was the only one who enjoyed the privilege. Oh, no. John Telich, Tony Rizzo and I shared it. In fact, Telich and I did most of the sharing and the Rizz did most of the flying. John and I would usually take a couple of flights a season and Rizz took the rest.

"That's because the helicopter and I came to Fox 8 together in 1997," Rizz rationalized. "I never knew what it was like to be a Beatle, but after the first night in the chopper, I knew. We'd land right next to the stadium and a thousand kids would surround us, trying to touch us. I felt like a rock star. What a rush! Some schools would beg us to fly there."

Cameraman Doug Herrmann's favorite stadium was Hudson. He pleaded to make it a regular stop on the Friday night tour.

"Because the first time we were there a woman was so wasted she lifted her shirt and flashed us her headlights—no bra," Rizz explained. "Doug wanted to come back every week and look for her."

We would cover three games each night in the helicopter. We would buzz the stadium to get everyone's attention and set it down as close to the field as they allowed. If we weren't within a few steps of the main gate, they would pick us up in a golf cart and drive us to the 50-yard line. Timing was critical. We would shoot the first quarter of the first game, jump back in the helicopter and fly to the next game. We would fly again at halftime to the third game. We love a good band performance as much as anybody, but we never wanted to be on the ground during halftime. We needed highlights. One night Rizz and cameraman Tim Roskey had no choice. It was halftime when they landed.

"We were sitting on the home bench," Rizz recalled. "Roskey had his camera turned off and I had some kind of hunch. I said, 'Tim, turn your camera on.' About the same time I heard a gasp from the crowd. I turned around and I saw this kid wearing only tennis shoes. That's all! He ran the whole length of the field. We were so surprised Tim didn't get him in focus until the last 20 yards but it was enough. He was a high school kid but he was no kid. He made some men feel inadequate. The ladies never took their eyes off him. We used the highlight, of course, but we had to digitize his image."

I remember thinking how proud his mother must have felt.

Our sports producer Tommy Bruno flew only once and it was an equally memorable flight.

"I wanted to experience Sky Fox—all of it—the take off, the landing, the pilot Captain Earl, not to mention the incredible rush of coming back to the station with a handful of tapes, a scribbled notepad with dozens of poorly written time cues—and less than 35 minutes to tell the story," Bruno said later when I asked him to reminisce about our aerial circus.

"Off we go, photographer Tim Roskey, Captain Earl and me. Our first game was Uniontown Lake. Tim and I were on the fifty-yard line. Out of the corner of my eye I saw what looked like a streaker. He was coming right at us. The boy was tall, wearing a large clown wig and Doc Martin leather boots. Best of all, he was doing a high step, his knees way up in the air. It added to the chaos. He was completely naked and he was moving fast. He went over a chain link fence and into the woods. The police chased him for several minutes. Eventually he was caught and he faced expulsion, but instead he got a long suspension. We used it. We had to blur his image, of course. That was unfortunate. The kid could have been a star. We fed it to CNN and Fox News and they used it. That was the only time I flew and I was on cloud nine. I had the highlight of the year."

Rizz and Roskey were in the air the night a red light began blinking in the cockpit.

"Uh, oh," said Captain Earl.

"I never heard him say that before," Rizz said later. "I looked down and for the first time I felt fear."

"We're gonna have to put this thing down right now," said Captain Earl.

And he did—in the parking lot of a strip shopping plaza in Warren. After the show that night a production assistant drove to Warren to get them. Their highlights never made air.

Doug Herrmann and I encountered the same problem one night while flying with Captain Bobby Koenig. We were returning home ahead of schedule when I noticed that the lights were still on at Olmsted Falls. We landed unannounced in a dark unpopulated area behind the school. We worked quickly. I mooched a roster from a visiting parent and picked up a couple of bonus highlights. But when we got back to the helicopter Bobby said we couldn't take off. That pesky red light was on again. I hope Bobby wasn't offended. We ditched him. Doug and I called a cab and got to the station in time to get our highlights on the air. Captain Bobby called a mechanic who fixed a minor problem and got him airborne by midnight.

"If you disconnect the red light it will solve a lot of problems," I told him.

Rizz and Roskey had other problems one night in Willoughby. We always alerted the schools in advance when we were coming and their athletic directors usually passed this information along to their police and fire departments. That was standard operating procedure. On this night, however, the Willoughby police and fire departments never got the memo. Some safety departments are more finicky than others about helicopters landing at their local football games and nobody was more finicky than Willoughby.

"The police pulled up with their flashers going and we thought they were the welcome wagon," said Rizz. "They got out of their cars with their guns drawn and we thought they were our body-guards. They started chasing me and I thought they were just trying to catch up to us to escort us in. They did catch up to us. Next thing, they've got me surrounded and my hands are in the air. I thought I was going to jail."

Sometimes I would set up their flight schedules, such as the time I sent Rizz and Roskey to Huron.

"You told us to land next to the long jump pit but I guess I didn't hear you say, the long jump pit at the practice field," said Roskey. "There were two long jump pits. The other one was right next to the end zone in the stadium and from the air that looked pretty good. 'There's a long jump pit,' I said. 'That must be the one.' So we buzzed the stadium and landed right next to the field. They had to stop the game while we landed. We jumped out and shot the game. Nobody complained."

When they buzzed the Brunswick stadium a lineman from the opposing team was startled and stood up. Out came the referee's flag and he was penalized for a false start. It came at crucial time and directly influenced the outcome. The *Medina Gazette* reported the next day that Fox 8 helped Brunswick win.

At Strongsville they were told to land on a baseball field behind a shopping plaza across the road where a car met them and drove them to the stadium. When it was time to leave, Rizz, Ros-

Cameraman Dave Bradford and I cover a Glenville-East Tech football game. We may look calm here, but by the time we went on air, every Friday night got a bit crazy. *(Akron Beacon Journal / Jocelyn Williams)*

key and Captain Earl could not find their driver and they set out on foot in the dark, not realizing there were ten baseball fields behind the shopping plaza. They wandered in the blackness like a trio of burglars up to no good. Along came the police.

"What are you guys up to?" the curious officer said while blinding them with his industrial strength police flashlight.

"We are looking for our helicopter. We lost it," Roskey said.

They should have been arrested on the spot for that answer, but once again the firm of Rizzo, Roskey and Sandlin won an acquittal.

Rizzo almost was banned from Paul Brown Tiger Stadium in Massillon.

"We were shooting a Massillon-St. Ignatius game," Roskey said. "An Ignatius kid made an interception but the referee ruled his foot was out of bounds. Rizz asked me, 'Do you have it?' I

backed up the tape in the camera and looked. 'Yeah, he was in,'
I said. Rizz told the Ignatius coaches our tape showed he was in
and the coaches were yelling at the officials that Channel 8 says
he was in. The referee blew a gasket and then he blew his whistle.
He ran over and told Rizz to shut up or he'd be thrown out of the
stadium. There was no instant replay in high school football."

*   *   *

At Hoban High School in Akron the baseball diamond behind
the visiting bleachers was a convenient landing pad. Captain Earl
swooped low over the stadium and settled the chopper next to
the pitcher's mound. The infield was bone dry. It had not rained
in a couple of weeks. As we landed, the chopper touched off the
biggest dust storm I've seen since *Lawrence of Arabia*. It was em-
barrassing. The dust wafted over the stands and across the field.
Fans coughed. Players gagged. The referee glared at us when they
stopped the game briefly to let the dust settle. While we waited
for the action to resume, I spotted the Walsh Jesuit wrestling
coach, Bill Barger, leaning against the fence and I trotted over
to pay my respects to him. Barger had fought in Vietnam during the worst times of the war and he came home with a reputation. When people spoke of him, they did so in a low, confidential
voice, as though he might be listening. "He's a trained killer," they
said. "Rambo was based on Bill Barger."

I don't know how true all of that was, but I wasn't going to say,
"Hey, Bill. I understand you're a tough guy."

When I got to the fence, I noticed that Barger had a faraway
look in his eyes. It was a look you never want to see in the eyes of
a trained killer.

"When your helicopter came in, with the sound and the dust,
it reminded me of Vietnam," Barger said softly, the way he might
have talked back in the jungle when he was armed with a knife
and a rifle and several clips of ammunition.

That was not a good time to reminisce about the war.

"The game is starting. Gotta get back to work," I said.

* * *

"Every week was an adventure," said John Telich, who rattled off a list of misadventures.

Tapes would get mislabeled and mixed up. Some games had no rosters. Storms cancelled most of the opening night schedule one year. We drove like mad men from school to school looking for any game being played between raindrops and lightning bolts. The on-off trigger on a camera got reversed. We had no highlights but we had shots of the huddles. Oops, no sound. That's the beauty of television. The audience never knew when all hell was breaking loose behind the scenes.

Nothing was easy. It was stressful. Tempers were tested. Sports producer Tommy Bruno and Rizzo almost had a fist fight behind the station in 1997.

"It was chaos," said Thom Thompson, our sports intern that year. "Scripts were late. The video would roll and nobody knew what they were watching. Rizz was screaming at nobody in particular. Tommy had enough. As producers, we were busting our ass. The last thing we wanted was his bitching and moaning. 'I'm sick of it,' Tommy said after the show. 'Let's go into the parking lot.' Of course, they didn't but it would have been an interesting rumble. Rizzo was bigger, but Tommy was a pretty tough high school wrestler at St. Vincent-St. Mary."

The first night we did an expanded version of high school football was 1997, first Friday night of the season. The Indians were in a tight pennant race and they were at home. I did a live shot from Jacobs Field on the six o'clock show and then met my football photographer outside the ballpark. He picked me up on Ontario Street and we raced to the western suburbs and shot three games. Back at the station I personally edited my three games, wrote the scripts for the teleprompter and then literally ran down the hall to the studio. I told our sports intern to bring me my scripts. They hadn't come out of the printer yet.

"Come right in the studio and hand me my scripts," I told the intern. It was his first night. I'm not sure he knew where the studio was. That was the last time I saw the kid. He never returned. He never set foot in the station again.

Rizz did his three games and Mark Schroeder was due up next with his games from the Akron bureau, but there was a glitch. Schroeder's microphone wouldn't work. Somebody had disconnected it. There was Mark on his hands and knees groping around for a loose cable and he never found it.

"Go to Coughlin," somebody screamed in the control room.

So they went to me. I was standing there with no scripts. Those were not my words in the teleprompter. On the black and white TV monitor in the studio, I didn't even know if those were my games. The show was suddenly out of order. I heard nothing in my earpiece from the director. I signaled to the control room to move the teleprompter up, to find my scripts. I'm sure that chaos reigned there. I hoped the natural sound of the games at least would cover up the monumental screw up.

The next week Lou Maglio said, "I was watching at home. Rizz tossed to Schroeder and then he said, 'Oh, we don't have Mark. Let's go to Dan Coughlin.' I could see you standing there with no scripts and I thought to myself, 'This is gonna be good.' But, you know, people watching at home didn't think anything about it. They have no idea how live television works, and sometimes doesn't work."

The news director put a letter in my file saying I screwed up. He had no idea what went on that night except for what the director in the control room told him and he didn't know, either.

*   *   *

"We came out of Revere once and took the wrong turn. We got lost and got back late," said Telich. "But nothing beats it. Friday night football. One night I flew to Kent Roosevelt. When we got there it seemed everything stopped. A golf cart was there immediately to drive us into the stadium. It was like I was Barack Obama."

Except that John Telich had a higher approval rating.

Telich, incidentally, was in better physical shape than any high school football player he ever covered. When he was 57 years old he entered a 100-mile race and completed 75 miles. The next day he came to work early and put in a 10-hour day.

I've got to give John and Casey Coleman credit for beefing up high school football coverage on Channel 8 as far back as 1984 with a half-hour highlights show which ran at noon on Sundays, just before the NFL pre-game show. Executive producer Tim Iacafano should share top billing because it was his idea. Tim, John and Casey would work through the night on Saturdays editing and recording the voiceovers for a dozen games. It had a nice audience. Channel 8 hosted a post-season banquet and honored its player of the year. It was good business. It strengthened Channel 8's position in the ratings.

However, they couldn't leave a good thing alone. Up in the executive offices someone thought we should include segments on the Browns and Ohio State. Before long, it was a Browns show, much like any other hometown pro football booster show. You can find that stuff almost anywhere. There's a glut of pro football shows on cable. The Internet has more pro football news than any sane person can absorb.

But you can find local high school football only on local television. It's the one thing we have entirely to ourselves. In 1997 Channel 8—known as Fox 8 by then—devoted the final 15 minutes of the Friday night 10 o'clock show to high school football coverage. In 2010 it expanded to a separate half-hour high school football show at 11 o'clock, 20 games in 30 minutes.

In 2011 Fox 8 made the greatest commitment to high school football in station history—thirty games in thirty minutes. It involved five reporters, ten cameras and another ten producers and editors behind the scenes, in addition to the usual directors and technicians in the control room. We actually held six afternoons of rehearsals. But there were no rehearsals for the camera people, score gatherers or editors. A week before the first show I actually had a dream that the show was going to blow up in our faces. It wasn't fast paced. It was supersonic paced. And it was put together in one hour. I worried. I imagined how Eisenhower felt the night before D-Day, when he prepared two speeches, one for a successful invasion at Normandy, the other an apology for a terrible failure. So there I was, ye of little faith.

Not only did it work, the first expanded "Friday Night Touchdown" was a nearly perfect production technically. The viewers liked it. The advertising department loved it.

* * *

One thing that didn't change from 1964 to 2011 was the deadline. Eleven o'clock was showtime at Fox 8. That also was the deadline for our home delivery edition at *The Plain Dealer*.

I always marveled at the paradox of a big city daily newspaper. Highly paid union writers, editors, photographers and printers assembled papers that were mass-produced on million-dollar presses, stunning mechanical wonders that automatically folded the papers and loaded them onto trucks driven by union Teamsters who delivered them into neighborhoods and tossed them on street corners where kids picked them up and delivered them to the readers' front doors.

The multi-million dollar operation depended on kids. If they didn't complete the final step, all that work by skilled professionals was wasted.

In sports we took it one step closer to lunacy. We relied on high school students to call in the final scores, stats, box scores and any other details from their games. The people who took the information and wrote the stories were part-timers from various walks of life who developed a unique camaraderie. The system worked, too, more than 99 per cent of the time.

There were exceptions. In the early 1960s we waited impatiently for the call from a game in distant Ashtabula County. The clock was running. The plates were on the presses. The foreman was poised to hit the green "start" button on the presses when Ed Chay, the scholastic editor at the time, reached our correspondent on the phone. The kid was at home.

Ed maintained his own school directories, with schedules, home phone numbers of athletic directors, coaches and student correspondents.

"Billy, what happened? Did you go to the sock hop?" Ed said sarcastically when the kid answered the phone.

"There was nothing to report," Billy said defensively. "They cancelled the game when the stands collapsed and they had to take a bunch of people to the hospital. They're gonna play the game tomorrow. I'll be sure to call then."

A few years later a prankster caught us with a phony high school swimming report. Fictional names and times turned up in the paper the next morning, to the surprise of the University School swimmers who were the targets of the benign stunt. That was harmless stuff. There was no defense against pranks. Covering the high school beat is based on trust.

* * *

We paid our correspondents two dollars a game. Those who were especially good got $3 and when Dick Zunt did the correspondents' payroll he tossed $5 bonuses around like after-dinner mints. Most were kids, although sometimes adults, even coaches and coaches' wives called in games. The two, three and five bucks added up. A full school year of football, basketball and baseball exceeded $100 tax-free dollars. In the mid-60s, that made two or three car payments.

Unlike television, we had to spell all names correctly, hundreds of them every night in agate box scores. A basketball player from East Tech in the 1960s drove us crazy. The correspondent read off the names in the box score, names that included Hill Dennis.

"Is that Hill, comma, Dennis?" I usually asked. "What's his first name?"

"Hill," came the reply.

"No, that must be his last name," I said.

"In the book it says Dennis, Hill."

"They must mean his name is Hill, Dennis," I said.

For most of the season we listed him as Dennis Hill.

By the end of the season we confirmed that his name was Hill Dennis. Who names their kid after a topographical feature? Only on the high school beat. I loved it.

*   *   *

How many people with almost no experience become overnight stars on the biggest radio station in town? That's me, raising my hand.

Maybe I'm stretching the "star" part, but only a little. In the fall of 1969 the owners of WIXY 1260 put me on the air each Friday night with high school football scores from my desk at *The Plain Dealer.* Among the teenage crowd, WIXY was not merely a dominant, blockbuster station, it was a hydrogen bomb compared to a cap pistol. Larry Morrow, the afternoon disc jockey, always claimed that when the kids got out of school at three o'clock his ratings soared to a 65 share. This would be like running a one-minute mile or a one-hour marathon. It isn't done. In a competitive market such as Cleveland, a 65 share is physically impossible. But WIXY did it day after day.

Everything about WIXY was new. It was the first top 40 station in town. In order to maintain their high energy, the disc jockeys stood and ran their own boards. They played their own records, twisted their own dials, and handled their own phones. Sitting down while on the air was absolutely verboten because the diaphragm can't suck in enough air. You're at full breathing power when you stand. The jocks at WIXY were at full power all the time.

The owners called and asked for a meeting. Bob Weiss, Norman Wain and Joe Zingale owned WIXY. They were all there.

"Can you do six phone reports every Friday night while you're covering your game?" Norman Wain asked.

Nobody had ever tried something like this before. Cover a game, drive to the paper, write the story and stop every 15 minutes to collect scores and make a phone call is really multi-tasking.

"Sure, it can be done," I said.

"We will pay you fifty dollars a night," Wain said.

"I was thinking seventy-five bucks. Let's compromise at sixty-five," I said and I stuck out my hand to shake on a deal.

They took my hand and we were in business. They had a sponsor, Arby's, which was new in the market with the best roast beef sandwich we've ever tasted. There's no comparison with the original Arby's sandwich, which cost fifty cents, and the product they sell today. They gave me a wad of coupons for free sandwiches, which I passed around to the guys who took the scores in the sports department and to the press box workers at the high school games.

It worked this way. I would call in a couple reports from the game I was covering. After the game I would drive like a fiend to the paper and without taking off my coat I would sweep through the sports department gathering scores for my next report. It became chaotic. I would write a few paragraphs and then run around the room getting more scores for the radio. I guarantee, a weaker man would have had a heart attack the first night.

There were probably 100,000 people at high school football games every Friday night in the WIXY listening area and they all listened to my reports. I was told that players would get on their buses for the ride back to their schools and the transistor radios would be tuned to WIXY. When I came on with scores, the buses would get very quiet.

"An upset in the Southwestern Conference," I would say dramatically. It was like Walter Cronkite with election results on the first Tuesday in November. The fact is, every Friday night was like Election Day in the sports department. Afterward we went next door to the Headliner bar and sat around a big table and patted ourselves on the back. We did OK. We never had Dewey beating Truman.

Rats' Nest Corners
and Other Fantasies

When *The Plain Dealer* was the biggest newspaper in the state, we had unlimited resources, especially on the high school beat. If we needed more part-time helpers to write games on Friday and Saturday nights, we hired them. I ran into Doug Clarke in a Lakewood bar one night in 1964 and hired him. He later became a sports columnist for *The Cleveland Press*. We had the space to give every school in our circulation area a headline and at least a paragraph in the Saturday and Sunday papers. That was a policy inherited from Ed Chay, who ran the high school beat from the mid-1950s until 1964.

Our Thursday high school page—a wide-open sheet uncluttered by those annoying ads—offered unlimited possibilities for creativity. We used it for some oddball things now and then. For example, one Thursday I teased cheerleaders for their silly antics, which led to a back-and-forth debate between the cheerleaders and me that went on for two weeks. Was it news? No. Was it fun?

Yes. In those days, nobody accused us of not having fun. I would walk in the building every day with a smile on my face. When the state basketball tournament began, we used that big Thursday page for predictions. Eight members of our staff picked eight different state champions and made an argument for each one. Essentially, they were informative profiles of the top teams in the state, ranging from as far away as Columbus, Dayton and Cincinnati, all on one page. According to our status as the state's largest paper, we took a statewide approach to the tournament. If you wanted a serious preview, we gave it to you. But we also had to do it with a different twist. For several years I picked mythical schools, so tiny that no one had ever heard of them. I took some liberties. Although my fictional schools were minuscule, I picked them to beat the biggest schools in the state. No one complained.

Wally Mieskoski, a friend from the old days, insisted that I include some of them. This sampler is for you Wally. I hope you're right, that others from four decades ago will appreciate the puns.

The Plain Dealer, March 6, 1969

It was by the merest accident I uncovered the only team capable of unseating Columbus East as the state high school basketball champion. I pondered the chances of John Adams and Maple Heights, Euclid and St. Joseph, Lakewood and Berea, but the old crystal ball didn't react. It went wild, however, over the long shot chances of the Fighting Fieldmice of Rats' Nest Corners Consolidated Local High School.

You may be unfamiliar with Rats' Nest Corners and its mystery team with an unbelievable record. The school is just coming off a long suspension for trying to recruit a nine-foot aborigine from Australia some years ago. That episode is a black mark in Rats' Nest Corners' history.

As you may have surmised, Rats' Nest Corners is a moneyed community. It used to be a boomtown in its fur-trapping era. Since the pelts petered out, it has more recently gained a considerable reputation in business and government circles with a thriving moonshine distilling industry.

This year the team did not have to recruit primates because it has reared its own. The five starters are all brothers. The sixth man is their sister, an oddity worth mentioning. They are the only students in the high school. Actually, Rats' Nest is a Class A school, but chose to enter the big Class AA tourney. This posed a problem for the Ohio High School Athletic Association, but in its wisdom the OHSAA gave permission.

Fieldmice coach Hymie Cohen, a former Italian who was a bigwig in the Mafia before he changed his name, is confident his Fieldmice will spring the surprise of the tourney. The Fieldmice have a lanky front line of 6-11, 6-10 and 6-9. They are the Frickard triplets, Frank, Fred and Fink. Fink is the highest scorer with a 27-point average. Fieldmice fans are wont to chant at appropriate times, "Fink is the King."

The guards are the Frickard twins, Nick and Mick. Each is only 5-2. A big play is for either Nick or Mick to dribble between the legs of Frank, Fred or Fink and sink a layup. Their sister, who confesses to being somewhat of a tomboy, is called Tom.

Rats' Nest Corners compiled an 18-0 regular-season record with much of its competition being semi-pro outlaw teams. Its only loss was in a secret scrimmage with the New York Knickerbockers in Scranton, Pa. "We took an early lead but they nibbled away at it and beat us, 120-119," recalls Fieldmouse coach Cohen.

When asked if East had a chance against Rats' Nest, one observer replied, "Gnaw."

When Columbus East coach Bob Hart learned of the Fieldmice entry in the big school tourney, he reportedly declared in agony, "Rats."

The Plain Dealer, March 4, 1970

A little-known school in southeastern Ohio with the improbable name of Echo Springs Consolidated Local is the surest shot to win the state Class AA basketball championship since Rats' Nest Corners, our ill-fated pick last year.

(Rats' Nest, you'll recall, was declared ineligible at the last minute because it scrimmaged against the New York Knickerbockers and each player lost his amateur standing.)

Echo Springs is only a two-year-old school located along the polluted banks of Carstairs Creek, named after a family of early settlers who were lynched for giving firewater to the Indians of that region. Echo Springs remained a backward community until the roaring twenties, when it became a favorite haven for bootleg truckers, who rested and gassed up on their way from the production centers of Kentucky and Tennessee to the consumer centers in the east. It was then that the community prospered and built a little red schoolhouse.

It fielded its first basketball team last year and Echo Springs went on an 18-game victory binge. Unfortunately, its coach, Jack Daniels, who had recently moved to Echo Springs from Tennessee, wasn't familiar with the high school rules and neglected to register with the Ohio High School Athletic Association.

Therefore, Echo Springs was ineligible for last year's tournament, which surely was a shame. "We had a corkin' good team," lamented coach Daniels, who is typical of most coaches in that he cries in his beer too much. Led by the Scribner brothers, who averaged 73 points between them, the team has the town of Echo Springs hopped up. As proof, Echo Springs mashed 18 straight foes this year with a smooth blend of offense and defense, pouring points through the bucket at an average of 98 a game and keeping their opponents thoroughly bottled up.

The Scribner boys' father also is sports editor of the weekly newspaper.

Because he ran their pictures in the paper every week, the townsfolk delighted in referring to the paper, the Echo Springs ECHO, as a Scribner and Sons publication. This brewed resentment, however, with two other families in town, the Simon and Schuster clans, whose sons also are starters on the team.

Thirsty for notoriety and anticipating a state championship, the giddy townsfolk have settled their petty differences and have funneled their efforts toward a common goal (except for the Wetz and Dries, two old German families who have been at each other's throats for generations). With a year of aging behind it, Echo Springs has the formula to go all the way.

The Plain Dealer, March 4, 1971

A tiny Ohio River town that has been kept a secret from the modern world will explode into the headlines later this month

when its high school basketball team wins the state championship.

My pick is Coffin Corners, a mysterious hamlet located near
the most southern tip of Ohio between Ironton and Ports-
mouth. Named because its main industry for more than a
century was providing wooden caskets for the legendary family feud between the Hatfields and McCoys across the river in
Kentucky, Coffin Corners was once a graveyard for coaches, as
well.

Last year, however, a new coach from Transylvania State
Teachers College in Lexington, Ky., was imported to instill new
life in the team. His name is Frank N. Stein.

"He's created a monster," moaned the coach of a rival team
that was buried by 59 points.

Stein took a group of dead-end kids and, through his elec-
tric personality and personal magnetism, changed them into
the most devastating machine in high school cage annals. Following extensive pre-season spadework and hours of experi-
mentation with intricate plays, the Galloping Ghosts, as the
team is called, nailed down their conference title and put the
lid on a perfect season in which they laid to rest 18 straight
foes. Each of the five starters is a deadeye shooter and they
have killed every opponent on the boards. Their skeleton key
to victory, however, is an adaptation of the box-and-one defense, which Stein calls the "one in a box."

It was almost the end of the trail for Coffin Corners in its
first tournament game, though, when the Ghosts came per-
ilously close to digging their own grave. They committed so
many fouls the other team enjoyed a procession to the foul
line. They survived a bone-chilling overtime thriller, however,
when a lanky center named Bill Lagosi shoveled in a field
ghoul in the dying seconds.

"We won't have a scare like that again," promised Stein.
"After that close call, we're going to take out revenge on every
team we play."

It looks as though there's only one thing the other teams can do—say their prayers. Coffin Corners is unbelievably terrifying. That is my grave prediction.

The Plain Dealer, March 9, 1972

Anybody who doesn't agree that Seville Junction can win the state championship should have his head examined.

Seville Junction is not to be confused with the town of Seville in Medina County or with Saville Estates in Montgomery County. Seville Junction of newfound basketball fame is an obscure little hamlet in southeastern Ohio almost completely surrounded by abandoned strip mines. For lack of work and because of the repugnant sight of the bald landscape, much of the population moved away in recent years. Even the former mayor of Seville retired and is now living in Washington Courthouse.

One of the few who remained is the barber of Seville. A stern disciplinarian, the barber always insisted that his five sons keep their hair closely cropped. He believed that the barber's sons should set an example for their shaggy-haired classmates. As a result, life has been miserable for the boys—12th grade twins, 11th grade twins and one 10th grader. Their classmates rejected them, especially the girls, who often pointed at them and called them "squares." The student council president, Dan Druff, even tried to get them suspended from school for having short hair. He came within a whisker of accomplishing the dastardly deed, too. Even at a young age the boys grew accustomed to finding their own diversions, which consisted mainly of shooting baskets in the neighborhood park. They never had trouble getting use of their town's one court because when they arrived everyone else left. As a result, they became the best basketball players in the school. They refined intricate plays with razor-sharp passing.

The basketball coach, Harry Lax, knew it would be a sticky situation when they came out for basketball practice in November. If he kept the barber's sons, the other players would quit and that would cause problems with other families. He also knew the only way to save his scalp was to keep the boys. Winless in four seasons, his job hung on a thin strand. He combed his mind for a solution.

Ultimately, the decision was easy. Although he hated to make waves, he believed that the barber's sons were a lock to win the state title. The five-man crew cut through their regular-season schedule like shears through lamb's wool. Their only close shave was a hair-raising 70-69 brush with elimination in their sectional finals. In the last second the 10th grader curled behind a zone defense and his shot from the side burned the cords.

Regardless of whether the barber's sons net the state championship, the self-styled snippets scored a major victory of sorts. As a sign of acceptance, the principal, Ms. Gloria Stineman, shaved off her beard.

Denny Marcin:
Never Out of Work

For a humble assistant football coach, Denny Marcin led an exciting life. He was hired in a bar, he was sprayed with mace at a wrestling match, he stepped into the bull fighting ring twice and both times was trampled by the bull, he was involved in a car chase through the Blue Ridge Mountains, he had to write a 21-page report to the NCAA on a recruiting episode, he was a mall Santa Claus and he was a prize on *The Oprah Winfrey Show*. Along the way, Marcin became one of the most highly regarded line coaches in the game on any level—high school, college and pro.

Nothing ever was ordinary about him. For example, he was recruited to play football by four different high schools even though he never played the game.

"I went to Our Lady of Lourdes grade school at E. 55th and Broadway and they did not have a CYO football team," Marcin said. "We didn't even live in the parish. We moved away when I was in the fourth grade. My parents made me take a bus from East 116th Street to East 55th Street every day for four years."

So how was he discovered?

"Our Lady of Lourdes did have a basketball team," Marcin said. "We played our games in the Benedictine gym. I was big and I was fast. Benedictine, Cathedral Latin and Holy Name recruited me for football. So did John Adams. I would hang around their practices and afterward I would hit their blocking dummies. At home I took an old mattress and taped it around a telephone pole. I would tackle the telephone pole."

He chose Benedictine and became one of the school's all-time best linemen. From there it was on to Miami of Ohio where he played for Bo Schembechler. In the spring of his senior year he met a high school coach from Youngstown named Jerry Hanlon who had just accepted the head coach job at St. Edward High School in Lakewood. Hanlon needed a staff and Marcin needed a job. They set up a date for an interview. It was at two o'clock in the afternoon on a Saturday at the G and H Bar on Detroit Ave., a block away from St. Edward. They had beers and burgers and talked a little football and after two hours Marcin had his first job.

"You'll coach the offensive line and teach driver's education," said Hanlon.

"Fine," said Marcin. "What kind of driver's ed program do they have?"

"They don't have a program," said Hanlon. "They don't even have a car."

Marcin spent 10 years at St. Ed's and thought he would be a high school football coach the rest of his life. He was content with that. He became the head coach for the last two years and produced St. Ed's first undefeated football team. When he registered his first victory over his old high school coach, Augie Bossu of Benedictine, one of his players snatched up the game ball and presented it to Marcin. It was Benedictine's home game and it was their ball. As the St. Edward team bus pulled away from West Tech field, Marcin looked out the window and saw Benedictine athletic director Joe Rufus looking for the game ball in the dark. Marcin still has that game ball carefully preserved among his treasures.

Hanlon spent only six months at St. Ed's. He left to take a job as an assistant coach at the University of Dayton. A year after that, Hanlon began a 25-year association with Bo Schembechler at Miami and then Michigan. He was Bo's number one assistant coach all that time.

"Jerry Hanlon broke me into the profession the right way," said Marcin. "He taught me to do hard work. He had coaches' meet-

ings until midnight. He made you feel like you were a coach. I
don't know if I ever thanked him. Jerry made sure there was no
profanity around the players. Instead of swearing, he would say,
'Cheese and crackers.' Augie Bossu was the same way. The stron-
gest words Augie ever said were, 'Hell's bells.' As for smoking,
Jerry said if you smoked don't do it around the kids."

Coaching at St. Ed's in those days was like a religious voca-
tion—the vow of poverty was involved. Marcin had a succession
of part time jobs and summer jobs on beer trucks and ice cream
trucks. He umpired baseball games in the summer and became
a wrestling referee. He even refereed pro rassling matches at the
old downtown Cleveland Arena.

"The first night I refereed pro rassling was on St. Patrick's Day.
The place was packed. All my students were there, busting my
chops," said Marcin. "In the main event I had Ernie (Big Cat)
Ladd, the old Kansas City Chiefs defensive lineman. For some
reason, I had to change the decision. We needed a police escort
of six or eight cops to get Ernie and me to the locker room. When
we got there I said, 'I can't see.' One of the cops said, 'Don't worry
about it. They sprayed mace on us when we were walking to the
locker room.' At least they didn't use tear gas. I imagined going
home that night and Betsey asking, 'How did work go tonight?'
and I'd say, 'Oh, just the usual. Mace and tear gas.'

"Another night I had the Fargo Brothers in the main event. A
lady hit one of them on the head with her umbrella. He just sort of
flipped a chair into the stands and that started a riot. They got us
all in the locker room and they bolted the door. Outside they were
trying to break down the door. It was like the mob scene in Fran-
kenstein when they stormed the castle with clubs and torches.
In the locker room, somebody pulled out a gun and pointed it
at the door. The first person who broke through was gonna get
shot. 'What am I doing here? I'm a high school coach,' I said to
myself. Then I realized what I was doing there. I was getting paid
a hundred bucks. That was a week's pay for a teacher at St. Ed's."

In 1974, Dick Crum was promoted to head coach at Miami of

Ohio and he needed a staff. Bill Mallory had just left for Colorado and he took many of the assistant coaches with him. Crum called Marcin. They had become friendly when Crum recruited the Cleveland area for Miami. That began a 14-year run with Crum as the head coach and Marcin his defensive line coach, first at Miami and then at North Carolina.

"I was there three years when Dick hired Chuck Priefer to coach special teams. Dick told Chuck to go with me on a signing," said Marcin.

In the 1970s, the recruiting rules were vastly different. There were more loopholes than actual rules. For the last forty years the NCAA's main job has been adding pages to its rules book and hiring detectives. Priefer, whose first coaching job was at Padua High School in Parma, went on to coach in college and the pros. He said high school coaching was the most fun and the NFL was the most rewarding "because I got to coach the best players at the highest level. The NFL is the epitome of my profession." His college coaching experience at Miami of Ohio and Georgia Tech was not what you might think, even though Georgia Tech won a national championship when he was there. "I got tired of the NCAA and its godlike approach," Priefer said.

In 1978, Marcin and Priefer set out to sign Dan Debevc, a prospect from Euclid High School. Debevc told Marcin he would sign his letter of intent with Miami. Marcin and Priefer were already in Cleveland. The official signing seemed to be a formality. They went to his house anyway to witness his signature and put the contract in their pocket.

"I'll pick you up at 6 a.m.," Marcin said to Priefer.

Priefer was surprised by the early hour.

"They're not allowed to sign until eight," he said.

"All kinds of things happen on signing day and the night before," Marcin told Priefer. "Some real nonsense. We've got to be ready for anything."

They got to Debevc's house in Euclid at seven o'clock in the morning and discovered they were not alone.

"There was a car in the driveway with official State of Ohio plates. All the coaches in the Mid-American Conference drove state cars. When we rang the bell, Nick Nicolau from Kent State answered the door with a cup of coffee in his hand," said Marcin. "So we sat there in the living room for an hour. Nick, Priefer and me. We knew each other. We got along. We all told stories until eight o'clock. There was a grandfather clock in the living room. When it struck eight o'clock, Debevc said, 'I'm signing with Miami.' Nicolau said, 'Thanks for the coffee,' and he left."

Today, coaches may not be anywhere near recruits on signing day. It's the rule. Coaches are in their offices on campus. But years ago even head coaches camped out in the living rooms of recruits the night before they signed. In one of the most famous vigils, Woody Hayes of Ohio State, Bo Schembechler of Michigan and Joe Paterno of Penn State stayed up until midnight with Tom Cousineau in his Fairview Park living room. The next morning, he signed with Ohio State and four years later he was the first player selected in the NFL draft.

When Crum, Marcin and the staff moved to North Carolina in 1978, national signing day really got wild.

"For me, recruiting was fun until the last couple of weeks," said Marcin. "You'd call a kid and they'd say, 'He's not here right now.' And you could hear his voice in the background. At North Carolina I was recruiting a very good receiver named James Brim from Mount Airy. It got down to Wake Forest and ourselves. At the end it was touch and go. The last two days I hung around the school. Two days before he could sign I saw the kid get in a car with the Wake Forest coach. I followed them. It was night and it was through the mountains and we were racing. The Wake Forest coach knew the mountain roads better than I did. He lost me.

"Back in town, Brim's high school coach told me he was going to sign with Carolina. The coach said they were going to pick him up and drive him to school. That's where he would sign. They were going to keep him hidden. On the morning of signing day they went to get him and he wasn't there. Brim's older brother worked at a plant and his boss was a Wake Forest guy. I knew where his brother lived so I drove over there and at the end of the street I could look down the back yards. There was a car hidden in the back yard of his brother's house. So I went down to the house and there were 12 people in the driveway. Four of them were college coaches. The kid came out and said, 'I'm not signing with anybody.' The rule was, everybody had to leave. Two days later he signed in a barbershop with Wake Forest."

Brim was worth the drama. In four years from 1983-86 he set the Wake Forest record for career receptions and he played one season for the Minnesota Vikings. But he never beat North Carolina.

"Dick Crum told me to write a report to the NCAA about the entire episode. I didn't want to do it. But he insisted. Dick abided by the letter of the law. He wouldn't tolerate any kind of cheating. The report was 21 pages long. I sent it in. Nothing ever happened," said Marcin.

In 1987, Crum and Earle Bruce of Ohio State were fired on the same day. Early in the afternoon of Monday, Nov. 16, the story moved across the wire that Bruce would be fired that coming Saturday after the last game of the season against Michigan. It wasn't a rumor. It was an announcement.

I jumped on my phone in the Channel 8 newsroom and dialed up Crum at North Carolina. He came out of a coaches' meeting to take my call.

"I don't know if you're interested in the Ohio State job, but it just opened up," I told him breathlessly. "They just announced that he's out after this Saturday's game."

"That's very interesting," said Crum. "This morning they told me the same thing. I'm fired after this Saturday's game."

I was astounded. Crum was the winningest coach in North Carolina football history and he still is. He had taken the Tar Heels to six bowl games in 10 years and won four—over Michigan, Arkansas and twice over Texas. In four years at Miami, he led the Redskins to Tangerine Bowl triumphs over Georgia and Florida. I considered Crum one of the stars of college coaching.

"What are they thinking?" I blurted out.

"They want to be Harvard on Monday through Friday and Oklahoma on Saturday," Crum explained.

North Carolina is good, but it never will be Harvard. As for Saturdays, North Carolina has never even played Oklahoma.

That's what happens to coaches who never stray outside the margins of the NCAA rulebook. Dick ended his coaching career with three disappointing years at Kent State and then retired. He and his wife, Shirley, have lived in Perry, in Lake County, for 20 years. In September 2011, he was inducted into the Greater Cleveland Sports Hall of Fame.

The North Carolina coaching staff scattered. Denny Marcin was hired by Illinois and eventually moved on to the New York Giants and New York Jets. Chuck Priefer was hired by Bobby Ross at Georgia Tech and moved with him to the San Diego Chargers and the Detroit Lions.

Marcin made quite an impact at Illinois, even drawing the interest of Oprah Winfrey. A female viewer of her show won a day with Marcin and the football team.

Marcin did not sail quietly into his sunset. He had many more adventures. When North Carolina played in the 1982 Sun Bowl in El Paso, Texas, the coaching staff was invited to witness a bullfight across the border in Mexico. Furthermore, they were invited to enter the ring and fight a bull.

"I think I'll try that," said Marcin.

The bull won, but it was a young bull. Its horns were not fully developed. Marcin was knocked down but he was not gored. He also was not discouraged.

When Marcin returned to the Sun Bowl in 1991 with Illinois, the bullfight was still on the itinerary of organized activities.

"Do you still have any of those young bulls?" Marcin asked.

"Si, Senor," said the boss of the bullfights.

"Sign me up," said Marcin.

Marcin strode confidently into the ring while the Illinois coaches howled. He deftly fluttered his red cape until he got the bull's undivided attention and then he braced for the collision, like a scatback trying to slow down a charging defensive end. Onward came the bull, downward went Marcin.

As usual, Marcin bounced up and brushed the dust off his uniform. John Mackovic was the Illinois head coach, but he left for Texas and Lou Tepper replaced him. Marcin was known as a teaching coach, something even Oprah Winfrey recognized. When two housewives on her show complained that they were football widows, she sent them to Marcin for a tutorial on football fundamentals. Marcin remained as defensive line coach until the entire Illinois staff was fired just before Christmas in 1996. After six bowl games in nine seasons at Illinois, Marcin used his Christmas vacation wisely. He worked one Saturday as a mall Santa Claus because he said it might be the only time he would be available.

"The guys I worked with played by the rules and most of them eventually got fired," Marcin said.

Denny, however, never missed a season. The New York Giants hired him as their defensive line coach and in his first official NFL game the Giants sacked the Philadelphia Eagles' quarterback nine times. Six of the sacks were by Marcin's linemen. After the game, Giants coach Jim Fassel said to him, "This is like falling off a rock."

After the season, defensive coordinator John Fox told him, "You'll never have trouble getting a job in the NFL."

When the Giants' entire staff was fired after the 2003 season, he was out of work for two days when the Jets hired him as their defensive line coach. He was 62 years old. He didn't even have to move. He retired from coaching at the age of 66, but still works for the Jets as a consultant from his retirement home in North Carolina.

Marcin lives in a development near the Atlantic Ocean. Priefer lives a few streets away and Joe Novak, who coached with them at Miami those many years ago, also lives nearby. Sometimes the sands of time flow backward. Marcin dusts his cherished game ball from his 1973 victory over Benedictine. Priefer still has all his

Padua baseball scorebooks. Marcin coached baseball at St. Edward at the same time.

"I got those scorebooks out not long ago," said Priefer. "We played each other twenty times. Believe it or not, we both won ten. Those were happy days. They were the happiest."

Kevin Mackey:
The Great Recruiter

Kevin Mackey arrived with a sizzle when he stepped onto the campus of Cleveland State University in the summer of 1983 to become its head basketball coach.

"He had the pedigree. He reminded me of Al McGuire," recalled Tom Bush, operations manager of WCLQ, an oddball independent television station located at Channel 61 on the dial in Cleveland.

Mackey was 37 years old and he talked like a basketball coach. He had that Boston accent and he had the credentials. As a high school coach in Boston, he won the New England Catholic championship at Cathedral High School and he won a state championship at the larger and more famous Don Bosco Tech. From there he was hired as an assistant coach at Boston College. His recruiting skill helped establish Boston College as a power in the Big East.

"In my mind's eye I could see big-time college basketball in Cleveland," said Bush. "Mackey could do that. I thought Cleveland State could become a big-time power."

Mackey was the most significant hire in the career of Cleveland State athletic director Bob Busbey, whose only concern until then was the swimming team. Even Mike Cleary, executive director of the NCAA College Athletic Directors Association, was intrigued. He picked up the phone in his Westlake office and called his friend Bill Flynn, the athletic director of Boston College, Mackey's previous boss.

"Who'd you send us?" Cleary asked, expecting to hear the usual platitudes. It was a conversation opener and Cleary never expected the answer.

"He's the best ghetto recruiter in the history of basketball," said Flynn.

"He'll have Cleveland State in the NCAA's in four years and on probation in four years."

It happened exactly as Bush had envisioned it. Unfortunately, it also happened just as Flynn had predicted. Television station WCLQ jumped on board immediately, agreeing to televise 10 Cleveland State basketball games in the season of 1983-84. Seven of them were road games in those little midwestern college towns.

Beverage Distributors, which handled Miller Lite, became CSU basketball's biggest television sponsor. Mackey himself made sales calls with WCLQ general sales manager Dennis Thatcher to close the deal. Beverage Distributors was owned, incidentally, by the John Conway family, one of the great Irish families on the East Side. This was a match made in heaven, an Irish coach, an Irish beer distributor and enough barley and hops to float the entire country of Ireland. "Kevin was great," said Bush. "They'd ask him questions and he talked basketball with that Boston accent and they signed on the dotted line. Eight minutes of commercials per game for Miller Lite."

This was getting good. In order to perpetuate the Irish theme, Bush brought Casey Coleman and me along as his basketball announcers. Casey was the play-by-play man, and I was the analyst. I protested.

"Get somebody else. I don't understand basketball," I said. "When I was in college I did Notre Dame basketball games on the student station and I was terrible."

"Don't worry about it," said Bush. "Nobody will be watching anyway. You need six-foot-long rabbit ears to pick up our station."

There was no backing out when Thatcher rang our front door bell and personally handed me my game uniform. On the air Casey and I wore matching blazers. Neither one of them fit but— what the hell? How could I say no?

"Don't get a flame anywhere near this garment," my wife warned me.

"Do you think it will catch fire?" I said.

"No, I think it will melt," she said. "This isn't wool. It's plastic."

It wouldn't be my everyday blazer. I had to squeeze into it only 10 times and, besides, nobody was watching. You needed a compass and a hyphen to navigate the terrain in the AMCU-8 conference. We traveled to Northern Iowa, Eastern Illinois, Western Illinois, Southwest Missouri State, Wisconsin-Green Bay, Valparaiso and Illinois-Chicago. After games we drank Miller Lite with Mackey in the Holiday Inn lounges until the bartenders blinked the lights.

As we enthusiastically supported CSU's biggest sponsor, Mackey mesmerized us with tales from the Big East. That's when I first heard the name Dave Gavitt, who founded the Big East in the 1970s and became its first commissioner. His concept was a television league. Gavitt's template banded together eight private colleges, each in a major television market. He went first to Holy Cross in Worcester, Massachusetts, about 30 miles from Boston. Holy Cross was a small school with high academic standards and a rich basketball history. Both Bob Cousy and Tom Heinsohn played there.

But the president of Holy Cross declined.

"It won't fly," he said.

So he turned to Boston College and they said yes. One at a time, Gavitt added commitments from Providence College, Seton Hall, St. John's, Villanova, Georgetown, Pitt and Syracuse. Prior to that, they were nice basketball programs with local and student support, but off campus hardly anybody noticed them. People paid attention to the Big Ten, the Atlantic Coast Conference, the Southeastern Conference and the PAC-10. Before long, the Big East was the most prestigious basketball conference in the country and Mackey watched it grow. He didn't merely have a front row seat. He helped build the Boston College program.

Now he was building something Clevelanders would never forget.

In Mackey's first year, the Vikings had a 14-16 record, nothing sensational, but Mackey's "run and stun" style of play caught our attention. His team was different. They ran a frantic full-court press for 40 minutes. He was different. He would get to work every day about two o'clock in the afternoon, still wearing his rumpled dark gray suit, just in time for practice. Most coaches I knew were in their office by seven in the morning, studying videotape and making phone calls to other workaholic coaches. Not Mackey. Here was a civilized man. I liked him immensely.

In his third year, Mackey put Cleveland State on the national stage. The Vikings won their conference championship to qualify for the NCAA Tournament and they won their first two tournament games in the Carrier Dome at Syracuse. They toppled Indiana, 83-79, on March 14 and two days later beat St. Joseph of Philadelphia, 75-69, to reach the Sweet 16. Mackey and the boys returned to Cleveland on St. Patrick's Day, and the coach's first stop was Public Hall where I was hosting a massive party featuring singer Pat Dailey and several Irish bands. Channel 8 did a live shot with Mackey and me during the six o'clock news. I named Mackey my Irishman of the year and presented him with a large framed map of Ireland. I don't remember many of the details, of course, because it was St. Patrick's Day and I had been going strong since noon. Channel 8 cameraman Ralph Tarsitano claims that he placed the Irish map on the floor and positioned Mackey and me on each side, using the frame to balance ourselves. Luckily, the wooden frame was well built.

It was four feet tall and two-and-a-half feet wide. The map was protected with thick glare-resistant glass. It was perfect for two Irish drunks to lean against.

"Both you guys could barely stand up," claimed Tarsitano, who was very proud of his ingenuity. "Viewers at home never knew."

While Mackey and I were laughing our way through the six o'clock news, the NCAA was taking a more serious view of Cleveland State. This always happens when an obscure team suddenly upstages the traditional giants. Five minutes after beating Indiana, Cleveland State had a target on its back and the NCAA investigators went hunting. They smelled blood.

The following weekend Cleveland State lost to Navy, 71-70, and what was called "The Magic Carpet Ride" was over.

Mackey had put together an interesting roster. The best player, guard Kenny (The Mouse) McFadden, had not graduated from high school. Mackey recruited him off the streets of New York City.

"I saw him score 40 points in an AAU game," Mackey recalled not long ago. "At the end of the game he moonwalked backwards with the ball, dribbling away the final seconds. The crowd went crazy. I said, 'I need to get him.'"

Two years later, Mackey did get him. Kevin did not subscribe to many of the silly rules that handcuffed the more conventional institutions, rules such as the requirement to graduate from high school before entering college. As Kevin explained it, the Mouse came to Cleveland to begin working his way through the maze of life. He landed a menial job at Cleveland State. He lived in an apartment house favored by other students near campus. But he wasn't a student.

He hung around practice with the basketball team while tutors helped prepare him for the GED test. He was 22 years old when he passed the test and became a college freshman in the fall of 1985. He was in the starting lineup by the middle of the season.

The leading scorer on that team, Clinton Smith from John Adams High School in Cleveland, transferred to Cleveland State after he was thrown out of Ohio State, and he established a pattern of playing Houdini with the criminal justice system. In June of 1985, Smith pleaded guilty to one count of forgery for stealing five official Cleveland State University checks and cashing them.

Cleveland attorney David B. Roth, a good guy who sympathized with underdogs, somehow persuaded Judge Stephanie Tubbs Jones to put Clinton on double secret probation for nine months. Put the emphasis on SECRET. So that Clinton M. Smith would not be identified in legal documents as the basketball player, he was identified as C. Michael Smith. By any name, Smith was lucky to find a lawyer as clever as Roth, who, coincidentally, also represented Mackey. Roth represented Smith pro bono, meaning no charge. How could a criminal be so lucky?

Mackey's team was difficult to explain.

While Mouse McFadden and Clinton Smith made interesting stories in their own right, two African imports brought down the Vikings. They were Manute Bol from the Sudan and Said Ibrahim from Somalia. Bol was a towering seven feet, six inches tall who weighed about 120 pounds. When he stood sideways he was invisible. Bol was Mackey's first international recruit, arriving on campus in the summer of 1983. Unfortunately, Bol could speak no English and his transcript was in shambles. Cleveland State had a problem. They had a political refugee on their hands. They could not send him back to his impoverished country. So Bol stayed and he was very visible. He was at all the home basketball games. Even at a basketball game, Bol stood out.

He lived in the Holiday Inn dorm, where other scholarship athletes lived, and he lived like a king. Bol did not work and he did not go to class. He didn't have to study and he had no homework. Bol would have been crazy to leave. CSU did enroll him in a class to learn to speak English. The class was at Case-Western Reserve University, which offered a special program for immigrants.

Mackey once said to me, "If I could have gotten Manute Bol in school, we would have won the national championship and we would have gone on probation the next day."

Eventually Bridgeport University in Connecticut managed to slip Bol past the admissions office and he played there until drafted by Washington in the NBA. He played in the NBA for seven seasons. Bol died in 2010.

The Said Ibrahim story is more complicated, as though that were possible. CSU inadvertently offered him a basketball scholarship sight unseen. Mackey's African scout described Ibrahim as seven feet, two inches tall, a star on the Somalia National Team. But when he got off the plane at Hopkins Airport in October 1984, he was only six feet, eight inches tall. Mackey had been swindled out of half a foot.

"This was not the young man who was described to me," Mackey said at the time. "I've been sold a bill of goods."

Ibrahim's visit had a 48-hour limit imposed by the NCAA. In order to get a student's visa for him, George Burke, associate dean of student life at CSU, sent a telegram to the U.S. Embassy in Somalia. Intending to strengthen the request, Burke indicated that CSU had offered Ibrahim a scholarship. Dean Burke, apparently unfamiliar with athletic department procedures, did not realize the implications of such a commitment.

Like Bol, Ibrahim also refused to leave and the drama moved forward. Associate athletic director Merle Levin suspected that Ibrahim switched places with the real player Mackey thought he was getting. There were other disputes. Mackey claimed Ibrahim already was a college graduate and had no eligibility left. Ibrahim claimed he was only a junior college graduate. Ultimately, CSU paid Ibrahim $7,000 as compensation for reneging on the scholarship offer and Ibrahim enrolled at Oberlin College, where he played basketball and was not very good.

In the face of these bizarre shenanigans, the NCAA investigators salivated like pit bulls at a family picnic. Meanwhile, the Cleveland State administration loyally stood behind its coach and for good reason. Having brought these young men here from Africa, CSU had a moral obligation to them. They shouldn't have been thrown out on the streets.

The NCAA, however, has never been tainted by compassion. In 1988, Cleveland State was put on probation for three years, which included recruiting restrictions and no post-season tournaments.

CSU hit the jackpot. It was in the big time. Neither Mackey nor CSU showed any remorse during the investigation, which was not wise. If you want to really make the NCAA angry, dig in your heels and fight back. Mackey even sought the advice of Nevada-Las Vegas coach Jerry Tarkanian, who also had waged a famous battle with the NCAA.

Despite the laundry list of sanctions, in the summer of 1990

Mackey was handed a new three-year contract at $300,000 per year. He never saw a dime of it. Two days later his life disintegrated.

He was arrested while stumbling out of a crack house with a prostitute, the moment that, sadly, defines his life. The Cleveland police were tipped off. The police alerted the media. TV cameras were waiting for him and Mackey woke up on national television again. Cocaine and alcohol were coursing through his system.

Within a week he was fired and his big contract was voided. In seven years, his coaching record at CSU was 144-67, the 13th-best winning percentage among active coaches in big time college basketball. The best career winning percentage at that time belonged to Jerry Tarkanian.

Two months later, Kevin pleaded guilty to drug charges and was sentenced to 90 days of confinement. He spent 60 of them in John Lucas' rehab clinic in Houston and then began an almost impossible task—putting his life back together.

"Before I got in trouble, the politicians and the movers and shakers asked me to make appearances for them all the time. When I got in trouble, they're gone," Kevin said recently. "Only one person stayed with me. Ted Stepien. He was great to me. The media made him a punch line, but I know about his charity. He was an unbelievable human being."

Stepien was an active member of Alcoholics Anonymous and helped many recovering drunks. Like Shakespeare's Caesar, bury his good deeds with his bones. Mackey then began bouncing around the minor leagues of pro basketball. Over 13 seasons he coached in six American cities—Portland, Maine; Miami; Atlantic City; Trenton, N.J.; Jacksonville; and Mansfield, Ohio—as well as towns in Canada, Korea and Argentina. He won four league championships and sent 39 players to the NBA. In the summers he picked up odd jobs at basketball camps.

"I tried to keep two jobs in order to make ends meet," he said. He never complained.

"I blame only myself," he said many times.

One winter he helped coach the Lorain Admiral King junior varsity. Athletic director Ray Ebersole had hoped to hire him full time as a teacher and a coach, but the school board would not allow it. One night Mackey saw Ben Roethlisberger, a six-foot, five-inch point guard for Findlay High School, score 40 points against Admiral King.

"He can play in the NBA," Mackey said to the Admiral King head coach.

Later when Roethlisberger was playing quarterback at Miami of Ohio, Mackey ran into Miami basketball coach Charlie Coles.

"Do you know who's the best basketball player in the Mid-American Conference?" Mackey said to Coles.

"Who are you thinking of?" said Coles.

"Your quarterback," said Mackey.

In the summer of 2003, Mackey answered his cell phone and the voice on the other end said, "This is Larry Bird."

"I thought it was one of my friends playing a trick," said Kevin. "Larry had been following my career. I didn't know that."

It actually was Bird, president of the Indiana Pacers. He offered Kevin a job scouting college players. It was a real job with real NBA pay. He lives out of a suitcase. He scouts a college game almost every night, driving from one game to the next in a company car, using a company cell phone and a company computer and sleeping in first class hotels. It took him 14 years to reach this point.

Many people would consider this a lonely life, but Mackey is a basketball junkie and as long as he has a game, he is never lonely. His three grown children moved back to Boston many years ago. Mackey's marriage is long gone.

Despite the chaos, Cleveland State remains Mackey's most cherished memory and the feeling is mutual. Mackey is responsible for the Wolstein Center, the 13,000-seat convocation center where CSU plays basketball. Original plans called for a 20,000-seat arena with ice-making facilities for hockey and ice shows. The Gund family, which owned the Richfield Coliseum, lobbied for a smaller building with no ice, which could not compete with them for events. They hired a full-time lobbyist in Columbus to work the state legislature, which controlled the purse strings and the Gunds got their way.

Mackey believed that an 8,000-seat arena was ideal for his basketball team and history shows that he was right. Actually, his preference was Woodling Gym, a glorified high school fieldhouse that had only 3,000 seats.

"That was a home floor advantage," Mackey always said. "Other coaches complained that I was playing my seven against their five."

I asked Mackey if he were ready to author a full-length book about his life, the good times and the bad.

"I don't know. A lot of people have asked me," he replied. "But the final chapter hasn't been written."

"You're 65 years old," I said. "You better start writing the final chapter."

It seems like a lifetime ago when Mackey and I were full of beer and laughter in those Holiday Inn lounges. If only Kevin had stopped at beer and laughter.

Al McGuire:
Self-Confessed Con Man

Al McGuire was only 48 and at the top of his game in 1978 when he gave up coaching at Marquette to become a college basketball analyst for NBC. He was a coaching legend. Sports announcers come and go. He had some explaining to do.

He grew up above his father's bar in Rockaway Beach on Long Island, and cherished his summer visits to his grandmother's house on the Jersey shore.

"At the end of my grandmother's street were steps leading down to the beach. I loved swimming in the waves. Every morning I would run down the street, down the steps and run into the ocean," he said.

"One morning my grandmother called me to come back for breakfast. She put a banana next to my cereal. I loved bananas, but I thought that if I ate the banana, I'd have to wait an hour before I went swimming. So I left it on the table and ran right back to the beach.

"But while I was gone the wind whipped up. The sand was blowing. The waves were getting higher and they were crashing on the beach. I sat down on the bottom of the stairs and I thought about what had just happened. I had bet on the if-come. I didn't eat the banana because I thought there was something better. I had the banana in my hand. It was a sure thing. Now I had nothing. I made up my mind right then. The next time, I'll eat the banana.

"That's what the television job was. I wanted to do it, but I also wanted to coach another year or two. I wanted them both. But maybe the television job wouldn't be available in a year or two.

That would be like betting the if-come. So I took the sure thing. This time I ate the banana."

Here was a pragmatic philosopher if there ever was one. He shared his views on several other subjects during a visit to Cleveland in 1976.

He advised his student sports information director Kevin Byrne about the secret to marital bliss.

"Only one person can be happy in a marriage," said McGuire. "Make sure that person is you."

McGuire shared his personal rules for coaching college basketball. "I'm a thief, con artist and hypocrite," McGuire said. "My players never take a towel out of a motel. They take the TV. We have a certain level of class to maintain."

McGuire called himself a hypocrite because he did not enforce discipline off the court. When a player violated curfew, McGuire didn't want to know about it. When a player was late for the team bus, McGuire wore blinders. To avoid confrontations, he waited in the motel bar until the student manager told him all the players were aboard.

"Don't issue ultimatums," he said. "I always leave a crack in the door so we can both get out with dignity."

He bristled when asked how he "handled" black players.

"I don't *handle* them," he said with a tone of contempt for the word. "I don't con them. They don't con me. In practice, I shout at them and they holler back at me. It looks like we're undisciplined, but actually we're the most disciplined team in basketball. On the court, I'm the boss. When the score is tied, 60-60, and there's a minute left, everybody is quiet. I'm a dictator.

"When we need to make the last shot to win a game, I tell them to take a 15-foot jump shot when we're on the road and drive to the basket when we're at home. Coaching is not a thinking man's game. I spend only twenty percent of my time on basketball and I never talk basketball at home. I never blow a whistle or use a blackboard. Sometimes I don't even show up for practice. They get tired of hearing my voice and I get tired of shouting at them.

We're all bricklayers. I don't want to scare the other coach out of a job. I just want to build a better house."

When recruiting, go to your strong side. McGuire was best in the inner city. That's where he found the best players. They knew that if McGuire recruited them, they would leave college with a big pro contract. His charisma was so powerful that players who never met him were attracted to him.

"I recruit best on concrete and in kitchens," he said. "I can't recruit on grass. I recruit one kid a year, one blue chipper. My co-coaches do all the recruiting. Sometimes I don't meet a kid we recruited until school starts."

He never believed coaching was a lifetime job.

"Hanging around with guys in short pants all your life would be OK if I were gay," he said.

Nothing wrong with being gay. McGuire preached tolerance.

McGuire's older brother, John, ran a nightclub on Long Island. When business went sour, John McGuire converted it into a gay bar, although he was straight. He was called the "King of Queens."

"My brother John is a thief. I'm only half a thief," said McGuire.

McGuire's father ran a saloon in Rockaway Beach.

"We'd take out the stools in the bar every weekend so the customers would become tired of standing and move somewhere else. After a guy's third drink, he's no good. He doesn't drink as fast and you get tired of looking at him. One time a lady said she stood up at work all day and wanted to sit down when she had a drink. She said she was tired. My father told her to quit her job."

Coaches should never forget they are in the entertainment business, he advised.

"The first thing I do when I walk onto the floor of our arena is to look up at the four corners of the building. There's one seat way up there in each corner. If somebody's sitting in each seat, I know I've done my job."

A good coach has two personalities. McGuire said that his game personality was "arrogant, surly and obnoxious." His friends said that off the court he was gentle, warm and empathetic.

"Did you ever know a free spirit?" McGuire asked me. "You do now."

You don't find any genuine free spirits in college coaching anymore. There's too much money and too much pressure involved. It's no longer a game.

Ken Carpenter:
Couldn't Hold a Job

Ken Carpenter was always scheming. While attending Cleveland State University and working part time at *The Plain Dealer* he read a story about a young middleweight boxer named Jeff Stoudemire who was ready to turn pro.

"They said he was the next Sugar Ray Leonard," said Carpenter.

Stoudemire won five Cleveland Golden Gloves championships, a national Golden Gloves title and a national AAU crown. Students of the sweet science believed Stoudemire was good enough to represent the United States in the 1980 Summer Olympics in Moscow, except that was the year the United States boycotted the Olympics to protest the Soviet invasion of Afghanistan.

I vigorously protested the protest. I remember the great sportswriter Red Smith writing an impassioned column that defended President Jimmy Carter's order to boycott the Games. I felt just the opposite. What did the boycott prove?

Nothing. It deprived American athletes of the chance to participate in the Olympics. For many, it was their only chance. The Soviets retaliated four years later by boycotting the Summer Olympics in Los Angeles. The dueling boycotts were indefensible. They were stupid.

Stoudemire was 22 years old. His only Olympic opportunity was sacrificed on the altar of international politics, so he signed a pro contract with Cleveland manager and promoter Carl Lombardo.

"Everybody wanted to sign him," said Carpenter. "Don King and Bob Arum wanted him. Stoudemire went with Lombardo because he was the only one who agreed to keep his amateur trainer, Clint Martin. That was important to Stoudemire.

Lombardo also paid him a salary of $80,000 a year. He gave him a car, an apartment and an expense account.

"After reading all this I picked up the phone and called Lombardo. I wanted to be his press agent," said Carpenter, who wasn't exactly a neophyte. He was only 23 but his resume already included three years as the publicity man at Northfield Park racetrack, a perfect stepping stone for the fight game. Lombardo was impressed.

"He hired me," said Carpenter.

"How much will I pay you?" Lombardo asked. He had never hired a press agent before.

"Three per cent of the gross of his fights," said Carpenter, who pulled a number out of the air. It was based on nothing.

"Two percent," said Lombardo, whose counter proposal also was based on nothing except his instinct to negotiate.

"That's fine," said Carpenter. They shook on it.

Carpenter's first assignment as Stoudemire's publicity man was to rig an election. *The Cleveland Press* was running a quirky "sexiest athlete" contest.

"I wish I could say it was my idea, but it actually was Carl Lombardo's," Carpenter said. "We bought up all the papers on the West Side and cut out the ballots. We bought them by the hundreds. No, by the thousands. Lombardo insisted that we pay for all these papers. He wouldn't let us steal any. He didn't want anything to taint the contest. We had secretaries from Lombardo's company clipping the coupons like crazy and mailing them."

Stoudemire won the contest and Carpenter arranged for a sexy photo shoot, which fortunately coincided with Stoudemire's first pro fight Sept. 18, 1980, in the Masonic Auditorium at E. 30th Street and Chester Avenue.

Lombardo brought in veteran promoter Don Elbaum to put together the card and he gave Elbaum specific instructions.

"He told Elbaum to get a white opponent for Stoudemire. He

did not want a pushover, either. No tomato can. He told Elbaum to find a white guy who would put up a decent fight," said Carpenter.

Elbaum did as he was told. He found a tough young kid named Mike Sacchetti from West Virginia. Carpenter recalls the night. It wasn't like a boxing match. It was like a coronation. There was a full house. Former heavyweight contender Jimmy Ellis was in the front row. Stoudemire paraded around the ring and posed for pictures.

Proclamations from all the politicians and labor unions were read and presented to him. The pre-fight introductions proved to be the highlight of Stoudemire's career. After that it was all downhill.

One minute into the fight, Sacchetti knocked him down. Stoudemire beat the count. He got up and was never in trouble again. But in a short four-round bout, there wasn't enough time to make up for a knockdown. The judges, all local men, gave the nod to Sacchetti. The judges had a problem. They were biased on the side of honesty.

"Lombardo was going crazy, screaming at the judges. How could local judges do that to a local fighter? He screamed at Elbaum for bringing in a kid who was too tough. Elbaum only did what Lombardo wanted," said Carpenter.

After one fight, the next Sugar Ray Leonard hit the comeback trail. Elbaum pulled bums off the street, lifted cripples out of wheelchairs and pushed them into the ring against Stoudemire. He built Jeff's record up to 14 wins and three losses but there were contract disputes, trainer changes and general chaos. He never had a big fight. He never had a big payday. After three years, Stoudemire left for California and disappeared. Many years later he returned to Cleveland and died on Dec. 5, 2008, at the age of 51.

"My dreams of Las Vegas riches went out the window," lamented Carpenter, whose boxing career lasted barely more than a month. He was fired after one fight, as though the publicity man had something to do with it.

*   *   *

The Stoudemire experience was not easy to digest. Carpenter was coming off a winning streak at Northfield, where he had a knack for picking winners. He had the touch. Although he was barely old enough to vote when he worked there, Carpenter enjoyed a night grizzled old horsemen don't have the audacity to even dream about.

Among the publicity man's duties was making the picks for newspaper handicappers when they took a night off. It was a common practice. Isi Newborn of the *Press* handicapped Florida tracks for the Miami Herald and when he was busy, he asked young Bob Roberts to handicap Gulfstream for him. Roberts later succeeded Newborn and became a celebrated handicapper himself for the *Press* and *The Plain Dealer*.

One Saturday night, Carpenter made Phil Hartman of the *Cleveland Press* a hero. Carpenter picked all 10 winners for Hartman, an accomplishment that is almost unprecedented. Although Hartman was off the clock, he was actually in the clubhouse with a group of his friends and neighbors from the Brush High School Athletic Boosters.

"After I went six for six, Phil came up to the press box and said, 'If you pick the seventh I'm gonna be elected mayor of Lyndhurst.' Everybody in Phil's group had his picks in their hands. They cut them out of the paper and brought them to the track. They saw what was happening. After the eighth race they were literally carrying Phil around on their shoulders," said Carpenter.

"I can't remember anybody carrying me on their shoulders. I can't picture racetrack people doing something like that. Besides, they were short-priced horses and you don't get rich on them," Hartman recalled decades later.

The workers in the press box, however, knew that Carpenter was responsible for the hysteria. When his 10th straight winner came home, the judges flashed the "Inquiry" sign as a gag.

Harness horses are easier to handicap than thoroughbreds because they are more consistent. It's their steady, rhythmic gait. They're frequently older and they always run the same distance— exactly one mile. Nevertheless, picking 10 winners in a row would justify a major story on Page One, not a tiny box on the racing page. At one time a man who picked nine straight winners at a thoroughbred track was in the *Guinness Book of World Records*. But there never was a word about it in the *Press* because it did not have a Sunday paper and by Monday it was old news. *The Plain Dealer* ignored the accomplishment.

"I'm sure that Phil Hartman's name was on the picks because that's how it was done," Roberts recalls. "But we should have carried a box saying a guy went 10 for 10 and the guy was Ken Carpenter. We didn't have to go into a long explanation saying he made the picks for Phil Hartman. That was irrelevant. Just say Carpenter did it. However, I wasn't in charge."

"I had a lot of big nights," Hartman said not long ago. "I had 5, 6, 7 winners lots of times. I had 9 winners once. But I never swept the card. I never had 10 winners except for that night."

Nobody printed a word. The greatest achievement in racing history went unacknowledged.

* * *

Carpenter moved on to *The Plain Dealer* in the 1980s as a part-time copy editor in the sports department but he still had the touch. In the summer of 1981, a nine-year-old pacer named Rowdy K was the hottest horse at Northfield Park and Ken was determined to buy him. Let's be clear. Rowdy K was only a cheap claimer, but when he won four straight $4,000 claiming races within a month he caught the eye of Carpenter. In those days nobody had four grand, certainly nobody who worked part-time on the sports copy desk at *The Plain Dealer*. Carpenter needed partners and he found four of them—his *Plain Dealer* co-worker Tony Grossi, Dave Dombrowski, who worked for the Cavs, and Cleveland State University hockey players John Wiegand and Marc Klecka.

But when Rowdy K moved up in class and won a $5,000 claiming race, his fifth win in a row, the price went up. Carpenter needed more partners. He called and I answered.

"I'm sure we put the deal together over beverages," Carpenter reminded me. I also worked at *The Plain Dealer*, which meant that I also had no money. Maddy and I were starting to have babies left and right. If I had sashayed into the kitchen with news that I had invested our last thousand dollars on a Northfield hay burner, I would have been hit in the head with a cast iron skillet.

But as the president of the Press Club of Cleveland, I represented a potential investor. There was one drawback. The Press Club also was almost insolvent. We barely had enough in the treasury to cover our bar bill at board of directors meetings. This was my philosophy. When the board met to conduct official Press Club business, our bar bill was an official club expense. Usually the only official business we discussed was how to pay our bar bill.

A horse such as Rowdy K, I reasoned, would guarantee our bar bill for at least a year, certainly until my term as president came to an end. I would have been hailed as a financial genius, setting a high standard for the next president. I called a board of directors meeting to propose the purchase of Rowdy K.

"How much is in the treasury?" I asked treasurer Pauline Thoma.

She rounded it off. "Twenty-five hundred dollars," she said.

"Then I propose we buy half of Rowdy K," I said, putting it in the form of a motion.

"Which half?" said Harriet Peters, the gossip columnist from the *Press*.

Harriet was nothing but trouble. She had not a drop of sporting blood in her veins. Furthermore, Harriet always was contrary. Instead of writing about Gib Shanley's wedding, for example, she interviewed one of his ex-wives.

For purposes of this story, John Sheridan, board member and two-term Press Club president, attempted to recall critical details of that fateful meeting because he claims to be the only one who seems to remember them. In the spring of 2011 he sent me an e-mail.

"My recollection is that there were only four of us at that board meeting—you, me, Pauline and Harriet. Not even a quorum. (But in those days, we never let a little thing like the club by-laws stand in the way of a crazy idea.) I think on the first vote, the one before you blackmailed me, the vote was 2-2, with myself and Harriet voting 'no.' Then, of course, you used a bit of artful persuasion to get me to change my mind. As I remember it, the final vote to buy that nag was 3-1, and Harriet remained steadfast in her opposition. Of course, I could be wrong."

Sheridan believes that Harriet's heroism in the face of lunacy is worthy of a Press Club Hall of Fame nomination.

"If nothing else, she deserves consideration for her insistence that we were off our rockers for buying Rowdy K. She is a woman of integrity," Sheridan wrote.

Of course, he could be wrong.

"We knew a trainer, Doug Hinklin, who put in the claim for us and our syndicate bought the horse from him in a private sale," Carpenter said.

The Press Club was now in the horse racing business. We sat back as a passive investor and waited to count our winnings. Carpenter's half of the syndicate handled the racing business.

"For a $5,000 claimer this was the biggest syndicate in history," said Carpenter. "First thing we did, we moved him to a new trainer—Doug Hinklin, the guy who put in the claim—and Hinklin changed drivers. Mel Turcotte had driven Rowdy K to five straight victories. The new driver was Gerry Bookmeyer, who had never driven Rowdy K before."

Rowdy K's training regimen was unusual but it worked for him.

"It was unprecedented," said Carpenter. "I never saw anything like it. Every day a girl rode him under saddle. She rode him for hours, all around Northfield Park, out in the country, over hills and dales. She put miles on him. But he hardly ever trained by pulling a sulky around the track."

Hinklin changed all that. He allowed the girl to ride him, but only around the track. They also began to attach a sulky to him. Rowdy K wondered what was going on. When horses begin to think, there's danger ahead. Rowdy K didn't know when he was training and when he was racing. He was confused.

"We were all out there for his first race," Carpenter said. "The horses came out for the post parade and there was no Rowdy K. Then the track announcer said, 'Rowdy K has been excused from the post parade.' That's not what an owner wants to hear. I never saw that before or since.

"Finally, he came out of a far corner and slipped into the warmup lap. He was covered head to toe in white, foamy sweat. I never saw anything like it. Foam all over him.

"Well, the race started and right out of the gate Rowdy K broke stride. He went off in a full gallop. Twenty seconds after he broke stride he put himself back in stride and he went like a bat out of hell. He caught the field and went into the lead. Bookmeyer wasn't driving the horse. He was holding on for dear life. Then Rowdy K broke stride again and he finished last."

Trainer Hinklin returned Turcotte to the sulky for Rowdy K's next two races and the horse did nothing. The owner collects on the first five places but in three races for the "syndicate" Rowdy K did not earn a nickel.

"After one month of craziness we sold him back to the original owner for $4,000," Carpenter said. "We lost a thousand dollars on the sale and it cost us another thousand dollars for training fees, food bill and entry fees. We split $2,000 in losses. In his first race after we sold him, he won."

As usual, Carpenter left an important legacy on racing. He proved that Cleveland was a one-horse town and that horse was Rowdy K.

The Press Club held a membership drive to pay Rowdy K's feed bill. The Press Club under my administration was like a Catholic Church—a lot of second collections.

*   *   *

Meanwhile, Carpenter was destined for greater acclaim. He went to Hollywood to get rich on the game show circuit in 1985. He was no novice. He had been on the South High School Academic Challenge Team a few years earlier. In fact, he appeared on the Channel 5 program two straight years under coach Frank Dillon. South High was the only school in Cleveland with a game show coach.

"Frank was a brilliant game show coach," said Carpenter. "He studied them. He knew exactly what questions they would ask. For example, he said there would be a question about the Heisman Trophy because that had been in the news and he was right. Don Webster was the host. He started reading the question. He said, 'In college football . . .' And I blurt out, 'John Cappelletti,' who had just won the Heisman Trophy. Webster was stunned. 'Yes,' he said. I saw Frank in the back of the room pumping his fist in the air."

When "Wheel of Fortune" held tryouts at the Renaissance Hotel on the Square, Ken caught the attention of the producers with another seminal performance.

"They ran practice games. The answer was 'a place.' There were a lot of letters in it. They didn't even finish putting up all the squares and I shouted, 'Boston, Massachusetts.' I was right. Oh, yes. They noticed me. So I got on 'Wheel of Fortune,' but not the prime time show at night. They had a low budget daytime version and that's the one I got on. I solved the puzzle, 'Porterhouse Steak,' and I won a set of patio furniture and some other small prizes. You didn't win money back then, only prizes. I was still living at home with my mom and dad. Gifts kept coming to their house for months. A case of Tuna Helper, a case of Faygo pop, a case of toothpaste."

*   *   *

Ken's game show career was over and he was still working part-time on *The Plain Dealer* sports copy desk. Late one night in

1986, he read a story about San Francisco's bid to host the 1996 Summer Olympics and he wondered, "Why not Cleveland?"

The next day he called the mayor's office and asked the same question. Nobody from Cleveland was interested, he was told. Well, Carpenter was interested. He called the United States Olympic Committee.

"Come on out to Colorado Springs and we'll show you how to do it," he was told.

"I was proud of what I was doing. I took it to our sports editor Gene Williams.

He said, 'You can't do it. Conflict of interest.' I said, 'I'm going to do it. I'm going to Colorado Springs.' After all, I was still working part time."

Carpenter's logic was unassailable. Most of *The Plain Dealer's* part-time employees had real jobs on the outside. Neither Williams nor anybody else had the right to dictate what they did on their own time. Gene Hersch, for Pete's sake, had been a full-time copy editor in the sports department and on the side handled publicity for Congresswoman Frances Payne Bolton. When he worked late night makeup in the composing room, he deftly slipped short items about his client in the final makeover edition.

Carpenter was acquainted with Mayor George Voinovich's press secretary, Claire Rosacco, who gave Carpenter an official letter of authorization from the mayor to be shown to the U.S. Olympic Committee. Essentially, Carpenter became head of the Cleveland Olympic Committee. He flew to Colorado Springs to attend a seminar on applying. He paid Cleveland's application fee of $50. They handed him a thick three-ring binder with hundreds of questions to be answered.

When he returned to Cleveland, *The Plain Dealer* fired him.

"Actually, that was good. I needed the time to complete the application," said Carpenter.

The application would have overwhelmed a committee. Carpenter breezed through it, researching such information as the number of hotel rooms, winds on Lake Erie for the sailing events, availability of venues such as Camp Perry for the shooting events. And it went on. Carpenter's key point was that 1996 would be Cleveland's bicentennial, which would be marked with fresh construction and heightened celebration. He completed the information, mailed the three-ring binder to the U.S. Olympic Committee and waited. Months went by. Carpenter forgot about it. So did the mayor.

"The next summer I was playing golf with my father at Punderson State Park and a guy came out of the clubhouse and asked, 'Are you Ken Carpenter?' He said there were nine phone messages for me. Newspapers, radio stations, TV stations were calling. They were all trying to reach me."

The United States Olympic Committee had just released the list of the five American finalists to host the 1996 Games and Cleveland was on the list, along with Atlanta, Nashville, Minneapolis-St. Paul and San Francisco. The story identified Carpenter as head of Cleveland's Organizing Committee. Mayor Voinovich received phone calls saying, "Congratulations."

"What for?" said His Honor.

Naturally, no one in Cleveland's political or power structure followed up and the newspaper stories focused exclusively on the one-man organizing committee. *USA Today* did a story on Carpenter. Writing in one of the alternative weeklies, Doug Clarke eviscerated *The Plain Dealer* for firing the one guy who cared. The *Akron Beacon Journal* also had a good chuckle at *The Plain Dealer's* expense.

"Instead of holding me up as a civic visionary, they fired me," Carpenter said, enjoying the irony these many years later.

"Down in Atlanta, Billy Payne invited 30 of his friends to his home and asked each of them to donate $100,000 to Atlanta's Olympic fund. He raised $3 million while I was filling out the paperwork."

Atlanta spent millions to land the 1996 Games. Billy Payne is now chairman of Augusta National, the golf course where they play the Masters. Carpenter spent 50 bucks and is still playing public courses.

* * *

Having lost the Olympics and his job, Carpenter got a call from an old friend in New York who hired him to join the copy desk of a startup sports daily called *The National*. Some big-time sports-writers and investors were involved.

"I was there from the first day to the last day," Carpenter said.

The National started in January 1990, and folded in June 1992.

"I haven't realized this before, but I guess there is a pattern here," Carpenter said.

* * *

He is now a professor of journalism at Valencia Community College in Orlando, Florida, where he teaches impressionable young college students how to find wealth and happiness in the media.

Name's the Same:
Who Are These Guys?

When I was a kid, people sometimes asked if I were related to Father Coughlin, the radio priest from Royal Oak, Michigan. They never used his first name, which was Charles. He was simply, "Father Coughlin." In my earlier years at *The Plain Dealer* several of my sports department colleagues kiddingly called me "Father Coughlin." We had nicknames for everybody back then. Over the years our hockey writer Richard Passan shortened it. He called me simply, "Father." Ironically, Father Coughlin was an anti-Semitic madman and Passan was Jewish. On the other hand, I called Passan "Maurice" after the great hockey player Maurice Richard. Over the years I shortened it to "Mo." Hal Lebovitz once asked me, "Why do you call him Mo?" I explained the hockey reference and Hal was satisfied. Later I learned that 'Mo' was a disrespectful term for Jews. How were we to know?

The last time we talked, I said, "Hi, Maurice."

He said, "Hi, Father."

In the late 1930s and into the '40s, Father Coughlin was infamous for his highly politicized network radio sermons on Sunday afternoons. It was estimated that at his peak of influence he had 30 million listeners and received 80,000 pieces of mail every week. He preached against communism, even though his thinking exactly paralleled the communists, and he was sympathetic to Hitler. Somebody should have told him to shut the hell up. The American bishops, the Vatican and President Franklin Roosevelt finally got together and pressured the archbishop of Detroit to silence him. Father Coughlin was ordered to turn off the microphone, get off the damn radio and confine his preaching to Paul's letters to the Corinthians. He gritted his teeth and complied. He pastored his parish until he retired in 1966.

When I was 12 years old, we took a family vacation in the car, our green 1941 Plymouth. We went north through Niagara Falls into French-speaking Canada and back home through Detroit, where we visited Father Coughlin's parish church, the National Shrine of the Little Flower in the suburb of Royal Oak. It was very modern, the first circular church I had ever seen. I think we went there because Father Coughlin was once a celebrity and my parents thought they might actually run into him, not because they endorsed what he stood for.

Afterward, when people asked about my connection to Father Coughlin, I would say. "Not related to him. Don't know him. But I've been to his church." The church, incidentally, is still operating. My son, Joe, once had a college roommate who grew up in that parish. In fact, he was an altar boy there.

"Do people still talk about Father Coughlin?" I asked him.

"Who is Father Coughlin?" he replied.

*   *   *

I have a fairly common Irish name, but people have a hard time pronouncing it. I must admit it's challenging. Even my father and his six brothers couldn't agree.

Some pronounced it with a "ck" in the middle. They said "COCK-lin." My Uncle Frank said it with an "aw" in the middle. He said, "CAWG-lin." I grew up saying, "COG-lin." The well-known football coach Tom Coughlin said he pronounces his name the same as I do, but when he coached at Boston College people in Beantown called him, "KOFF-lin," and that's the name that stuck.

"I got tired of correcting them," he said to me once during a telephone conference call.

*   *   *

When I was in high school at St. Edward in Lakewood, there was a kid two years older than me on the other side of town at Benedictine who had the same name. He also was Dan Coughlin and his name was in the papers frequently because he was an outstanding lineman on Benedictine's football team that played in back-to-back Charity Games at the Stadium in 1952 and '53.

Men who worked with my father on the railroad asked him if the Benedictine lineman was his son.

"No, he's not," said my dad, "and I'm not related to Father Coughlin, either."

The Benedictine Dan went on to play for the University of Miami Hurricanes and then went into college coaching, most notably at Memphis, Kentucky and Florida. Naturally, he recruited the Cleveland area, which caused no end of confusion. When he was a young football coach, I was a young sportswriter at *The Plain Dealer* and my job was the high school beat. When we called high school coaches on the phone, the coaches never knew if they were talking to the football recruiter or the newspaper reporter. That led to puzzling conversations. I called a coach for a routine feature story on a kid and he began by saying the kid doesn't test well and he would need a junior college and a tutor. "Huh?" I sometimes said.

I imagine there were times when recruiter Dan Coughlin was asked, "Do you want to come out and take a picture?"

"Huh?" he probably said.

Years later when I took a job with CBS in Miami, old timers there thought I was the former Hurricane football player returning to the site of his previous conquests. They were disappointed to learn otherwise.

One day at Calder Racetrack in Miami a press box attendant rushed up to me.

"You just missed Dan Coughlin," he said. "He was here not half an hour ago."

Dan returned to Miami occasionally because he liked the horses. We had much in common. Is it any wonder we were often confused with each other? That was our last chance to meet. I was out of there within a year in the spring of 1990 and Dan died of cancer eight months later at the age of 54. I regretted that we had never met. I always wanted to hear his side of the story.

We are linked forever in other ways. Years ago Abbot Father Roger Gries, O.S.B., who later became a bishop, made me an honorary alumnus of Benedictine and, to reinforce it, they send me an invoice every year. When they get my check I hope they credit the right guy.

"I'm going to find this guy," I said.

I didn't even have to try. We were tripping over each other with connections. He knew some of my cousins who went to high school with him at Padua. At one time he worked for Vince Hvizda, an old friend of mine. His mother knew my niece.

Best of all, we worked at *The Plain Dealer* at the same time in the early 1980s.

"I worked in the advertising department as a copy checker. It was my first job out of high school in 1980," he said when I reached him on the phone at his Middleburg Heights home.

"Did you ever become a writer, a humor writer?" I asked.

"Never did," he said. "I'm just a barroom humorist."

He's married with two children and he works as a printer at Admiral Products on West 150th Street in Cleveland.

"My mother was often asked if she was related to Dan Coughlin," Dan said. "She always said, 'Yes, he's my son.'"

My mother always said the same thing. What a coincidence.

* * *

In recent years a fellow named Dan Coughlin began turning up in Bud Shaw's columns in *The Plain Dealer*. Bud writes whimsical columns and encourages reader participation. Dan Coughlin was a frequent contributor. The guy was good. His items were clever. Everybody thought he was me. He didn't embarrass me, but I was uncomfortable with the message it seemed to convey, that I was so hungry to see my name in print that I was giving away my stuff. I'm a professional. This is not a hobby. The other Dan Coughlin, however, was a hobbyist just having a good time.

LeBron James:
No Names, Please

For all those years that LeBron James played in Cleveland, I never heard him call any of the local reporters by name. It's just sort of natural, isn't it, to occasionally say somebody's name in the course of a conversation, especially people you see regularly year after year? Even the president of the United States acknowledges his regular reporters by name. It's a courtesy in a cultured society. LeBron talks to network reporters like old friends, such as Jim Gray and Craig Sager. He's all over them, it's "Jim this" and "Craig that." But he dealt with the local people like the movie, *Fifty First Dates*, as though he never saw them before, even after 10 years. I don't think he watched the local news so he didn't know who was on television. He wasn't much of a reader, except for sports headlines in *The Plain Dealer* and Akron *Beacon Journal*, so he didn't know the names of the small-town writers.

I mentioned this a few years ago to some other reporters who were killing time after a Cavs practice while waiting for LeBron to finish his lunch, his shower, his nap or whatever that day's reason to inconvenience the local media. The coach and other players would do their duty with the media immediately after practice. Not LeBron, however. He liked to disappear and come back in half an hour or an hour later. Everybody would wait and grumble. Sometimes after a long wait a public relations person would come by and say, "LeBron's not talking today."

He liked to tweak the noses of the media, often in subtle ways. For example, when LeBron was in high school the media became apoplectic when his mother, Gloria, bought him a Hummer. Where, the media demanded, did his mother get the money for so lavish a car? Let me toss out some possible answers. For one thing, every sports agent in the world would have happily advanced her the money. There was nothing illegal about that. For another thing, any Hummer dealer would have been smart to set up a friendly finance plan, considering the publicity it generated. For a third thing, it was none of our business. Before the next basketball game at the height of the media commotion, LeBron entertained the crowd during warmups by playing with a remote control toy Hummer about the size of a shoebox.

"He called me by name once," Mary Schmitt Boyer of *The Plain Dealer* said.

I was taken aback. She said it happened in New York after the Sunday morning shoot around. He finished his interview with the New York writers and started to walk away.

"Lebron, could I ask you one more thing for a special story I'm doing?" Mary said.

"Sure, Mary. What is it?" LeBron said.

Mary Schmitt Boyer said she was caught by surprise. She was a beat reporter who covered the Cavs since LeBron arrived in the summer of 2003 and that was the first time he had uttered her name.

LeBron also never even said "Hi" to Cavs radio announcer Joe Tait. They even traveled on the same plane to away games, more than 300 away games in seven seasons. Never a "Hi, Joe. How you feeling?"

I can rationalize the fact that he never called me by name. I don't think he knew it, even though our relationship dated back to March 2000, when I interviewed him for the first time. That was the week of the state championship final four in Columbus. Fox 8 cameraman Chris Reece and I popped into the Akron St. Vincent-St. Mary gym for their final practice. They left that night for Columbus. We shot some practice video and I interviewed coach Keith Dambrot and two seniors. We had enough for 45 seconds on the air so Chris started to pack up.

"Time to leave," I said to Coach Dambrot. "Good luck in Columbus."

"Did you talk to LeBron?" he said.

"He's that freshman, isn't he?" I replied.

Dambrot said yes.

"No. I didn't get him. He's just a freshman. I got you and a couple of seniors. That's all I need," I said.

"You ought to get LeBron," Dambrot said. He almost insisted.

So I asked Dambrot to point him out. I didn't know what to ask a freshman.

"How do the older players treat you?" I asked.

"They treat me fine, just like I'm one of the guys," LeBron said.

That was perfect. I could use a six-second bite from the freshman. What I didn't realize was that LeBron was not this dinky little freshman. He was the star of the team. Somebody should have told me straight up instead of dropping veiled hints. We used that little sound bite many times over the years to remind viewers that we were the first station to discover LeBron James. Hell, Dambrot talked me into it. St. Vincent-St. Mary won the state championship that weekend and went on to win two more state titles over the next three years.

In the middle of the following summer, *Sports Illustrated* magazine put LeBron on the cover and labeled him the "Chosen One." I remember saying to athletic director Frank Jessie, "This is either the best day of your life or the worst." Maybe it was both. It changed all our lives. Speaking for myself only, I cannot say it was for the better.

Dealing with LeBron and his mother, Gloria, never was easy. One summer, LeBron broke his wrist playing in an AAU tournament in Chicago and he came home to Akron with his arm in a cast. By then, everything LeBron did was a major story. Our producers at Fox 8 wanted a picture of that wrist and that cast. They didn't have a clenched fist, jump-up-and-down tantrum, but it was moving in that direction. Television is a picture business. It's one thing to get the story first. It's a thousand times more important to get the picture first. This was the middle of summer so it was not a school issue. I called LeBron's mom and asked her if she would help us get that picture, perhaps walking down the street, at the park, at the Dairy Queen or some other benign location.

"Where'd you get my cell phone number?" she demanded.

"I don't remember," I said. "I have a lot of phone numbers in my book. It's my job to get phone numbers."

And so began one of the strangest phone conversations I've ever had. She wanted to know how I got her cell phone number and she wanted to know now. To this day, I remember exactly how her phone number found its way into my book, but I'll be damned if I would ever tell her, not with that attitude. She berated me for a good quarter of an hour, recklessly using up her cell phone minutes, and we never got back to the original question about the cast on LeBron's wrist. Did we ever get that picture? No, we did not.

From that moment on, I spent a lot of time in Akron. I was in a small group of reporters who interviewed LeBron after all his tournament games. Following four years of high school came seven years with the Cavs, where I would cross paths with him mostly after practice. That made 11 years without a nod or any other sign of recognition. That isn't normal. The mailman, the garbage man, the checkout person at the super market become familiar faces in one's life. Maybe you don't know their names, but they're not strangers. To LeBron, we were all strangers. But that didn't bother us. We noticed, but we weren't troubled. He wasn't abusive and threatening like Albert Belle. He wasn't rude like George Hendrick. He wasn't mean like Dave Kingman.

At the end, he treated Cavs owner Dan Gilbert the same way he treated the rest of us. He treated him as a stranger and that was unforgivable.

Since buying the Cavs in March 2005, Gilbert had granted privileges to LeBron that were unheard of in pro sports. LeBron's high school friends had privileged parking spaces in the basement of Quicken Loans Arena and their game tickets were directly behind the Cavs bench. In order to keep LeBron happy, all the players' meals—three meals a day—were prepared by the team chef. When LeBron wanted to attend a celebrity party in Hollywood after a game, the team plane waited several hours for him on the tarmac of LAX—with his coaches, teammates and radio announcer aboard.

Looking ahead to LeBron's free agent year, when money was virtually irrelevant, Gilbert knew he couldn't buy LeBron's loyalty; he could only create an atmosphere of entitlement for him unequaled in the NBA. LeBron shamelessly took every advantage of the situation. He was, after all, the King. He was the Chosen One. That's what his tattoo said.

Dave Plagman: Runaway Train

(This piece originally appeared in the Elyria Chronicle-Telegram *and other papers on May 20, 2001. It had nothing to do with Browns coach Chris Palmer, who also drove a runaway train.)*

Mr. Will Cover, the sports handicapper, was particularly interested in the story of the runaway train on the news the other night. Usually he watches only ESPN, but that night his eyes were glued to the real news on the big screen at the bar.

"I could have stopped that train," said Mr. Cover.

We scoffed. The 47-car freight train that got loose in Toledo with nobody in the engine rolled through towns such as Bowling Green and Findlay at 50 miles an hour. Nobody could have stopped that train. A comic book superhero might have had a chance.

"I could have," Mr. Cover repeated. "If you can steal 'em, you can stop 'em."

Because he is not certain about the statute of limitations for stealing trains—"I'm a handicapper, not a lawyer," he says—he insists on being identified only by his gambling handle, Will Cover. Early in his career he was known as Willie Cover (Will he cover?), but he wanted to remove all doubt that his picks would cover the spread. He wanted to put a positive spin on his handle. Now he's just plain Will. Long before that he was known as Dave Plagman from Cleveland's West Park neighborhood, but that name belongs to antiquity.

He relates the story.

In 1968, while a student at Hillsdale, the small liberal arts college in southern Michigan, and the sports editor of the college newspaper, Cover and four fraternity brothers from the ATO house drank beer in Martin's Bar until 2:30 a.m.

"We came out of the bar and we were real hungry," Cover stated. "One of our fraternity brothers, a rich kid from Grosse Point, said if anybody could get us to Jonesville he would buy breakfast for everybody.

"There was an all-night truck stop called Ma Bell's in Jonesville on U.S. 12, which was a main highway between Detroit and Chicago. It was seven miles away and we didn't have a car."

As they walked toward their frat house, they passed a small railroad yard where a diesel engine idled tediously. Diesel fuel was cheap in those days and trainmen routinely left their engines running, often for hours, when they were not in use. Cover knew there was no third shift. The engine was unattended all night.

"I knew how to run a train. My summer job was working as a fireman on diesels in the Collinwood yards," he said. "It was a great college job. I paid my way through college. So I said, 'I'll take you to Jonesville.'

"We all got in the cab of the engine. We had a couple of six packs. I pushed a couple of buttons and put it in gear and we pulled out. We were pulling five or six boxcars and a flatcar. It was a small railroad yard. There were several tracks, but when we got out of the yard, the main line was a single track through the woods to Jonesville."

In Jonesville they stopped the train on the single track and enjoyed a fine smorgasbord breakfast and a beer, which they smuggled into Ma Bell's. After breakfast, Cover put the train in reverse and backed it seven miles to school.

Just thinking of the possible consequences sends chills up one's spine. An unscheduled train parked on a one-track main line in a truck stop town could give a yardmaster a heart attack. Then driving backward with an unlighted flat car and six boxcars leading the way is an absolute railroad nightmare.

Although the train was unattended, it was not exactly unguarded. A night watchman eventually noticed that the train was missing and alerted the railroad police.

How the watchman explained that a train had been purloined from under his nose is left to your imagination.

"In the paper the next day we read that the New York Central police were investigating a report of a train taken," Cover said. "In the brief time that we were gone, the state police were hunting for it. I'm guessing that while they were on the road to Jonesville, we were on the way back through the woods and they didn't see us.

"It was the stupidest thing I ever did, except for betting on the Baltimore Colts over the Jets in the Super Bowl later that year. At class reunions they still talk about it.

"They ask me what would happen if we were caught. I always say, I'd be getting out of jail Monday—this coming Monday."

John Lowenstein:
Model of Consistency

John Lowenstein might have been the most eccentric character who ever played baseball in Cleveland. While other players
had fan clubs, Lowenstein said he had an "Apathy Club." He was
proud of it.

When *Cleveland Press* baseball writer Bob Sudyk heard that
line, he thought he had just found a hundred-dollar bill on the
sidewalk. Sudyk, one of the cleverest wordsmiths ever to caress
a keyboard, picked it up and ran with it. Sudyk turned "apathy"
into the mantra of Lowenstein's career in Cleveland. When Lowenstein played left field, as he often did, fans in the lower deck
behind him often held up "Apathy Club" signs.

In reality, Lowenstein was anything but apathetic. He was
hard working, ambitious and humble.

"I don't want to be a star. I only want to twinkle now and then,"
he said.

You had to be humble when you played for the Indians in the
1970s. The Indians paid their players peanuts and the checks
barely cleared. Lowenstein was forced to seek a second job in his
early years here.

"Lowenstein and Ed Farmer, one of our pitchers, got part time
jobs at the zoo shoveling manure," recalled Dino Lucarelli, the
Indians' public relations director at the time.

The job fit in nicely with their baseball schedule. They worked
at the zoo only when the Indians were at home, of course. Most of
their games were at night and they worked at the zoo in the early
mornings.

"Gabe found out about it when both Lowenstein and Farmer failed to appear at a Wahoo Club luncheon," said Lucarelli.

They were both scheduled to be part of the program at the luncheon at the Statler Hotel. The Wahoo Club was the Indians' official booster club and headed by the most prominent civic leaders, advertising executives and media exemplars. Players usually made a few opening remarks and then one of the Indians radio or television announcers interviewed them. On this particular day, there were no players. Indians president Gabe Paul filled in and smoothly tap-danced for twenty minutes.

"Gabe was fuming," Lucarelli said. "He came back to the office after the luncheon and demanded to know where they were. I told him they were at the zoo shoveling shit."

Gabe reacted to minor issues by flying into a rage. For instance, when he saw his grounds crew throwing a football around instead of cutting the outfield grass, he called down to head groundskeeper Marshall Bossard and ordered him to command the grounds crew to throw a baseball.

Upon learning that Lowenstein and Farmer were shoveling manure, he almost had a seizure. Gabe gasped for breath. He pounded his fist on his desk. The Stadium shook to its foundation.

Lowenstein could do that to people. It was enjoyable to watch him work. Small pleasures amused him.

Each year the Indians' PR department sent out a personal questionnaire to each player.

"One year Lowenstein listed his nationality as German Catholic. Another year he was Jewish. Another time he put down American Indian," said Lucarelli.

"He drove public address announcers crazy," Lucarelli continued. "If they pronounced his name Lowen-STINE, he would correct them the next day and say it was Lowen-STEEN. The next trip they would pronounce it STEEN and he would tell them it was STINE."

He sometimes tormented his teammates.

When Buddy Bell and Jack Brohamer were roommates on the road in the early 1970s, Lowenstein sneaked into their room and hid in their closet for an interminable length of time for the perverse pleasure of surprising them when they opened the door.

"John asked me to arrange a car deal for him," recalled Lucarelli. "Many of the players had car deals. I told him he would have to cut commercials for them. He said that was fine. I got a car for him from Miller Pontiac in Ravenna. I picked it up, a beautiful Pontiac Catalina. I gave him the keys. The next day the keys were on my desk. 'I don't want it,' he said. 'It doesn't have air conditioning.' I said, 'It's a convertible, for Pete's sake. Just put the top down.' He said that wouldn't do when it rained and it rained a lot in Cleveland."

Lowenstein played 16 years in the Major Leagues, the last seven with the Baltimore Orioles, where he did twinkle. One year he hit .320 with 24 homers. The next year he hit .281 with 15 homers. He played in the World Series twice with Baltimore.

In those days, good things usually happened to players only after they left Cleveland.

Lowenstein, however, did leave an indelible mark on the Indians. He was a model of consistency. In fact, he was the most consistent player who ever pulled on the Indians' double-knits. In the four seasons between 1974 and 1977, Lowenstein hit exactly .242 three times. Such a modest batting average in itself is nothing special, but three times in four seasons is unique. In the long history of the game, no one has accomplished such a feat.

(Cleveland Press Collection, Cleveland State University)

Bob Cain:
Pitched to a Midget

It was the single most unusual moment in baseball history. Nothing else ever came close. St. Louis Browns owner Bill Veeck signed a midget to a contract and actually used him as a pinch hitter in an official Major League game in 1951.

Having purchased the moribund Browns the previous year, Veeck was losing his shirt. The Browns were draped in indifference and he went to great lengths to attract attention. His strolling bands and wild promotions, which had worked so well in Cleveland just three years earlier, didn't generate a ripple of interest.

Veeck's fundamental problem was that St. Louis had two teams sharing one ballpark and fans cared about only one of them, the tradition-rich Cardinals. Old Sportsman's Park crackled with excitement when the Cardinals were home. When the Browns were home, hardly anybody noticed. The Browns were always last in attendance in all of Major League baseball, with the second-worst team sometimes outdrawing them 2-1 and 3-1. In 1950 the Browns drew 247,131 fans.

The Cardinals had Stan Musial, one of the greatest who ever played the game. For one day the Browns had Eddie Gaedel, the greatest midget in baseball history, and people finally noticed. This is the story of that one day, based on a column that originally appeared in *The Plain Dealer* on June 16, 1980.

In a six-year Major League career that embraced 1949 to 1954, Bob Cain had his moments.

A slim left-handed pitcher who toiled for the Chicago White Sox, Detroit Tigers and St. Louis Browns, Cain compiled an unimposing 37-44 career mark. But he collaborated on some classic duels with Cleveland Hall of Famers Bob Feller and Bob Lemon. On those special nights, Cain was every bit as good as those great Cleveland pitchers.

For example, on July 1, 1951, Cain was the opposing pitcher when Feller threw his third no-hitter to beat the Tigers, 2-1. Two weeks later in Detroit, Cain was the 2-1 loser to Lemon's one-hitter. Vic Wertz hit a home run in the ninth inning to spoil Lemon's perfect game.

Cain gained a measure of revenge the following season while pitching for the Browns. Cain and Feller threw one-hitters at each other with Cain winning, 1-0.

"In my first Major League start," Cain pointed out, "I beat the Yankees, 15-0, their worst beating ever in Yankee Stadium up to that time. I beat the Yankees four times that year."

Hardly anyone remembers those moments when Cain approached greatness. "All they remember," said Cain, "is me and the midget."

Cain's fame was shaped by the strangest of circumstances, but he will take it. On Aug. 19, 1951, Cain was the Detroit pitcher when Veeck sent a midget to the plate, the first and only certifiable midget in baseball history.

It was the second game of a doubleheader in St. Louis between the eighth-place Detroit Tigers and the seventh-place Browns. Detroit already had taken the first game, 5-2.

Between games, Veeck had a large cake pulled onto the field at Sportsman's Park on a four-wheeled cart. Out of the cake popped a midget named Eddie Gaedel, 26 years old, three feet, seven inches tall, weighing 65 pounds, and dressed in a Browns' uniform with the number 1/8 on his back. Gaedel scurried into the Browns' dugout to enthusiastic applause from the sparse crowd.

Cain laughed heartily and soon forgot about it. He went to

the bullpen to warm up. He was Detroit's starting pitcher in the second game.

After the Tigers went out in order in the top of the first inning, Cain strode to the mound to face the Browns' leadoff hitter, centerfielder Frank Saucier. Cain took his eight warmup pitches. He toed the dirt in front of the pitcher's rubber, took a deep breath and looked up, but Saucier was not there. Out of the dugout came Gaedel, carrying a tiny bat. Gaedel told plate umpire Ed Hurley that he was pinch hitting for Saucier.

"Hurley's neck got redder and redder until he exploded," Cain recalled. "Hurley demanded to see Gaedel's contract. Browns' manager Zack Taylor trotted out from the dugout and pulled the contract out of his pocket. Hurley looked at it and said, 'Play ball.'"

"It was funny," Cain continued. "I thought Veeck would have his laugh and then put in another pinch hitter."

But, no, as everyone knows, the midget, a right-handed hitter, stepped into the batter's box and dug his spikes into the dirt, presenting the smallest strike zone Cain had ever seen. Catcher Bob Swift knelt down on both knees to give Cain a target, but his efforts were futile. Cain walked him on four pitches.

"Veeck was up on the roof of the stadium," said Cain. "He said that if Gaedel so much as tried to swing, he would shoot the little SOB. Early Wynn said that if he ever faced a guy like that, he would knock the guy down. Wynn was like that."

When Gaedel arrived at first base—it took almost a full minute for him to walk the ninety feet—Jim Delsing was dispatched as a pinch runner and finished the game in centerfield. The Browns failed to score that inning and Cain went on to beat them, 6-2, as the Tigers swept the doubleheader.

American League president Will Harridge was incensed. The following day he ruled Gaedel's contract invalid and banned midgets from the American League forever. Furthermore, Harridge ordered Gaedel's blasphemous existence stricken from the box score and the record books.

Veeck fired off an angry letter to Harridge demanding that
he define a midget. "Is it three feet six? Is it four feet six? If it's
five feet six, that's great. We can get rid of Rizzuto."

Yankees shortstop Phil Rizzuto was an even five feet, six
inches tall.

Veeck went on to ridicule Harridge for purging Gaedel
from the record books.

"They couldn't balance the books if they didn't put Gaedel
in," Veeck blustered. "Somehow they had to account for his being on first base and someone running for him and the walk
Cain gave up. So they had to let him in the box score and the
record books."

And so, to preserve the integrity of baseball's sacred balance sheet, Gaedel remained in the box scores in hundreds of
newspapers, a giant in agate type, and in the Baseball Encyclo-
pedia forever. His career on base percentage is 1.000, tied for
best in baseball.

Veeck was in a typically devilish mood when he talked
about this in an interview earlier in 1980.

"I made my point, discharged my obligation to Falstaff
(the Browns' radio beer sponsor) and stuck a few pins in a few
stuffed shirts," he said. "Eddie Gaedel tried harder than anybody else on our team. He got on base and that's something
very few of our athletes could claim. If I had any courage and
we'd used eight other fellows like Eddie, we might have won
a game or so. We'd have run around and around and might
never have finished the game."

Veeck reached deep into the Old Testament to deliver his
final volley.

"If little David hadn't belted away big Goliath, you'd never
have heard of either of the bums," he said. "One of the things
about baseball is that it's the only game left for humans. To
play basketball, you have to be seven feet six and in order to
play football, you have to be the same width."

Cain always felt inextricably linked to Gaedel and the other
two members of the oddest quartet in baseball history—plate

umpire Ed Hurley and catcher Bob Swift. Cain and Swift, incidentally, were from the same hometown, Celina, Kansas.

Gaedel was paid $100 for his one game but he made $17,000 the rest of the summer appearing in rodeos, circuses and minor league games. Product endorsements and interviews on radio and television added to his income. He turned down movie opportunities because he was afraid to travel. He was most comfortable in his native Chicago.

Fame was not good to Gaedel, however. He drank too much and became belligerent when he was drunk. He was murdered on June 18, 1961, in his hometown of Chicago. He was 36. The coroner's report attributed death to a heart attack brought on by a beating. His assailants never were apprehended. Cain and his wife, Judy, went to the funeral in Chicago.

"We met his mother," Cain said. "She told us he fell in with bad company. She said he was despondent and had taken to heavy drinking. She found him in his room at four o'clock one morning foaming from the throat. A gang of boys had beaten him up.

"We went to the funeral because we felt we were part of the deal. We felt we should be there. There was a church service. There were two bouquets of flowers, one from Veeck, the other from a ballclub. I forget which one. Veeck was in the Mayo Clinic at the time. There were about 100 people there. I thought it was very, very strange, though. There was not one representative from baseball there."

It was a natural extension of baseball logic. Having pretended that Gaedel never existed, it was easy to pretend that he never died.

Veeck's promotional genius had little effect on the box office in St. Louis. In 1951 eight Major League baseball teams drew more than one million customers, including the rival Cardinals. The Browns were dead last in attendance with 293,790. The Eddie Gaedel stunt, in fact, had long-term consequences. Veeck's intention from the start was to move the Browns to Baltimore (readers in Cleveland pause here to appreciate the irony), but the other American League owners spitefully voted against the move. They resented Veeck's disdain for convention and wanted to force him out of the game. Permission was granted to move the Browns to Baltimore in 1954 only after Veeck sold the team.

*   *   *

I visited with Bob and Judy Cain several times over the years. Bob never played for the Indians, but he settled in Cleveland after he and Judy got married. They met when he was pitching for the Tigers and Judy worked in a flower shop downtown. Cleveland was her hometown. In 1952 they bought a house on E. 226th Street in Euclid and never moved. After his playing days ended Bob worked quietly in the Indians ticket office.

Periodically over the years I updated the story of Bob Cain and the midget, usually on the anniversary. He was unfailingly gracious and enjoyed reminiscing about it. Bob was interviewed on network TV live from his basement recreation room on the 40th anniversary.

Bob Cain died on April 8, 1997, at the age of 72. Judy asked me to deliver the eulogy at Bob's funeral Mass at St. John's Cathedral in downtown Cleveland. I noticed that I was the only person in the church with any connection to baseball other than the guest of honor. The Indians were opening the season up the street against the California Angels.

Richie Scheinblum:
Hit for Reverse Cycle

Richie Scheinblum almost scoffs at the suggestion that he deserves a chapter in this tome. Only a chapter? He says he is worthy of an entire book. Look at the panorama of his baseball career, which started with the Indians in 1965.

"I am the only player in baseball history to hit for a reverse cycle. I was thrown out at every base," he said proudly.

"But it happened in spring training in Tucson," I said.

"It counts," he insisted.

It was in spring training of 1969. Scheinblum hit a ground ball and was thrown out at first base on a routine play by the second baseman. He singled to right and was thrown out at second trying to stretch it into a double. He blasted a shot into the gap in right center for extra bases and was thrown out at third trying for a triple. He hit another gapper. The center fielder slipped as he was running it down. Richie circled the bases. He was thinking inside the park home run. But he was slowing down as he rounded third and his gas tank went empty halfway to the plate.

"The catcher had to come up the line to tag me. I couldn't make it to him," Richie said.

In the dugout, his teammates were howling.

"Everybody except Alvin Dark," said Richie.

Dark was the Indians' humorless manager.

It was in that same spring training that baseball experimented with a softball rule. In an attempt to speed up the game, batters who were intentionally walked were automatically awarded first base without any pitches thrown.

"Juan Marichal was the pitcher. Umpire Ed Runge pointed to first base. He told me to go to first base. I didn't know what was going on. Marichal had not thrown a pitch. The next day they called off the experiment. I was the first and only player ever who reached first base without a pitch being thrown. These are the things to hang your hat on," Scheinblum said.

That also was the worst year of Scheinblum's career. He was coming off two sensational minor-league campaigns and the Indians expected him to blossom into greatness at the age of 26. In fact, the Indians made a choice between Richie and Lou Piniella, the two stars of their farm system. With Kansas City and Seattle coming into the American League in 1969, each current team could protect only 15 players in the expansion draft. The two new teams then took turns, picking players to fill out their rosters. The Indians chose to protect Scheinblum and risk losing Piniella. Both the Royals and Pilots had their scouting eyes on Piniella, who could hit but was known for his temper. Seattle drafted him and he hit. He also had a couple of tantrums and so the Pilots dealt him to Kansas City for two players on April 1. It certainly was April Fools' Day for the woeful Pilots. With the Royals, Piniella became the American League rookie of the year. He played 16 full seasons, managed until the cows came home and spent more than half a century in the grand old game.

Richie remembers having a strong spring training in 1969. He played every inning of every game and hit nine home runs in the light air of Arizona. The Indians were certainly vindicated for choosing Richie over Piniella. Richie was the opening day right fielder and he batted third.

"We opened in Detroit against Dennis McLain, who had won 31 games the year before. I had never seen him before. It was 10 degrees out. We had just come from 80 degrees. I never played well in cold weather. I went 0-for-4 but I did not strike out. We lost. In the second game we faced Mickey Lolich, who won 17 games the year before. I had never seen him. I went 0-for-4 but I did not strike out. We lost. The next day we came home to Cleveland. I don't remember the Boston pitcher but I went 0-for-3, no strikeouts. We lost."

Richie was too hard on the weatherman. The official game-time temperature was 68 degrees for the opener. As for strikeouts, he did fan against Lolich, but left out his own heroics. His first-inning sacrifice fly gave the Indians a 1-0 lead. It wasn't enough. The Tribe lost, 12-3. And forgive Richie, who turned 69 years old in 2011—but he short-changed himself in that home opener against the Red Sox. He went 0-for-7 with two strikeouts. He did throw out a runner at the plate in the 14th to keep the score tied at 1. Alas, the Red Sox scored in the top of the 16th. With two outs in the bottom half, who was the Tribe's last hope? Richie. He struck out.

That was the beginning of the end of Scheinblum as the No. 3 hitter. The Indians got off to the worst start in franchise history. To this day it remains the worst start. They lost 15 of their first 16 games.

Ten days into the season, the Indians acquired Ken (Hawk) Harrelson in a trade from Boston. Harrelson took over right field and went on to hit 30 homers and drive in 92 runs.

Scheinblum moved farther down the bench. He extended his hitless streak to an eye-popping 0-for-35. Manager Alvin Dark only glared at him. He never talked to him.

"That entire season he said only one sentence to me. 'Nobody ever went an entire season without a hit,' he said."

That may have been Dark's version of a pep talk or his way of showing support and encouragement. On the other hand, it sounds a lot like, "Even a blind squirrel sometimes finds an acorn."

Richie's playing time decreased. Eventually he was used only as a pinch hitter. He led the league with 54 pinch-hitting appearances and he had 14 pinch hits for a respectable .259 average coming off the bench. Overall that season, however, Richie hit .186 in 199 at bats.

That winter the Indians sold him to Washington for $25,000 and a player to be named later.

"Later, Washington wanted to make me the player to be named later," Richie said.

The Tribe turned down the offer and never did get a player in return, settling just for the cash.

Kansas City picked him up in 1972 and he caught fire. When he had five straight pinch hits early in the season, the Royals installed him permanently in right field. Kansas City then had both of the Indians' former top prospects in the same outfield, Lou Piniella in left and Richie Scheinblum in right. Piniella batted .312. Scheinblum batted .300 and made the All-Star team.

Over the next two years, Richie was traded to California, Cincinnati, back to Kansas City and to St. Louis. He wound up in Japan with the Hiroshima Carp, where he helped the Carp reach the Japanese World Series for the first time after finishing last 29 times in the previous 30 years. He became the second foreign player to hit .300 in Japan.

He missed a Japanese World Series game, however, because of Yom Kippur, the most solemn of the Jewish holy days. Nobody plays baseball on Yom Kippur. They're not even supposed to play cards. Here in the United States this is understood. Even Sandy Koufax once missed a start in the World Series because of Yom Kippur. But the Shintoists and Buddhists in Japan thought this was quaint.

"Fifty Japanese reporters came to my apartment to watch me pray," he said.

His career ended after two seasons in Japan when he severed his Achilles tendon playing basketball back home in the States.

"It felt like I was shot," he said. "Everybody in the gym dove for cover."

Bob Roberts:
Nude Beaches and the Derby

You don't hear much about soccer in the mainstream media and for good reason. Millions of kids between six and 16 play it, but, except for the World Cup, hardly anyone watches it or reads about it.

The exception to this generalization, however, is Bob (Railbird) Roberts, who was revered as the horse racing writer and handicapper for *The Plain Dealer* and *The Cleveland Press*. One by one, they fell on hard times. The *Press* folded and *The Plain Dealer* downsized. Roberts then performed public relations duties at Thistledown Racetrack until the track started laying off everybody except the horses and the jockeys. Shed no tears for our intrepid handicapper, however, because he'll always have soccer.

Roberts, whose real name is Randazzo, says he first noticed the local Italian club kicking the ball around on the grounds of the Baldwin Water Plant at the top of Fairhill Rd. That was in the 1960s, when all the ethnic groups had their own teams. His curiosity turned to passionate interest when he discovered you could bet on soccer. All around the world they gamble on pro soccer the way we bet on college and pro football. Maybe that's what makes a scoreless tie interesting.

"I started listening to the BBC to get the scores from the English First Division. I would buy the English newspapers at Erieview News downtown and at Schroeders bookstore on Public Square," he said.

This is a man who covered one of the greatest rivalries in sports—Sunday Silence versus Easy Goer. The great colts met four times in 1989 in the Kentucky Derby, Preakness, Belmont

Stakes and Breeders' Cup and each time they finished first and second, with Sunday Silence winning three of them. Roberts covered every one of those races, which would be the career highlight for most sportswriters, especially those who chronicle the Sport of Kings. But not for him.

No, it was covering the World Cup of soccer in France in 1998. He spent four weeks in France drinking wine and eating escargot. At the Kentucky Derby he spent four days eating Colonel Sanders and drinking Natural Light. It didn't take a Ph.D. to make that call.

"Actually," he said, "I covered two World Cups. I covered the 1994 World Cup that was played here in the United States. I particularly remember Italy vs. Ireland in Giants Stadium. The crowd was three-quarters Irish. They saved for years to come here and it paid off. Ireland did not have a great soccer tradition but they beat Italy. Ironically, Ireland was coached by an Englishman, Jackie Charlton."

Any conversation with the Railbird takes pleasant side trips and abrupt detours.

"I once went on a vacation with two other guys to Buenos Aires for horses, soccer and steaks," he said. "In Argentina, when the home team wins, you are not allowed to leave until the visiting fans leave. It cuts down on the riots. In Argentina they are also known to turn fire hoses on the fans. They make home fans and visiting fans enter the stadium from different directions. On game days the sports newspaper, *Ole*, prints maps. When reporters apply for credentials to cover the Argentine League, they are asked for three things: their name, their affiliation and their blood type. A guy named Grant Wahl wrote that in *Sports Illustrated* a few years ago."

How the Railbird cajoled his wife, Joanne, to turn him loose in Argentina for a couple of weeks will remain his secret. But he made up for it in 1998 when he took Joanne and their daughter, Maria, to France for five weeks to cover the World Cup.

"Everybody in the sports department complained that soccer

was boring. 'How boring is it now?' I said to them. 'See you in five weeks.'

"By the way," he added, "that broke your record for the longest foreign trip in *The Plain Dealer* sports department history."

That is true. I took a three-week trip in 1967 to cover Stoke City in England and the Formula I Grand Prix of Monaco, which my colleagues were still trying to rationalize decades later—those who were still alive. It was their sweet mystery of life.

"When the United States was eliminated, the French refused to credential the American reporters for the final week of the tournament. They wanted room in the press boxes for the European reporters. But I found things to write about anyway," Roberts said.

They took a side trip to Torino and gathered up a bag of Italian soil, which they brought home and scattered on the grave of Roberts' mother, who was born in this country and never visited Italy, to her great disappointment.

"Joanne and Maria and I went to Normandy. Omaha Beach. We visited the cemetery where all our troops were buried. We walked along the beach. We walked among the grave markers in the cemetery. The grass was like a putting green. That was the opening scene in the movie *Saving Private Ryan*. I wrote a column about it, which they took on Page One. I also wrote a soccer column which they took on the first sports page."

The next beach they visited was far different.

"The topless beach at La Baule," Roberts said with enthusiasm and appreciation.

"It was six miles long. All topless. Mothers and daughters. Boyfriends and girlfriends. It was nothing to them. My daughter asked if we could walk along the beach. 'We can walk all day long,' I said to her."

Six miles of female pulchritude staring him in the face. That balanced out all the nil-nil soccer draws he ever saw. To quote Mister Roberts once more: "How boring is it now?"

D'Arcy Egan:
Catch and Release

As the outdoors writer for *The Plain Dealer*, D'Arcy Egan has spent more than 30 years telling his readers how to kill things and he might do it for another 30 years.

"There is no age limit," said Egan, who turned 65 in the spring of 2011. "A 100-year-old woman in Pennsylvania got her first deer last year."

That answers the question, "What does an outdoors writer do when he retires, go to the office?"

The office? Never!

In the first place, Egan has no intention of retiring. As long as *The Plain Dealer* continues to print newspapers, he's going to tell his readers where the walleye are biting, where the grouse are nesting and where the deer herds are thickest. Egan's office is the entire world. You'd have to point an elephant gun at his head to get him inside the newspaper building. He and his wife, Laura, moved to Marblehead 10 years ago, close to the water and far from the city where he grew up in the Old Brooklyn neighborhood of Cleveland.

He is also a dinosaur. When Steve Pollick of the *Toledo Blade* retires in December 2011, Egan will be the last full-time outdoors writer in Ohio. There probably are not more than a couple hundred left in the country. Newspapers can't afford them. There are many part-time outdoors writers who crank out a column on the first day of deer hunting season and cover an occasional fishing tournament but you don't hear from them the rest of the year. Egan does it every day.

Personally, however, his taste for blood has waned in recent years. He does more shooting with a camera than with a gun. On the lakes he's a catch and release guy.

"There's a mantle in my house against a 22-foot high wall. It's perfect for a couple of trophies, but I don't want trophy heads on the wall," he says.

But there was a time, he admits, when he envisioned a kudu on one side of the mantle and an American elk on the other.

"The American elk is the most magnificent trophy of them all," he says. "The kudu is the largest African antelope, known for its majestic corkscrew antlers."

The kudus and American elks can relax. He won't shoot them. He won't shoot bears, either, partly out of professional courtesy.

"Bears are predators. I won't shoot predators. We're in the same business. Besides, I don't like bear meat."

* * *

There are risks attached to a business that involves wild animals and guns. D'Arcy had his moments, such as during a trip to South Africa.

"I was visiting my brother, who lives in Johannesburg," he said. "I did a little hunting, but mainly I was taking photographs. We were in a game preserve in high grass. A Zulu park ranger was our guide. He carried an old .308 rifle that he had never shot. The stock was painted with white house paint. I can't say he never shot a rifle, but I know he never shot that rifle.

"Suddenly there was a rustling in the high grass ahead of us. This baby rhino came crashing through. Right behind him, here came mom and dad to protect their baby. I raised my Nikon and started firing off pictures. Click, click, click with the motor drive. Rhinos can't see very well but they have very good hearing and they can smell real good. With all my clicking, the rhinos knew exactly where we were. The rhinos were only about 10 feet in front of us. I looked around and our Zulu guide with the rifle he had never shot was gone. He evaporated. One of the other guys in our group said, 'Be real quiet and back up very slowly,' which we did until the rhinos lost interest in us. The other guys were not happy with me at all."

His most momentous adventure occurred in the mid-1990s when *The Plain Dealer,* gushing with money like an Oklahoma oil well, sent him fly-fishing to the rain forest in Nicaragua. He arrived like somebody from the Peace Corps, with a box of shiny new baseballs to give to the kids. But that is not why they still remember Egan in Nicaragua.

"I had an old American guide. His name was Pete. I studied the way he cast. What I noticed was the way he kept rubbing his arm. He also complained of indigestion. These were the classic symptoms of a heart attack. I know. I had a heart attack and open-heart surgery about eight years before that. I told Pete I had to get him out of the rain forest and to a hospital. He said he didn't have any money. I told him I'd take care of it. I got him out of the rain forest to an airstrip and flew him to San Jose, Costa Rica. I called an old friend, Jerry Ruhlow, the editor of the magazine *Costa Rica Outdoors,* and asked him to meet me at the airport in his van. He was there. We took Pete to the hospital and while he was in the emergency room he had a heart attack. They saved him. Last I heard, he was still alive and he tells everybody down there that I saved his life. That's true. If he had had the heart attack in the rain forest he would have died. I wish I could remember his last name."

From Costa Rica near the Equator to the Arctic Circle, D'Arcy traveled across much of the Western Hemisphere writing his "Adventure Series" for *The Plain Dealer* in the 1990s. When I went on the road with the Browns, I packed an overnight bag. When D'Arcy went on the road, he packed for a month.

"My greatest fear was forgetting something," he said. "For example, was I prepared for snow in July in the Northwest Territory of Canada? I fished some lakes there that were so pristine, no fisherman had ever been there before. The mosquitoes and black flies tormented us so much; they drove us north to the Arctic Circle. No mosquitoes or black flies there. Black flies get under the wristband of your watch and they bite you. Their bites last for days and weeks. What you watch out for in the Arctic Circle are bears. The black bears and brown bears shy away from people, but not the polar bears. They're fearless."

He was in upper Quebec when a bus transporting some prisoners broke down. The bus driver got out to see what the problem was and all the prisoners escaped and ran away toward a swamp. The bus driver reached a phone and called the prison.

"Stay where you are," he was told. "They'll be back in four hours."

Right on schedule, they all came wandering back. They realized they could never survive in the Canadian swamp. They would rather go to prison.

As D'Arcy recalled his adventures, I felt embarrassed. During the 1978 World Series, I was annoyed when the hotel dining room in New York served only unsalted butter. I really don't like unsalted butter and I complained to the commissioner's office, which hosted the dinner. But D'Arcy never complained. He gave sportswriters a bad name. And he is a sportswriter. His stuff is carried in the sports section.

"I am part of a team sport," he pointed out. "When you hunt game birds, you and your dog are a team. My smartest dog was a German short hair. My most graceful was an English setter. I had them when I was in my twenties. They taught me how to hunt. And my Labrador is everybody's pal."

D'Arcy's traveling days are over. He stays close to home. *The Plain Dealer* no longer has the budget to support him in the manner in which he was accustomed. He has added a television show on STO, the cable channel owned by the Indians, and has had some classic segments with Browns tackle Joe Thomas, an avid fisherman and deer hunter.

"At West Branch Reservoir near Ravenna, Joe Thomas and I threw in our lines. We were looking for muskies. I said, 'Joe, you can have the first one.' Well, before long we had a nibble. It was a big one, a three-footer, and it put up a good fight. It made great television. We had it all on tape, from start to finish. Joe landed him, he took the hook out, we took a picture and released him.

"We threw our lines back in the water. Joe's musky had barely disappeared under water when we got another nibble, another musky, and this one turned out to be a trophy. I said, 'Joe, do you want this one? He said, 'No, we made a deal. I got the first one. This one's yours.' So I fought him and what a fight he put up! Joe helped get him in the boat. We took the picture and released him. He was four feet long. When you're doing a fishing show on television, you need luck. You hope the fish give you a great story.'"

D'Arcy's most satisfying accomplishments came not with a gun or a fishing pole, but with his keyboard.

"When I became the outdoor writer in 1978, the Cleveland area was not very interesting. We didn't have much. No walleye, no pheasant and it was rare to see a deer in Cuyahoga County," he pointed out.

While he was on the job, walleye proliferated and so did deer. He didn't have anything directly to do with that, but he did influence the outdoor life in other aspects.

He campaigned for a 12-inch size limit on bass to protect future generations and his efforts paid off. It is impossible not to notice the growing number of Lake Erie bass tournaments.

He worked to eliminate gill nets on Lake Erie. He calls gill nets "rape and pillage" because they kill indiscriminately.

He campaigned for a dove hunting season, against the wishes of animal rights groups who spent millions of dollars opposing him on the grounds that doves are migratory songbirds.

He has a solution to the Canada geese problem: "Unlimited shooting of Canada geese as long as you eat them. Cut strips off their breasts. Marinate them for two days in orange juice. Cook them medium rare and they taste like filet mignon. If you cook them too long, they taste like burnt liver."

* * *

D'Arcy actually was born into a hockey family. A younger brother, Kelly Egan, still plays in adult leagues and a nephew, Riley Egan, was the high school hockey player of the year in 2011 at St. Edward High School. D'Arcy's father, Gale Egan, a native of Canada, came to Cleveland in the 1940s to work for the old Barons hockey team as a scout, radio broadcaster and public relations man. Oddly, hockey was the only sport D'Arcy did not play at St. John Cantius High School.

"I was in grade school when I got a bamboo fishing pole and would walk to Edgewater Park to fish. Later a man befriended me and drove me to the East Ninth Street pier to fish for perch. I would scale the perch for him. I would nail bottle caps to a board for scaling fish. My dad thought I was crazy. He had never fired a gun and he had never caught a fish," D'Arcy said.

He graduated from St. John Cantius High School in 1964. Congressman Dennis Kucinich was one of his classmates and they both went into the newspaper business. Kucinich became a copy boy at *The Plain Dealer*. D'Arcy went right to work as a newspaper reporter for the *Parma Post*, and then it was on to the *Coshocton Tribune*, the *Medina Gazette* and part-time work at *The Plain Dealer*. Gale Egan eventually became public relations man for Northfield Park racetrack and when he died in 1976 D'Arcy was offered the position. It lasted only a year because he clashed with general manager John Phillips. D'Arcy had the bad manners to say what was on his mind.

In 1978, *The Plain Dealer's* outdoor writer Lou Gale walked into sports editor Hal Lebovitz's office and announced he was retiring.

"Hal knew I wanted to come back to *The Plain Dealer*," D'Arcy said. "He called me and said, 'Put in your application.' I got the job in the spring of 1978. Lou Gale took a lot of movies, which he showed when he gave talks. He called me and wanted to sell me his movie equipment. He said I could make a lot of money with it. I told him I wasn't interested. He never talked to me again."

Les Levine:
Voice of Truth and Reason

When Steve Liverani called Les Levine about a job, he did not realize the dangers involved. Les is broadcasting's demolition man. He usually puts stations off the air and teams out of business. He should have been Bishop of Cleveland. He could have shut down the entire diocese.

Les, a native of South Euclid and a product of Brush High School, graduated from Ohio State in 1968 with a degree in political science and intended to become a lawyer. But he wanted to think about it. While he was pondering, he taught school for two years—one in Lorain, the other in Cleveland's inner city.

"Years later I drove my daughter around and showed her where I started," Les said when I interviewed him for this chapter. "Both schools no longer exist."

He was establishing a pattern.

"In those two years I decided to change careers and become a sportscaster. I thought I'd be happy doing it," he said.

Why not? When he was a senior second baseman on the Brush baseball team, the Arcs had a precocious junior right-hander named Steve Stone who later won the Cy Young Award while pitching for the Baltimore Orioles. Stone became a television broadcaster for the Chicago Cubs. Maybe there was something in the water at Brush.

Les' first job was at a radio station in the southern Indiana town of Jasper.

"My plan was to spend a year in Jasper, then go to Indianapolis and then to Chicago," Les told me.

That sounded like a good plan. Small towns are great places for play-by-play announcers to start. In fact, they're a good place for anybody to start.

In Jasper, Les did one season each of high school football, basketball and baseball, averaging three games a week, on station WITZ. To get that job he sold ads during the day and he was a disc jockey at night. He coined one of radio's great station ID's: "We're WITZ. Wits' end."

"I did a game that Larry Bird played in. Bird's school was Springs Valley High School in French Lick, Indiana. I wish I could tell you that I knew he was destined for greatness, but I can't say that. He scored maybe 12 points, maybe only 10," Levine recalled. "But he was only a freshman.

"I wasn't in the movie, *Hoosiers*, but I did games from three gyms that were in the movie. I did the state championship semifinals and finals from Hinkle Fieldhouse in Indianapolis. That's Butler University's home court. The semifinals and finals were played on the same day. East Chicago Washington won the state championship with a team that included Junior Bridgeman, Pete Trgovich and Tim Stoddard."

All three played college ball, Trgovich for UCLA, Bridgeman for Louisville and Stoddard for North Carolina State. Trgovich and Bridgeman played against each other in the 1975 NCAA national championship game won by UCLA, 75-74, for coach John Wooden's ninth and final championship. Stoddard was a starter on N.C. State's 1974 national championship team and later pitched in the Major Leagues for 13 years. For several seasons he was a teammate of Steve Stone with the Baltimore Orioles. It is not known if Stoddard and Stone ever discussed Levine's influence on their careers.

That summer, Les also played outfield for the Jasper Reds, a semi-pro team, and recalls, "I got the game-winning hit on a Sunday and the next day on the radio I said that the Jasper Reds won, 4-3. A ringing double by Les Levine drove in the winning run. This is Les Levine reporting."

The Jasper Reds no longer exist and shame on them for never inviting Les back for old timers' day.

Nevertheless, the year in Jasper went so well that Les decided to skip the Indianapolis part of the plan and go directly to station WKNT in Kent, Ohio, which was an upgrade because he did not have to pull a disc jockey shift. He concentrated on announcing sports and selling ads. For eight years he honed his craft doing high school games and Kent State University games.

He stepped up to the big leagues when Nick Mileti hired him to broadcast all the Crusaders' home hockey games from the old downtown Cleveland Arena into Akron on Warner Cable television to build up interest in that market while the Richfield Coliseum was under construction. He also did some Cavaliers games. When the Coliseum opened in 1974, both teams moved there but not Les. His job was finished after two seasons. So were the Crusaders. The hockey team folded after four seasons.

Les then called Cleveland Jaybirds and Cleveland Competitors professional softball on the radio.

"I'm sure we had five or six listeners. Ted Stepien owned the Competitors and to get paid I had to go down to his lingerie bar in the basement of the Statler Office Tower," he said.

Both the Jaybirds and Competitors went out of business after only a few years.

In the 1990s, Les and former Browns linebacker Eddie Johnson were the radio play-by-play radio voices of the Thunderbolts indoor football team at the Coliseum, a scenario that turned tragic. Not only did the Thunderbolts go defunct, their owner committed suicide in a motel room in Canfield, Ohio. A few years later Eddie Johnson died of cancer.

Les always had Cleveland State University, however. For 23 years he was the voice of CSU basketball, including the glorious Kevin Mackey era.

"I didn't put them out of business, but they did go on double secret probation," Les said proudly.

In 1991, Les opened a window and a door flung open. He

started an afternoon drive call-in sports show on WERE (1300 AM). Les called it *More Sports & Les Levine* and actually introduced humor into sports talk. People listened and he developed a following. Those were the final days of news-talk on WERE, which once was a broadcasting giant in Cleveland. He worked with such legendary conversationalists as Merle Pollis, Joel Rose and Jim McIntyre. But in 1994 the owners abruptly ended it. They cleaned house.

Les was not off the air long. In 1994, Art Greenberg and Phil Levine, who were running WHK (1420 AM), invited Les to move his show down the dial to their station, where his audience continued to grow. (The Levines were not related, by the way.) Les bantered easily back and forth with his producer, Pat McCabe. He introduced gimmicks, such as "How Come Quickies," which brought out the humor in his callers. He hired football writers Tony Grossi from *The Plain Dealer* and Ed Meyer from the *Akron Beacon Journal* to dissect the Browns and named them "Doom" and "Gloom." Not only did Browns owner Art Modell have to read Grossi and Meyer in the morning, he had to listen to "Doom" and "Gloom" driving home at night. Art wasn't the only listener. Les began with a cult following and built it into a broad based audience.

Tony Rizzo also did an hour of sports talk in the mornings on WHK. You can find people today who claim WHK in the mid-1990s was the best sports talk station in Cleveland history.

You know what happened next. It's what always happens. In 1996 the station was sold. The new owners changed the format, the staff hit the bricks and nobody has listened to WHK since.

Like everything else about his radio career, Les had an unconventional contract. He was not paid. His arrangement with WHK permitted him to sell the commercials and keep all the money. Les set his own ad rates. The station was allowed a few commercials each hour, but Les had the bulk of what radio people call "inventory." He made a nice living.

Les' agent, Armond Arnson, was puzzled.

"Les, if they don't pay you, there's nothing to negotiate," said Arnson.

"That's right," said Les. "Think of something. That's why you're an agent."

So Armond threw a little clause in there that said if and when the station is sold, Les would be paid a rather large sum of money in one hellaciously big check. There was no objection. Maybe the station never would be sold. Why argue about something that may never happen?

And so, when WHK was sold, Les Levine was handed the biggest check he had ever seen in his life. He had the check in his pocket when he attended Armond Arnson's funeral later that morning.

* * *

Armond Arnson was a brilliant lawyer. In the chaotic 1970s, he was the Indians' attorney and he saved them from bankruptcy several times. When Indians managing partner Ted Bonda walked in the front door of the bank, loan officers slipped out the back door. The Indians careened from one economic crisis to another. Financially, it was the last of the ninth for the Indians when Arnson accompanied Bonda to an appointment with a bank to plead for more money. He knew they would be denied. The bank had already loaned them too much money.

"Give me your keys," Arnson said to Bonda before leaving the Stadium.

Bonda was puzzled.

"Just give me your keys," Arnson demanded.

Bonda turned over his key ring, which included keys to the Stadium offices.

After a cordial 20-minute meeting with the bank vice president, their loan request was declined. It was, in the lexicon of the day, "Business, not personal." After all, the bank was a season ticket customer and a loge holder.

Bonda and Arnson stood up and turned toward the door. As

they walked away, Arnson tossed Bonda's keys on the banker's desk.

"What's this?" said the surprised banker.

"They're the keys to the Stadium. You own the ball club now," said Arnson.

"Wait a minute," exclaimed the banker.

Arnson and Bonda sat down and signed the papers for a new loan.

* * *

Within a month in 1996, Les received a phone call from a man he did not know, Steve Liverani, the general manager of SportsChannel, the cable channel that carried the Indians games at the time.

"I was a listener. I am a big fan of yours," said Liverani when he introduced himself to Les over the phone. "Can we talk?"

"That's what I do," said Les.

"I have an idea for a sports call-in show on television," said Liverani. "It's called 'More Sports & Les Levine.' Would you please apply?"

Les happened to be between engagements so he applied and got the job.

SportsChannel was desperate for programming. The Indians filled only about three hours on game days. Liverani envisioned pioneering new ground—a radio call-in show on television. No one had done that before. It seemed to defy logic. It sounded like a Bob Newhart comedy sketch.

"You point the camera at a man talking on the phone and people will watch that. How long will they watch? An hour? Have you run this past the programming department?"

Liverani *was* the programming department. Obviously, it worked because Les made it work. Les Levine was Liverani's Ponce de Leon. "More Sports & Les Levine" has run continuously for 15 years, moving from SportsChannel to Fox Sports Ohio to Adelphia cable and now to NEON (Time Warner), the largest cable company in northeast Ohio. Liverani remained with Fox

Sports Ohio until he was transferred to run its Florida operation. He retired two years ago and now lives in Charleston, South
Carolina.

"He's been my savior," said Les. "You're only as good as the guy
who hires you thinks you are."

"A savior?" said Liverani. "I respectfully decline that. He's been
on TV for 15 years now because he's Les Levine. The first thing is
his sense of humor. He's very funny and knows his sports. He has
a wonderful way with words. He's very clever. He's a true Cleve-
lander, very proud of his roots."

When we last looked, "More Sports and Les Levine" was seen
on Time Warner cable between 6 and 7 p.m. each weeknight under the same financial arrangement that served Les so well on
WHK. He sets his own ad rates and sells his own commercials.
He still hires sports writers for guest appearances. His viewers
are the most loyal in all of sports. So are his sponsors. Sokolowski's University Inn in Tremont has been an advertiser for 17 years.

"I'd like to go another 17 years with Les," Mike Sokolowski said.

Mike should be loyal. Les sacrificed his body for Sokolowski's.
There are several levels in the sprawling restaurant, where you
step up or down a couple of steps. One day while carrying his tray
of food, Les took one step down when he should have taken two
steps. The EMS responded quickly. Les tore the ACL (anterior
cruciate ligament) in both knees, quite an achievement. Nobody
has ever managed to do that in a pro football game. That was several years and several surgeries ago. When asked about the food
at Sokolowski's, Les said, "It's to die for."

He never has a full plate. Despite the pain in his knees, he's
always ready for more. He and I did a noontime talk show for
several years for Joan Andrews of Lake Effect Radio. That was a
good experience.

He also was talked into doing standup comedy at the Improv
in the Flats. It was not a good experience.

"Once. I did it once," he said. "In all these years on radio and
television, I have never been nervous, not for one second. But for

ten minutes that I was up there, I was shaking inside. I've never been so nervous in my life. There were about 100 people. I made some people laugh and felt stupid and scared to death. It's not as easy as you think."

He does make it look easy, however. He is 65 years old and seems financially secure.

"I have enough to live on as long as I don't buy anything," he said.

Ken Coleman:
Loyal to an Old Friend

Ken Coleman and John FitzGerald were giants of the Cleveland television industry. They operated with style and class.

Coleman broadcast Browns' games for 15 years and he probably would have stayed for another 25 years except he refused to take another man's job. He was the Browns' play-by-play man on radio station WTAM (1100) in 1952 and '53 and then he switched to television as the lead announcer of the Browns on WJW (Channel 8) from 1954 to '65. He also was the Indians' television announcer for 10 years from 1954 to 1963.

He had only one eye. Maybe you knew that. He was 12 years old, a kid growing up in Quincy, Massachusetts, near Boston, when a friend shot him in the eye with a BB gun. But he could always see right from wrong.

In 1965, Ken was offered the lead sports anchor position at WJW-TV Channel 8. It was an enticing opportunity. It would double his income and provide predictability and stability for his family. At the time he was broadcasting Browns games on television—14 regular season games and five exhibitions. He also hosted the weekly "Quarterback Club" on television, another 14-week gig and a 15th if the Browns made the NFL championship game, which they often did. But that was all. It was a part-time job. This was Cleveland local television. It wasn't New York and it wasn't the network. Coleman had a long off-season and in television you don't get paid when you don't work.

The other stations had solidly established sports anchors. Jim Graner was on Channel 3. Gib Shanley was on Channel 5. John

FitzGerald was on Channel 8. Those jobs did not become available often.

But Coleman didn't like the sound of this one.

"What about John FitzGerald?" Coleman asked.

"We're taking him off the air," he was told.

"John's a friend of mine. I'm not taking his job," said Coleman.

"We're taking him off, anyway, whether you take the job or not," they said.

"Then you better find somebody else. It won't be me," he said.

Channel 8 was punishing FitzGerald for his union activities. After 15 years as sports director, he wasn't being fired; he was simply being hidden away in the booth announcer's closet, reading station identifications all night. He did that for the next 18 years, until he retired. FitzGerald's first replacement was the Texan Frank Glieber for three years and then Dave Martin, Jim Mueller, John Telich, Casey Coleman, Mark Schroeder, Tony Rizzo and Telich again.

In 1953, FitzGerald helped organize the Cleveland chapter of AFTRA, the broadcasters' union (American Federation of Television and Radio Artists). He was president of the Cleveland chapter for 10 years and a national officer for another 40 years. Union men revered FitzGerald. He fought for pensions, vacations and health benefits. Sometimes those fights were bare-knuckle battles. There were long strikes and bitterness. But working conditions at the two union TV stations, Channel 3 and Channel 8, were the best in Cleveland.

Ken Coleman respected that and he was grateful. When he turned down the job at Channel 8, he packed up his family and moved to Boston, where he landed on his feet. He joined the Red Sox announcing team that included Ned Martin and Mel Parnell in a three-man rotation on both radio and television. The opening was created when Curt Gowdy left to become a network announcer on NBC. Ken Coleman was the voice of the Red Sox from 1965 to 1989, except for five years when he broadcast the Cincinnati Reds on television.

In 2005, Channel 8 shocked the industry by voting out the AFTRA union. Tom Merriman, a lawyer and an investigative reporter, led the revolt. He quietly lobbied, especially with inexperienced young reporters, telling them they no longer needed the union. He pointed out that union dues were expensive. The employer's contribution to their 401(k)s were a better retirement plan than the AFTRA pension, he said. In a union of just under 40 members, he won by a single vote. When the station was sold, their 401(k)s and other benefits were eliminated, which was the trend nationwide.

Soon afterward, Merriman left television. He now works for a Cleveland law firm but he's still on the air. You probably have seen the ubiquitous commercials for his law firm.

Bambi Gone Berserk:
Overrun With Deer

Deer are now having lunch in our backyard. On Memorial Day, 2011, we watched a doe and her live-in boyfriend turn our flower garden into a salad buffet. Hostas to a deer are like chocolate to a princess. They spent the next couple of nights in our neighbor's backyard and a day after that she gave birth to a fawn in another neighbor's backyard. A few days later we watched the fawn nurse from its mother.

I mention this because we live in the city.

Actually, we live in the suburb of Rocky River, Ohio, but it is totally urban. The Cleveland city line at Kamm's Corners is maybe two miles away. I could walk there. I won't but I could.

That same week a wild turkey sashayed down our street and put on quite a show, spreading his colorful tail feathers. I think that meant there was a lady turkey in the vicinity. And it wasn't even Thanksgiving. It was summer.

I wouldn't be surprised if a bear showed up next. I'm serious.

It made me realize how life had changed, even in my lifetime.

A century ago there wasn't a single deer in the entire state of Ohio. The farmers had eradicated them to protect their crops. The farmers also wiped out the wolves, cougars, mountain lions, bobcats and bears to protect their chickens and livestock.

Ohio must have been a sterile environment a century ago.

Then it got worse. To control the parasites, the farmers sprayed DDT, which got into the water and that took care of the eagles. It rendered their eggshells too thin to produce live babies. There were no more bald eagles.

The industrialists came along and dumped every chemical

they had into the rivers and the lake to go along with the sanitary sewers that emptied directly into the nearest streams. Signs went up along Lake Erie that said, "No swimming." The lake was crawling with germs. Parents were afraid their children would catch polio. Some of my classmates caught it.

We finally woke up and discovered the environment is like a computer. We clicked on "undo" and turned back the clock. We got the chemicals out of the rivers and the sewage out of the streams and we cleaned up the lake.

In the 1920s, Ohio hunters had itchy trigger fingers. They wanted to shoot something and there wasn't anything other than rabbits and squirrels to shoot. It wasn't very heroic to mount the head of a rabbit on the wall of your rec room. So, in 1922 Ohio's state legislature authorized the purchase of 9,000 acres of forestland in Scioto County for a deer preserve. Named the "Teddy Roosevelt Game Preserve," it was located in one of the most remote areas of Ohio. Draw a line directly south of Columbus to the Ohio River and you're there. Coincidentally, "Sciota" is a Shawnee Indian word, which means "deer." A man named Simon Labold, who owned the land, sold it to the State for $31,835.45.

The only known documentation of this landmark event was F. B. Chapman's doctoral dissertation in 1938.

A 700-acre corral was fenced off and 200 deer were imported from neighboring states and from private farmers. Between 1922 and 1932, those 200 deer increased to almost 1,000 and they were released into the wild. The Ohio River was a natural boundary on the south so they slowly dispersed north into Ohio. Five years later, in 1937, the number of deer had doubled to 2,000 and they were found in 28 counties. By 1956, the deer had reached all of Ohio's 88 counties and the first official statewide hunting season was held. There has been a hunting season every year since except for 1961.

What began with 200 deer has grown to 800,000. There are an estimated 500,000 deer hunters in Ohio, which sounds high, but that's what the Ohio Department of Wildlife claims, and the hunters usually kill 250,000 deer each year. They spend $266 million a year on guns and ammunition and $19.5 million on hunting licenses.

The deer are now breeding in our back yards and raising their children on our patios. Motorists are dodging them on their way to work. Interstates are littered with their carcasses. Some communities have hired professional sharpshooters to cull the herds.

The deer even affected the 1995 high school football playoffs. Brunswick had lost in the state semifinals to Colerain but was reinstated when it was discovered that Colerain had used an ineligible player.

"We got a call on Monday morning that we were back in the playoffs. We were to play St. Ignatius that Saturday for the state championship," said Gerry Nowak, an assistant coach at the time. "We couldn't reach our players. Most of them were not in school. It was the first day of deer hunting season."

At schools such as Brunswick, which is located in rural Medina County, the first day of deer hunting season is almost like a national holiday. Brunswick lost the state championship game to St. Ignatius, 41-21.

There should be a warning when you click on "undo." When the deer were brought back, their natural predators were not. Nobody is bringing back the wolves, cougars, mountain lions and bobcats. Coyotes have worked their way into Ohio from the western states, but they're not going to bring down a full-grown deer. In 1932 seven black bears were released into the wild in Ohio. Occasionally a bear is spotted, but usually they're tourists from Pennsylvania.

DDT was banned and the bald eagles have returned. Several are nesting nearby. In 1979 there were four nesting pairs in Ohio. By the year 2011 there were almost 200.

Between the walleye and the perch, we have some of the best eating fish in the world, but commercial fishermen from Canada are poaching our fish.

I would like to click on "undo" one more time and go back on the hunt with the *U.S.S. Cod*, the submarine docked near East Ninth Street. The volunteers who care for her tell me the engines could be fired up. The wiring is unreliable, but, what the hell? With a few torpedoes we could end the poaching.

Life is good. We're still in the process of correcting our mistakes. We're not done, but we're getting there. The deer get in our way, but if that's the worst they do, I can live with them. I'm also grateful that the legislature, in its wisdom, did not import 200 caribou.

Punxsutawney Phil's Untimely Demise

I've been fortunate to cover almost every major sporting event in this country except the Kentucky Derby, the Masters and Groundhog Day in Punxsutawney, Pennsylvania. Frankly, the Masters is not on my bucket list but Groundhog Day is, even though it's not exactly a sporting event. Ever since the movie with Bill Murray, I've been intrigued.

"Then you know about the sad demise of Punxsutawney Phil," said Mike Wagner, a realtor in Mayfield Heights, Ohio.

"What?!!!"

"Yes, he froze to death in 1970," said Wagner. "Grave robbers stole his corpse."

I was speaking at the Mayfield Chamber of Commerce luncheon and Wagner was there to introduce me, but this revelation suddenly dwarfed my prepared remarks. I was talking about my first book and discovering a chapter for my next book.

Wagner was a student at St. Francis College of Loretto, Pennsylvania, which is about an hour's drive from Punxsutawney. He was the first to discover Punxsutawney's dirty little secret.

"I believe it was Pete Sentren's girlfriend who invited us to Punxsutawney for Groundhog Day in 1970. She lived near Punxsutawney. She said we could sleep in the basement of her parents' home," said Wagner.

So Wagner and half a dozen of his fraternity friends from St. Francis made the trip, arriving in late afternoon of Feb. 1. Groundhog Day was the next day, Feb. 2. It is one of the few major holidays celebrated on the same date every year, like the Fourth of July, Christmas and New Year's Day.

Among them was Mike Asselta, whose nickname was "Goody" because he was always looking for a good time. The boys went out partying, drinking, riding toboggans and then they slept in blankets on the floor of the Roberts' basement, which was fine. They were college lads. Early the next morning they dragged themselves off the basement floor and drove to Gobbler's Knob, where the ceremonies took place. The members of the prestigious Groundhog Society were dressed in their traditional top hats and morning suits. Phil was in his box with the tiny door.

"There were a couple of hundred people there," Asselta recalls. "We were half hung over and it was cold. I bet it was zero degrees. The time came and they tapped on Phil's box with a stick or a cane or something. He didn't come out. They tapped again. He still didn't come out. We're all saying, 'Get that sucker out. We came all the way from Loretto. We want to see the rodent.' They tapped his box again. 'He doesn't want to come out. Six more weeks of winter,' said the president of the Groundhog Society. Then they all left to get pancakes and bloody Marys at the Punxsutawney County Club. They just left Phil there."

That was not the end of the story for the expeditionary force from St. Francis, however. They were young, they were out of town, they were adventurous and they were thirsty. And the Franciscan monks at St. Francis were a good hour away.

Mike Wagner worked the crowd at the pancake breakfast, making small talk with one morning suit guy after another.

"One of them confided his suspicion to me that Phil was dead, that he froze to death," said Wagner, who passed the word to the others.

"So we went back to Gobbler's Knob to see if he was still there," said Asselta. "And there was Phil's box, abandoned, alone, unguarded."

Another of the Unholy St. Francis Seven, a chap named Steve Gill, looked into Phil's box and found, exactly as advertised, one groundhog, frozen solid. Here was a case of morbid indifference, a felony, but nowhere on the Punxsutawney web site will you find any reference to the passing of Phil in 1970 or to the mysterious disappearance of his corpse.

"Steve Gill reached in and pulled him out," said Asselta. "Steve had a big winter parka on. He put Phil in his pocket. Later that day we drove back to St. Francis. Steve put Phil in his freezer. He lived in a house off campus. We thought about getting Phil stuffed, but that was too expensive. So Steve left Phil in his freezer."

Time passed. Winter turned to spring. Summer was just around the corner and so were finals.

"I had to give a speech for my final in Helen Carroll's public speaking class," recalled Ray Ward, another of the Seven. "The subject was local history."

Ray approached Steve Gill.

"Steve," said Ray, "do you still have that groundhog in your freezer?"

"Yeah, I do," said Steve.

"Can I borrow him?" said Ray.

"You can keep him," said Steve.

And so, on the morning of his final, Ray Ward picked up the frozen ground hog and brought him to class. Ward concealed the dead body behind the rostrum and he began his speech, ten minutes on the tragic and bizarre demise of the frozen Punxsutawney groundhog.

"The other students in my class thought I was doing a comedic presentation," said Ward. "Helen Carroll was a native of the area and she was skeptical of us who were from eastern urban areas. I was from northern New Jersey. She thought I made the whole thing up. She questioned my validity and thought I was ridiculing local history. And then I held up the carcass and she was incredulous."

Ray got an A in the class and returned the rodent to Steve Gill's freezer. Shortly afterward Steve grew tired of the groundhog staring at him every time he opened the freezer to get a frozen pizza so he left Phil on the porch to defrost. When Phil began to ripen, he disappeared.

Steve Gill's adventures took him to Alaska and most recently to Seattle. Ray Ward, who made such an impressive speech about a frozen rodent, lives in Morehead, North Carolina, and is a salesman for a company that—get this!—makes cold storage facilities and walk-in freezers. It is natural that you should wonder what attracted him to that business.

Mike Asselta, a retired schoolteacher from Fairport, New York, returns to the scene of the crime periodically. Because of the popularity of the movie, crowds of 30,000 now are typical on Groundhog Day at Punxsutawney. Parking is a mile away and you ride shuttle buses to Gobbler's Knob.

"Come on up. I'll show you around," said Asselta, who seems unafraid of any pending legal action for abuse of a corpse.

"I was only a witness," insisted Asselta, who claims protection from prosecution by the statute of limitations.

Bill Baker, another of the Unholy Seven, is now a lawyer and says the statue of limitations does not apply in this case.

"I understand there is a nice reward offered for your capture," Baker emailed Asselta.

Frankly, I think the whole gang should be rounded up and forced to spend a night at Gobbler's Knob in an unheated box.

Consider the ultimate irony of this sordid saga. St. Francis College is named after St. Francis of Assisi, the patron saint of animals. He was an animal lover! That saintly man has been spinning in his grave for more than forty years. The Unholy Seven should have been expelled for desecrating the corpse.

Nevertheless, I might accept Asselta's offer. But I won't sleep in anybody's basement.

Cats and Rats:
Hold Your Breath

I never had a problem with cats until a Siamese thought I was a hot lunch in 1970. I was visiting friends on Lake Avenue in Lakewood when I noticed a Siamese cat in the corner of their living room staring at me, giving me the evil eye. "Here's something to stare at," I thought. I scratched the back of the chair. Scratch. Scratch. Scratch. His glare intensified. I smiled to myself. That will drive the cat crazy, I mused.

I turned back to the conversation with my arm draped over the back of the stuffed living room chair and I forgot about the cat. I neither saw that feline creep toward me nor heard its velvet paws glide across the Oriental rug. Suddenly it struck like a viper. I snapped my head around to see the cat clinging to the back of the chair by its claws with its four incisors dug deep into my flesh, through skin, through muscle, almost to the bone. The attack lasted only a cat-like wink. He let go and bounded away, licking the blood off his lips.

My hosts were horrified. "No need," I said. "It's just a little nip." I took out my handkerchief and wiped away the blood from the four puncture wounds in my arm. I kept dabbing at them until they stopped bleeding. The holes in my arm healed quickly and I forgot about the attack.

Several months later I was visiting my sister, who was excited to show me her new kitten. It was a Siamese.

"Give your Uncle Dan a kiss," she playfully said, holding the kitten against my face.

It was as though that cat was radioactive and I was a Geiger counter. I broke out in hives. My nose started to run like a spigot. My throat tightened up. I couldn't swallow. From that moment I was allergic to cats. The medical diagnosis was that the saliva from the Siamese cat had entered my bloodstream and activated a latent allergy.

For the next 40 years I could walk into a house and within less than a minute tell you if they had one cat or multiple cats. Indoors or outdoors, it was the same. I could talk to somebody on the street and I knew. Their cat's dander would be on their clothes.

At an Indians opening game I turned around and said to the woman behind me, "You look like a cat lover. How many cats do you have?"

"I have three cats," she said proudly.

I knew that. That's how it went for four decades.

On May 20, 1976, the Cleveland baseball writers honored our Indians' Man of the Year at a small dinner party with a couple of informal speeches at Swingo's Keg and Quarter at E. 18th St. and Euclid Ave. Considerable drinking was involved. I went at it pretty good that night. When the party broke up it was off to the Theatrical Grill for one more. I persuaded our sports cartoonist Dick Dugan and his wife, Jean, to join me.

So we had one more at the Theatrical and when they blinked the lights at closing, I insisted that we needed another one. Across the street a cheap joint called The Seven-Thirty Lounge was still open.

The Seven-Thirty Lounge turned out to be a dirty go-go bar with a tired, disinterested dancer gyrating on a raised platform behind the bar. We had barely sat down at the bar when my throat got tight, I couldn't swallow and my nose started running.

My computer-like mind, fueled by Budweiser and Drambuie, solved this case in a wink.

"Do you have cats?" I asked the bartender.

He ignored me. I asked him again.

"Do you have cats?"

He paid no attention.

I knew they kept cats in the bar and I knew why. They probably had rats. They probably had rats as big as cats. So I moved on to the next question.

"Do you have rats?" I said.

I was polite. I merely wanted confirmation. I knew he heard me but he said nothing, which annoyed me. Even the go-go dancer was now listening. I was out of patience. I turned sarcastic.

"Hey, Mr. Katz," I said. "Do you have rats?"

I asked him twice more. "Mr. Katz, do you have rats?"

Now he was annoyed and he started to make a move toward the end of the bar. I knew what was happening. He was going for a gun. Many downtown bartenders working alone late at night had guns stashed behind the bar. If he got his gun, we were all in danger because he was one angry bartender. I had lured Dick Dugan and his wife into a shootout. I had to prevent the bartender from reaching his gun.

In a flash, I was off my stool, on my feet and around the corner of the bar. As he reached for it, I grabbed him and dragged him from behind the bar out into the open where we began fist-fighting. I was down. He was down. We were bouncing up and down like tennis balls. The go-go dancer stopped dancing. Dick Dugan and his wife watched in awe. They had never been out drinking with me before and they certainly would never make that mistake again, if they lived. This entire plan was not going well. He broke loose. He ran behind the bar. He got it and he let loose. "Crack. Crack. Crack." I threw my right arm up defensively and it stung my hand and forearm.

But it wasn't a gun. It was a whip. He kept a whip back there and he knew how to use it. He came out like a lion tamer flailing away with the whip. I tried to get inside and lay a few punches on him, but the whip kept me away.

I picked up a chair, a cheap, old-fashioned cane chair. The chair was light and I could use it as a shield against the whip and I also tried to hit him in the head with it. But he was more skillful

with the whip than I was with the chair. Blows landed were probably two to one in his favor.

This couldn't go on all night, him with the whip and me with
the chair. It was time to go. I motioned for Dick Dugan and Jean
to go for the door. They made their escape. I threw the chair at
the bartender and followed them out into the warm May night.
I didn't really expect them to say, "Thanks for a wonderful evening," but I didn't expect Mrs. Dugan to be crying like that. I'm
sure she felt better in the morning.

The next day I had to throw away my light-colored tan sports
coat and pants. Dirt from the floor was permanently ground into
the knees and elbows. I guess I was up and down a few times.

I never went back to that bar. It was out of business and vacant a year later. I wasn't surprised. It was dirty, it had rats, the
bartender was rude and the customers had to fight their way out
of the joint.

Willie Mays and 3.2 Beer

On any list of the great heartbreaks in Cleveland sports history you will find the usual suspects—Red Right 88, the Drive, the Fumble, Michael Jordan's shot, Game Seven of the 1997 World Series, losing three straight playoff games to Boston in 2007, LeBron James quitting against the Celtics in the 2010 playoffs, the dispirited Indians losing the 1940 pennant to Detroit by one game because of their rebellion against hated manager Oscar Vitt. It's an interesting list.

Include the 1954 World Series.

The '54 Indians, managed by Al Lopez, snapped the New York Yankees' streak of five straight American League pennants and in the process set an American League record with 111 victories. The previous record of 110 was held by the 1927 Yankees, the year Babe Ruth hit 60 home runs and Lou Gehrig hit 47.

There were three 20-game winners in the American League in 1954 and the Indians had two of them—future Hall of Famers Bob Lemon (23-7) and Early Wynn (23-11). The other starters were Mike Garcia (19-8), Art Houtteman (15-7) and Bob Feller (13-3). The Indians led the league with the lowest team earned run average at 2.78 and their staff had an astounding 77 complete games. That was exactly half of their 154-game schedule.

Relief pitchers were not clearly defined at that time. There were no labels. There were no setup men or closers. Even the term "long man" didn't come into use until the '70s. The only American League teams with relief specialists were the Yankees with 36-year-old veteran Johnny Sain (22 saves) and Boston with 39-year-old Ellis Kinder (15 saves), both savvy former starters.

The Indians were a spectacular exception. They alternated three closers, depending on the situation, and two of them were raw rookies, left-hander Don Mossi (7 saves) and right-hander Ray Narleski (13 saves). The third was 33-year-old lefty Hal Newhouser (7 saves and 7 wins in relief). Newhouser enjoyed a long earlier career as a starter in Detroit and eventually was voted into the Baseball Hall of Fame. When makeup doubleheaders left the Indians short of starters late in the season, Lopez turned to his three bullpen aces, each pitching three innings. The Indians won that game, Mossi getting the win and Narleski getting the save.

Look at the Indians' pitching staff this way. The five starters combined for 93 wins and 36 losses. The three relief specialists combined for 27 saves and a 14-3 record coming out of the bullpen. It was the greatest pitching performance by any team in history.

From beginning to end, that season was magical. Second baseman Roberto Avila won the batting crown at .341. Centerfielder Larry Doby led the league in home runs with 32 and runs batted in with 126. The Indians led the league in home runs and were second in runs scored. When the Indians needed a pinch hit late in a game, backup second baseman Hank Majeski usually came through. He batted .301 as a pinch hitter.

The Giants had a slight edge in home run power but otherwise were similar offensively. Centerfielder Willie Mays was the National League batting champ at .345 and he clubbed 41 home runs. The Giants had Dusty Rhodes, the best pinch hitter in baseball. He batted .333 as a pinch hitter and .341 overall with 15 home runs. Left-hander Johnny Antonelli had a 21-7 record and led the league with the lowest earned run average. The Giants' staff also led the league in earned run average and they used a two-man closer tandem, 36-year-old Marv Grissom (19 saves) and 31-year-old Hoyt Wilhelm (7 saves).

Where they differed most dramatically was in their managers. They called the Indians' Al Lopez the Silent Señor. The Giants were managed by Leo (The Lip) Durocher.

The World Series opened on Sept. 29 in the Polo Grounds, the Giants' home field in Manhattan, and everything that happened after that was strange and impossible to explain.

In the first game, with Bob Lemon and Sal Maglie locked in a 2-2 tie, the Indians threatened to break it open in the eighth inning. With runners on first and second bases, and only one out, Cleveland first baseman Vic Wertz hammered a monstrous drive to dead centerfield in the oddly shaped Polo Grounds. Willie Mays turned his back to the infield and ran at full speed until he caught up with the ball and caught it over his left shoulder almost 460 feet from the plate. Most historians call it the greatest catch in World Series history.

With the score still tied, 2-2, and right-hander Lemon still pitching in the last of the 10th inning, Durocher sent left-handed hitting Dusty Rhodes to the plate as a pinch hitter for right-handed Monte Irvin and he lofted a fly ball down the right-field line where the seats were only 257 feet from the plate. The ball cleared the wall for a three-run homer and the Giants took Game One, 5-2. It was probably the time to bring in Mossi to face the lefty Rhodes, but matchups were not yet part of ordinary baseball strategy. Durocher, however, seemed to have a handle on the lefty-righty thing.

By the way, I'm curious about the man who designed that ballpark. He must have been a sadist.

Al Smith led off Game Two for Cleveland with a home run on Antonelli's first pitch, but the Indians managed only three hits the rest of the game and the Giants beat Early Wynn, 3-1. Rhodes drove in a tying run with a bloop single to center in the fifth inning. Once again, Rhodes was pinch hitting for Irvin, the 35-year-old left fielder who was enjoying a fine season in his own right. Rhodes stayed in the game in left field and hit another home run in the seventh, this time an honest blast over the roof in right field.

Rhodes delivered the big hit again in Game Three as the Series moved to Cleveland. In the third inning with runners on second and third, Rhodes pinch hit for Irvin for the third time and delivered a sharp two-run single against Mike Garcia for a 3-0 lead. The Giants won the game, 6-2. Rhodes drove in seven runs in the Series and went 4-for-4 as a pinch hitter.

The Series ended on Saturday, Oct. 2, when the Giants completed a shocking four-game sweep by beating the Indians, 7-4.

Many years later, Indians third baseman Al Rosen postulated that the Indians lost the World Series because they placed too much importance on breaking the Yankees' record for most wins in a season. He claimed they lost their momentum after they won their 111th game. Emotionally, that was their impossible dream. Vic Wertz stood alone as a valiant soldier. He hit an even .500 with four singles, two doubles, a triple and a home run. And a 460-foot out.

Nobody in Cleveland, however, cried in his beer like Ignatius McIntyre, owner of Pat Joyce's Tavern on East Ninth St., one of the busiest joints in downtown Cleveland. It was on a stretch between Superior and Chester Avenues where the sporting crowd congregated. Kornman's was a few steps to the south and a few steps beyond that was the Roxy Burlesque house, where the top strippers in the country appeared. Across the street from Joyce's was Jean's Fun House, where you could play arcade games and buy risqué trinkets. High school kids got a kick out of it. Not far from there was a strip tease bar where girls coaxed traveling salesmen and naive visitors from the suburbs into buying them watered down drinks. If you turned west on Short Vincent Ave. you found the Theatrical Grill, a classy joint that featured entertainment but no strippers. Gamblers, bookies and other sharpies fancied the Theatrical. Also squeezed onto that block were several other bars with no distinguishing features. In good weather you could stumble upon gamblers and bookies hanging out on the corner of East Ninth and Short Vincent. Also in bad weather. They were never in their cups because they lived by their wits. Many of them survived to an old age if they didn't do something to get bumped off. Cleveland was a hot town in those days. It was exciting. Athletes and entertainers liked coming here. We were the sixth biggest city in the country.

Joyce's was the best. Visiting ballplayers and umpires appreciated it because you could get a meal after a game. Newspaper people liked it because the food was good and it wasn't too expensive. The downtown office workers liked it because you weren't embarrassed to be seen there.

Unlike most of the other spots on East Ninth Street, Joyce's was open on Sunday. The Victorian liquor laws in Ohio at that time mandated that only 3.2 beer could be sold on Sundays, no wine or liquor. Three-two referred to the amount of alcohol in the beer, 3.2 percent. Supposedly regular beer had more alcohol although I don't know anybody who could tell the difference. The only way to distinguish them was by the bottle cap. Three-two had a red cap; regular beer had a blue cap. I believe it was the same beer. All they did at the brewery was change the bottle cap. That's my theory.

The point of all this is that Game Five of the World Series was to be played on Sunday, Oct. 3, at Cleveland Stadium and a large portion of the crowd of 86,000 was expected to descend on Pat Joyce's after the game. In anticipation, Ignatius McIntyre, whom everybody called Iggy, laid in enough 3.2 beer to slake the thirst of the entire 82nd Airborne Division. You could barely move in the basement of Joyce's. There were cases of 3.2 beer stacked floor to ceiling. It was like a submarine at the beginning of a cruise with every passageway crammed with cans of food.

Not everybody shared my theory about 3.2 beer. Many thought there was a difference and they didn't want to drink it except on Sundays. Bartenders had to be careful when opening bottles of 3.2 beer so that the customer could not see the red cap.

So Iggy was stuck with 3.2 beer until the following St. Patrick's Day, which, unfortunately, fell on a Wednesday.

The Indians spent most of the next four decades rebuilding and so did the City of Cleveland. In the 1960s, urban renewal leveled the entire block. There went the Roxy, there went the strip joint, there went Jean's Fun House, there went the gamblers and there went the fun. Joyce's moved to East Sixth Street and St. Clair Avenue. The McIntyre family later opened a second restaurant downtown and third and fourth restaurants in Rocky River and North Olmsted. That was progress but downtown Cleveland never was the same.

The Theatrical:
Characters Welcome

The movie about Cleveland gangster Danny Greene, *Kill the Irishman*, featured several references to the Theatrical Grill on Short Vincent Avenue in downtown Cleveland. The restaurant closed in the early 1990s, but in its heyday it was the smartest joint in town.

Having mentioned the movie, let me clarify something. I never saw Danny Greene in the Theatrical. I don't know where he hung out, probably in the Collinwood neighborhood. As for Shondor Birns, he only ate lunch there, always at the first table to the left. That was Shondor's table. He was never there at night. I never saw Cleveland's leading Italian gangsters at the Theatrical, either, and I was there a lot. They favored the Murray Hill neighborhood and other East Side Italian spots.

But this isn't about them.

My denizens of the night included gamblers, detectives, lawyers, sports figures, broadcasters and other characters, including the most colorful figures in Cleveland history, and you would find them at the Theatrical. That's where *The Plain Dealer* sportswriter Bob Dolgan fought a draw with boxing trainer Richie Giachetti. When the New York Yankees were in town, they signed their tabs and the bill went to George Steinbrenner. When Dick Jacobs was riding high as owner of the Indians, he picked up the tab for the entire joint for three hours one St. Patrick's Day. Imagine, wall-to-wall Irishmen drinking on St. Patrick's Day. The bill could have financed the first Gulf War.

Among professional drinkers, nobody rivaled Dick Lamb, heir

to a trucking fortune. He slept until two o'clock every afternoon and then began his nightly rounds. He had a regular routine. In the early evening he joined his best friend, Creighton Miller, and other pals at the Pewter Mug downtown, always at table 14. From there he would move on to the Theatrical. Dick never needed a big introduction. He announced his arrival in a loud, gravelly voice that carried a great distance.

"Gentlemen, start your engines!" he usually bellowed as he walked into the bar.

This from a tall, lanky, gray-haired man wearing glasses and a business suit. Everyone looked up. He could be heard even above the din of the band.

He sometimes varied his anthem. "Prepare to dismount and fight on foot!" he would declare.

Sadly, Dick died when he ran his Bentley into the railroad trestle at E. 55th St. and Euclid Ave. at two o'clock in the morning. Several bartenders were grief-stricken. Dick usually bought drinks for everyone present and he was a big tipper.

He never should have let his chauffeur go. Dick lost his license a few years earlier for driving with a snoot full. He spent 30 days in jail. They treated him well in jail. He had a television and a small bar set up in the doorway of his cell, which was usually left open. He was the first inmate in that suburban pokey to host happy hour every afternoon.

I once called the jail and asked to speak to Dick Lamb.

"I'll see if he's available. Whom shall I say is calling?" said the desk sergeant.

When he was released, he was not permitted to drive for a year but life didn't change. He hired a chauffeur who picked him up in the afternoon and they made their rounds from bar to bar. His chauffeur usually found a chair off to the side and watched Dick drink. When the year was up the chauffeur handed Dick the keys to his Bentley.

*   *   *

Notre Dame and the Naval Academy have met in football every year since 1927 and 11 of those games were at Cleveland Stadium. Notre Dame was a big draw in Cleveland. Two days before the 1976 game I entertained the two sports information directors at dinner. They were my old friends, Roger Valdiserri of Notre Dame and Tom Bates of Navy, the publicity men for their respective schools. Bates, in fact, was my old college classmate from Notre Dame. It was Thursday night, Oct. 29. The teams didn't arrive in town until the next day.

I made a reservation at the Theatrical and we sat at Shondor Birns' table. Valdiserri, who didn't drink, had a Coke while Bates and I tossed back a beer and looked at the menu. We were barely settled when I noticed sports agent Ed Keating in a far corner negotiating a player's contract with Ted Turner, neophyte owner of the Atlanta Braves. I waved at Ed. He waved back at me. When they finished dinner and made their deal, Turner agreed to pay an outlandish sum to free agent outfielder Gary Matthews, far more than he was worth. Then they headed over to our table and sat down. The adjacent table was empty so we pulled it up against ours.

I made the introductions. Keating was frequently in the news but Turner was a relative unknown. He had owned the Atlanta Braves for only a few months. His various cable television networks were in their infancy. He had neither skippered the sailboat *Courageous* to the America's Cup victory nor married Jane Fonda.

While everybody was getting acquainted, boxing promoter Don King wandered by and he sat down. I performed the introductions. King knew nothing about college football but he liked the sound of the Notre Dame Fighting Irish. King, a convicted killer, had been out of prison only about three years and already was an important boxing promoter. At that very moment he was putting together a professional boxing series and he needed venues. Notre Dame sounded like a good place.

King moved closer to Valdiserri and soon had him against the ropes. The last person in the world Valdiserri wanted as a business partner was Don King. Valdiserri kept fighting him off. King was relentless.

Turner, meanwhile, having discovered that Bates was from the Naval Academy, launched into a long, boastful monologue about his own sailing expertise, such as racing on Annapolis Bay. Bates, unaware that Turner actually was an accomplished seaman and that he was captain of the Brown University sailing team during his college days, did not believe a word of it.

"Who is this guy? He's full of bullshit," Bates whispered to me.

Bored with Turner's boasting, Bates turned his attention to King, who was going nowhere with Valdiserri. I'm not saying this was a major career mistake by Bates, but it did not gild his résumé. Some people see dead end roads. King sees eight-lane super highways. A heavyweight boxing series on the flight deck of an aircraft carrier was even better than a fight at a football school. King was on Bates like a mongoose on a cobra.

Cleveland Cavaliers owner Nick Mileti sashayed by and he sat down. We pulled up another table. Everyone was getting paired up. Mileti talked to Turner about pro basketball. Keating talked to Valdiserri about Notre Dame football players. King talked to Bates about the aircraft carrier. I sat back and waited for the next guy to sit down.

All this time we were ordering dinner and drinks and appetizers. The next guy to arrive did not sit down. He was the waiter and he handed me the bill. I stared at it a long time. It would not bankrupt *The Plain Dealer* but it would get special attention from the accounting department.

"I suppose you expect me to pick up the bill," said Turner. Keating had bruised him so badly that Turner was conditioned. He actually expected to get my bill, as well.

"It never occurred to me," I said. "But since you brought it up. I'll flip you for it."

I dug a quarter out of my pocket and flipped it. I caught it. I peeked. I won.

I won a $500 bar bill.

Here's how it ended. Keating paid the bill. His monthly bar bill at the Theatrical exceeded $1,000 anyway.

The following summer Turner skippered *Courageous* to victory in the America's Cup and he wound up on the cover of *Sports Illustrated*, July 4, 1977.

Don King staged his boxing series at the Naval Academy, at a naval installation in Florida and on the aircraft carrier *Lexington* docked at Pensacola, Florida, all thanks to Tom Bates. It did not go well, however. There were allegations of fixed fights, phony records, contract violations and generally every possible ethics violation, which in boxing is a long list. One fight on the hallowed grounds of the U. S. Naval Academy was so obviously rigged that the losing fighter, heavyweight Scott LeDoux, stormed around the ring and inadvertently knocked off Howard Cosell's toupee. LeDoux, after all, had just outpunched the inept Johnny Boudreaux, 50-1. One of the judges, Carol B. Polis, explained the decision. "Johnny Boudreaux threw possibly 10 punches and Scott LeDoux threw maybe 500," she said. "But Johnny's were effective. We had a unanimous decision for Johnny Boudreaux. It's not the amount of punches you throw. It's how they land."

The FBI investigated the judges. ABC cancelled the TV contract and *Ring Magazine*, which rigged its ratings to support King, backed away in disgrace.

When Turner bought the Atlanta arena, he hired Keating to handle contract negotiations with promoters who booked the building for ice shows, conventions and other events. Turner had learned the hard way that night in the Theatrical that Keating was the best.

* * *

Historic events often began at the Theatrical. That's how Art Modell bought the Browns and former Browns running back Fred (Curly) Morrison earned a fat commission on the deal.

Morrison told me the story many years ago. After his seven-year NFL career with the Chicago Bears and Cleveland Browns ended, he went to work as an advertising salesman for CBS television. Because he was from the Columbus suburb of Upper Arlington, had played at Ohio State and spent three years with the Browns, CBS assigned him to handle the accounts of the Akron rubber companies.

"Whenever I called on the rubber companies, I would come through Cleveland and stop in the Theatrical Grill. That's where you found out what was going on in Cleveland," Morrison said.

In January 1961, Morrison had dinner at the Theatrical before catching the last Capitol Airlines flight back to New York. That night he learned that the Cleveland Browns were for sale and his interest was piqued. He made some inquiries and learned that Dave Jones was the point man for the owners.

For the previous eight years, a syndicate of wealthy Cleveland investors including Jones, insurance man Ellis Ryan, Saul Silberman and Homer Marshman had owned the Browns. All were sportsmen. Ryan had once been president of the Cleveland Indians. Silberman owned Randall Park Racetrack. Marshman was an attorney who had founded the Cleveland Rams in the National Football League in the 1930s and later owned a piece of Northfield Park Racetrack. They were making money on their investment each year, but they felt they wanted to move their funds elsewhere. A minor investor was Bob Gries, whose family owned the May Co. department store.

Morrison reached Jones on the phone.

"He told me they already had an offer of two million dollars from a Cleveland investor," said Morrison.

They were happy with that. It represented a nice profit. They had bought the Browns for $600,000 in 1953 from Arthur B. (Mickey) McBride, who had paid $50,000 for the original franchise in 1946. The value of pro football teams was escalating.

"But I told him I could get him more. I said I could get him three million," said Morrison. "I knew something they didn't. I knew that CBS had just agreed to a new contract with the NFL that would pay each team another one million dollars per year. It hadn't been announced yet. The owners didn't even know."

"You've got thirty days to find a buyer," said Jones.

Morrison went back to his office in New York. He was on the clock. At stake was a 10 percent finder's fee, enough to set him up for life. The days turned into weeks and Morrison had nothing. Less than a week remained when Art Modell picked up the scent. Modell was a degenerate pro football fan. The Giants were his team but the Browns also made Modell's heart skip a beat.

At the age of 35, Modell had accumulated a modest fortune in the advertising business. He had become executive vice president and partner of the H. L. Hartman Company and he also owned a television production company.

Modell hungered to buy the Browns. He sold his production company and borrowed to the max from banks. He was still more than a million dollars short.

In an unusual deal, Gries agreed to increase his shares in the team. Instead of selling, he bought back in at the new price. Essentially, Bob Gries became Modell's partner. Gries owned almost 40 percent of the Browns, but he was content remaining in the background.

The selling price was $3,925,000. The price of the Browns had increased almost 80 times in 15 years.

Curly Morrison walked away with nearly $400,000 and started a television production company in California. He never set foot in the Theatrical again.

The Blue Fox:
Under Siege by the FBI

The Blue Fox was one of the finest restaurants on the West Side, with exquisite food and exciting clientele, but now it's a drug store. We can thank Carmen Loparo for that. Loparo led the FBI raid on the elegant eatery that closed it permanently in 1984.

"It was the day after the Super Bowl," said Loparo, who remembers the date as though it was his wife's birthday.

In those days, the FBI always pulled its gambling raids on Super Bowl weekend for an obvious reason. The Super Bowl was always the biggest gambling day of the year and it still is.

"It's Christmas Day, the Fourth of July and the Senior Prom all rolled into one," said the prominent handicapper Will Cover.

And so on Jan. 23, 1984, Loparo led a team of eight FBI special agents and two Lakewood policemen into the Blue Fox in the middle of the day. They had two specific targets—bartender Marty Rini, who ran a bookie operation, and Joe (Spags) Spagnola, a Cleveland mafia figure who picked up the money from the bookies each Monday for the mob.

"We already had an agent inside sitting at the bar. He was watching Marty Rini," said Loparo. "He had to make sure that Marty wasn't able to throw the betting slips in a bucket of water. The betting slips were made of rice paper. Rice paper dissolves when it hits the water."

All the FBI agents were wearing jackets with "FBI" in big letters across the back. When they struck, they didn't do it quietly.

"We went charging in the front door and I almost knocked down Roger Berry. 'Roger, get out of here,' I said to him," Loparo recalled. "We hit the bar and we told Marty Rini, 'Don't move.' He

Diners at the Blue Fox restaurant probably did not know about the high stakes poker game going on directly above them. *(Cleveland Press Collection, Cleveland State University)*

did not give us any problem. He stood still. He never had a chance to throw the rice paper in the bucket."

Then they nabbed Spagnola.

Roger Berry's presence was providential. Berry, the funeral director who ate and drank at the Blue Fox, seemingly presided over the restaurant's death. Berry hurried out the door and never returned because the Blue Fox never re-opened. There were no services, unless you count the proceedings in U. S. District Court.

Its closing changed many lives. For example, after the Wagon Wheel moved from Shaker Square to Solon, the Blue Fox became my restaurant for special occasions. I took my wife to the Blue Fox on our first date. It was around the holidays and it was crowded. I heard a familiar laugh from the other side of the restaurant. My ears perked up and I leaped to my feet.

"Harry! Harry, is that you?" I said loudly over the noise of a busy dining room.

"Over here," Harry shouted back.

It was Harry Leitch, Gib Shanley's spotter on the Browns' radio broadcasts. He was celebrating his birthday. I stood up and led the entire restaurant in singing "Happy Birthday, dear Harry."

My wife, who wasn't my wife yet, thought she had been transported into a surreal world of lunatics. She has regretted marrying me many times, I suspect.

It was at the bar of the Blue Fox where I engaged in lengthy conversations with Monsignor Edward Seward, a Catholic priest who talked to horses and to God. We never brought up religion, unless you consider horse racing a religion. The Monsignor spent his Wednesday afternoons in the clubhouse at Thistledown Racetrack and most of his evenings at the Blue Fox. He considered it missionary work.

The young widow, Ellie Mangan, took her last breath at the Blue Fox. She was sitting at the bar next to the Monsignor when she suffered a fatal heart attack and tumbled off her barstool. The poor widow had led such a sad life. Her husband, a Cleveland policeman, also died young. He succumbed to a gunshot wound from his own service revolver. When the gun fired, it was in the hand of the widow herself. No charges were filed. The prosecutor, John T. Corrigan, believed that Ellie was justified. He always had a soft spot in his heart for widows.

"She came to me for counseling. The poor thing was deeply troubled. I did my best," said the Monsignor, whose dedication to his parishioners almost equaled his devotion to horses.

As for the Blue Fox, it didn't need a priest. It needed a lawyer.

Mike Carney:
A Bullet Saved His Life

Remarkably, Mike Carney is still alive, which defies all the natural laws.

You can still find him at his old saloon, Carney's at the Top of the Flats, at 1329 Washington Ave. around the corner from St. Malachi's Church and across the street from the Stella Maris alcohol rehab center, the most incongruous intersection in Cleveland.

In its day, Carney's was a tough Irish bar. If you wanted to live on the edge, you stopped in Carney's for a beer and a knuckle sandwich. On a hot summer evening in the mid 1970s, I was on my way home from work at *The Plain Dealer* and succumbed to a lingering temptation to peek behind the green door. Inside was a tiny horseshoe bar with about 16 stools and a couple of tables. I was pleasantly surprised to see an old friend, Gracie O'Donnell, tending bar. The only other people there were three young roughnecks facing me from the opposite side of the bar. They already had a few beers in them and were feeling cocky and aggressive, emboldened by a three to one advantage. They decided to have some fun. "Who's the guy in the suit?" they asked each other in loud voices. Since I was the only person wearing a suit, I was required to respond. It went this way: "Hey, morons. Shut up."

Obviously, this was not going to end well and Gracie knew it.

"Closing time," she said. "Everybody out."

That was smart. Gracie was using her head. She didn't want anything broken. We would take the fight to the sidewalk. She opened the door and nudged them outside, one at a time.

"Not you," she said when she got to me.

She slammed the door and locked it.

"Sit down and finish your beer," she said.

"Gracie, I think you just saved my life," I said.

"I know I did," she said.

It was almost closing time anyway. Carney's closed at about nine o'clock in those days. I sipped my beer and allowed time for the three musketeers to lose interest. Finally, Gracie unlocked the door and I left. All was quiet. I walked across the street to my car when they raced up the street toward me in their noisy old junker. They had not lost interest. They had been waiting to ambush me. They came straight at me as I was unlocking my door. I pressed myself against the side of my car and they missed me.

About two weeks later I learned that one of them had jumped into the Cuyahoga River while running from the police. Here's how stupid he was. He forgot that he didn't know how to swim and he drowned. I did not rejoice at the news, but I wasn't sad, either.

Mike Carney himself was behind the bar almost 25 years later on January 26, 2001, when Benford Curry got up on the wrong side of the bed. Curry, who was a regular customer, pulled a gun to settle a beef with another patron who had the temerity to sit on his regular barstool. Curry always sat on the same stool and in his typically charming manner, ordered the man to move. There is no better way to start a fight in a bar.

"Go to hell," said the interloper.

Out came the gun. In a flash, Mike wrestled him to the floor and took the gun away. He threw it in a wastebasket behind the bar.

"Sit down and drink your beer," Carney commanded.

Oh, no. Not this guy. Curry went back to his office down the street and got another gun. This time he barged through the door shooting. He sprayed lead all over the bar. Two men sitting at the bar were wounded. He put four rounds into Carney, hitting him in the forehead, the arm, the neck and the back.

"He was having a bad day," Carney said.

It got worse. Police and ambulances descended on the place. Curry fled and the police followed his tracks in the snow to his building down the street. A standoff lasted for several hours. Curry never surrendered. Tired of the standoff, he finally held the gun to his head and put a bullet in his brain. He was an excellent shot to hit something that small.

Carney was taken to MetroHealth Medical Center where they patched him up and he was back at the bar 72 hours later when Fox 8 television reporter Jack Shea sought him out for a follow-up story.

"I couldn't believe it," said Shea. "There he was relaxing in his recliner in the bar after getting shot four times. All you could see was a bruise on his forehead."

"One bullet hit me in the eyebrow, right here, and bounced off my hard Irish head," Carney said earlier this year, pointing to a spot above his left eye.

"The bullet in my arm didn't hit a single bone or tendon. They took out the bullet in my neck. They left the one in my back until about five years later when I felt a pain in my stomach. The bullet had moved. So they just made a little cut and took it out."

Carney then said something amazing.

"Getting shot was the luckiest thing that ever happened to me. It saved my life," he said.

What!!! After all these years he never mentioned that.

"When I was in the hospital, they found out that I had an aneurism on my aorta.

They told me to keep an eye on it. So I would get it checked every six months.

After about a year and a half they noticed that it was getting bigger, so they put a stent on it. That's why I'm alive today. If I didn't get shot, they never would have found the aneurism and eventually it would have burst and killed me."

He turned the bar over to his nephew, Dave Flowers, a few years ago. Carney is now 72 years old and in good weather drinks with friends in the courtyard of the bar and enjoys the companionship of two trusty old brown dogs. He'll be fine as long as he stays near the bar. It has the power to save lives.

Lakewood Village:
Home of the Calder Cup

The Lakewood Village was a neighborhood bar with a powerful sports tradition in the 1960s. It was your typical corner tavern, literally on a corner at Elbur and Madison Avenues, smack in the middle of Lakewood. It sponsored your usual assortment of adult men's softball teams and it had a basement clubhouse for the J. Schrader Co. men's baseball team. Its adult flag football team, quarterbacked by Jack McCafferty, was famous for an 88-game winning streak and several national championships.

The Lakewood Village was unique, however, because it was home to the Calder Cup, the second most important trophy in all of pro hockey.

The bar was owned by Sally Bright, a lawyer, who was married to Paul Bright, who owned the Cleveland Barons of the American Hockey League. This is the epitome of the match made in heaven, nothing less than rapturous. One family owned both a bar and a hockey team. The Hand of God had to be involved.

At the risk of insulting my readers, let me state the obvious. When they are away from the rink, hockey players have an all-consuming hobby—drinking. Look at the words. The word rink is contained in the word drink. They like drinking and they like bars. And so, it was both good business and good recreation for the Barons players to patronize the bar owned by their boss's wife. The Barons were nothing if not loyal. Wisely, Sally and Paul rarely set foot in the bar. That would have made the players uncomfortable. The bar was run by Sally's brother, Larry Jorgensen, and his wife, Lois.

I spent many happy hours drinking there with hockey icon

Gail Egan, a Canadian who came to Cleveland in 1945 as the public relations man for the Barons. Later he scouted for them. He did some radio and television work and handled publicity for all the events at the old Cleveland Arena, such as the ice shows, boxing, pro wrestling, Globetrotters, circus, etc. He was busy, but never too busy to share a pint with me at the Lakewood Village. He was my buddy and my hockey mentor.

When the 1963-64 season rolled around, nothing was expected from the Barons. The year before they had lost 15 of their first 18 games, but rallied in the second half behind player-coach Fred Glover to finish with a 31-34-7 record. It was the first season that Glover, the team's best player, had added the duties of coach. The off-season was marked by tension and turmoil. Several partners in a fragmented ownership wanted to fire club president Paul Bright and general manager Jackie Gordon. Glover held the owners in contempt. He retorted that if Bright and Gordon were fired, he would quit.

Glover was irreplaceable and the owners were not. Confronted by Glover's ultimatum, the owners not only backed down, they backed out. They sold the team to Paul Bright who retained Jackie Gordon as general manager and the 1963-64 season was the best in Barons history, despite the loss of star goalie Les Binkley.

Goalies did not wear masks or helmets at the time and Binkley suffered a serious concussion when he was hit in the head by the puck on March 20. Because the Barons had a working relationship with Montreal, that's where they looked for a replacement goalie. Montreal sent them Jean Guy Morissette.

Despite poor eyesight, Morissette rose to new heights. He was an anchor on defense as the Barons built momentum for the playoffs. They rolled through the playoffs with nine straight victories. They won the first three-game series, 2-0. The next series was best of five and they won it, 3-0. And they swept the final series, 4-0, winning the final game at home.

Naturally, the post-game celebration was held in the Lakewood Village and when the sun began to rise on a warm May dawn, the front door was still wide open and the bodies were strewn all around. They were crumpled in booths and one even was stretched out on the bowling machine. On the bar was the Calder Cup, one of the most revered baubles in pro hockey at the time. It was the ninth and last time the Calder Cup was displayed in Cleveland. Fred Glover was involved in four of them.

The National Hockey League's Stanley Cup overshadows everything in hockey, of course, but the Calder Cup was next. From the 1930s until the late '60s the American Hockey League was the highest minor league. Because the NHL consisted of only six teams, the winner of the Calder Cup was considered the seventh-best team in all hockey.

The precious Cup was displayed in several locations that summer. It was in the window of Higbee's downtown department store for a while. It was in the main lobby of National City Bank downtown. And it was on the back bar of the Lakewood Village.

Thinking hockey fans would want to visit the humble tavern and venerate the Cup, I trumped up a letter to sports editor Hal Lebovitz asking where the Cup was. When Hal sought help, I gave him the answer. He had a funny reply in his column and that was it.

Tom Place was outraged, however. He was the hockey writer and he didn't drink. He sent a photographer to the Lakewood Village to get a picture of the Cup and then he wrote a scathing diatribe about the indignity of the Cup stuck "between the cash register and a pickle jar."

It was the most prominent story on the first sports page that day. It was great publicity for the Lakewood Village, but Sally Bright didn't see it that way. She dialed me up and exploded with righteous indignation. "What are you doing to me?" she screamed.

"That's the last time I'll do a favor for somebody," I thought to myself.

A few years later the Calder Cup lost its luster. In 1967 the NHL expanded from six to 12 teams and in 1972 the World Hockey Association came along with 12 more teams. There were now 24 franchises higher in the hockey pecking order. The beloved Calder Cup now represented the 25th best team in hockey. In 1972 Nick Mileti bought a franchise in the World Hockey Association, a team he named the Crusaders, and Cleveland hockey entered its swinging door era. Hockey teams here were like tourists. They never stayed very long. But they kept coming.

In order to make room for the Crusaders, the beloved Barons moved to Florida and eventually folded. The Crusaders lasted only four years and then moved to Minneapolis where they merged with the Fighting Saints and went bankrupt in the middle of the following season.

In 1976 Cleveland entered the National Hockey League when the California Golden Seals moved to Cleveland and changed their name to the Barons but two years later they also moved to Minneapolis.

Under owner Mel Swig, the Seals were perennial cellar dwellers on the West Coast and nothing changed when they moved here. Swig missed payrolls, begged the league for handouts and eventually the players' union contributed the money to pay the players. After one year Swig sold the Barons to George Gund III and the financial picture did not improve, prompting Gund to merge them with the Minnesota North Stars. Gund owned the North Stars and their arena in Minneapolis. Two years in Cleveland, two last-place finishes. For the franchise, that made seven last-place finishes in eight years.

The merged team didn't stay long in Minneapolis, however. They moved along to Dallas. What followed in Cleveland was a succession of minor-league hockey teams, beginning with Larry Gordon's Lumberjacks. One after another, they pulled disappearing acts. But the Lakewood Village is still there, hockey's only remaining symbol of continuity. If you mention this to anyone sitting at the bar, you will notice their blank stare.

Buddy Langdon:
Memories Forever

"Morgana was like a county fair, like a carnival. I couldn't wait to get there," said Buddy Langdon, who played slow pitch softball at Morgana Park for about 20 years.

Nobody at Morgana Park was normal back in the 1960s and '70s. In those days the tiny ballpark at Broadway Ave. and E. 65th St. was home to the *PD*-Major, the most intense slow pitch softball league in the world. One night Joe Nato, the pitcher/manager for the Star Motel team, was in a nose-to-nose argument with Hall of Fame umpire Frank Dillon.

"You've got one minute to get off this field or I'll forfeit the game," Dillon threatened.

"You've got one minute to get in your car and get the hell out of here," Nato roared back at the umpire.

Nobody fooled around with Nato, an imposing and ill-mannered person whose face could have been surgically improved with a steel crowbar. He once went into the stands and bloodied the nose of a heckler, and then calmly walked back to the mound and resumed pitching. The fans gave him a standing ovation.

Get this. Nato owned Star Motel, which was located in Greensboro, North Carolina. He worked as a mutuel clerk at Thistledown Racetrack during the day and he managed his softball team at night. Nato's picture is in Merriam-Webster's next to the word "multitasking."

"I drove around Cleveland for two years looking for Star Motel," said Chuck Webster, who covered softball for *The Plain Dealer*.

Nato also had strange players and his roster was in a continual state of flux. He had a right fielder who wore Levis for six weeks because Joe did not have uniform pants to fit him. He had a shortstop who always wore a watch.

Opposing teams continually asked him what time it was.

When Otis Chapman quit the team, he did a strip tease as he left the field. He tossed his uniform over the fence at Nato, one piece at a time. There went his cap, there went his shirt, there went his pants, there went his socks, and finally, there went Chapman.

Umpire Frank Dillon was not cut from your ordinary bolt of cloth, either.

In real life he taught history and coached baseball at South High School in Cleveland, but he also umpired softball, refereed high school basketball, worked part time in *The Plain Dealer* sports department and had an inordinate fascination for television quiz shows. He appeared on many of them and won a lot of money. He was a five-time winner on *Jeopardy.* He was "The Man" well before Ken Jennings came along. After one show stiffed him on the money he won, Dillon wrote an exposé in *The Plain Dealer* and never was invited to appear on a quiz show again. When Dillon died, he told nobody. A lifelong bachelor, Dillon left instructions for the funeral home to keep his passing a secret for 30 days. No runs, no hits, no services.

Umpires had to be a little crazy to work in this maelstrom for eight bucks a game and many of their wives also were off the grid. Joe Vulich never had a driver's license. His wife drove him to games every day for 50 years. In 1990, Vulich was inducted into the Greater Cleveland Softball Hall of Fame. His wife drove him there. She should have been inducted into the Auto Club Hall of Fame.

Umpires were under severe pressure because of all the money bet on games. It started with situation bets. Will this guy get a hit? Will they score this inning? Before long there were actual betting lines on games, just like pro football.

"Sometimes guys had to work and they'd miss a game. Before games guys would ask if this guy or that guy was going to make it that night. That was important inside information," said Buddy Langdon, an outfielder on the Pyramid Cafe team in the '60s and '70s.

"One time I brought $1,000 to bet on Pyramid Cafe against Non-Ferrous," said Langdon. "It wasn't my money. The players never gambled. I won't say who was betting the thousand dollars. All that betting was done by the team sponsors and fans and they bet a lot."

Langdon doesn't remember who won that particular game, but as a rule of thumb it was never wise to bet against Non-Ferrous Metal Fabricating, which had a hellacious lineup of sluggers.

In 1975, Non-Ferrous was invited to the July Fourth Invitational in Louisville, Kentucky, and in their first game they faced the Kentucky state champion.

"Before the game their manager said, 'We'll give you seven runs and we'll bet you $500,'" recalled Shelly Hoffman, a Non-Ferrous outfielder.

Whereupon George Opalich, who owned the Non-Ferrous company and sponsored the team, countered, "You give us seven runs and we'll bet you $5,000."

So, that was the deal. Five-thousand bucks on the line.

Hoffman remembered that in the first inning Mack Chandler hit one out. Preston Powell hit one out. Dave Watson bounced one off the air conditioning unit on the roof of a distant concession stand.

"We scored 25 runs in the first inning," said Hoffman. "I batted three times in the first inning alone. After the first inning the manager of the Kentucky team came over and gave us $5,000."

Opalich was one of the biggest spenders in softball. They called it amateur softball but he treated his players like pros.

"We were at the national tournament in Jacksonville in 1974," Hoffman said. "George Opalich chartered a private plane for 160 people. Some people paid, but the players and their wives were free and he gave us 50 dollars for expenses that weekend and he rented us cars.

"In the third or fourth inning we were losing, 32-14 to Little Caesar's from Detroit. We used four pitchers in four innings. They bring me in from left field to pitch. We come back to win, 34-32. We just beat the best team in the country. We didn't win the tournament, but we had a party all the way back. We even had a three-piece band on the plane."

* * *

It was a trite expression to say that slow pitch softball was an obsession 50 years ago.

"It was life and death," said an old player.

"No," argued another. "It was more important than that."

Actually, it really was life and death. During the 1972 Stroh's Tournament at Rose Field in Cleveland, Buddy Langdon of Pyramid Cafe made a sensational catch on the dead run with his back to the infield. As he caught the ball he crashed face-first into the outfield fence. The umpire thrust his right arm into the air and shouted, "Out."

A fan watching through the fence took issue with the umpire's call.

"He trapped it!" the fan shouted. "He trapped it against the fence."

Langdon was annoyed. Instead of throwing the ball to an infielder and trotting back to his normal position in left field, Langdon rifled the ball at the fan, barely missing him.

This, of course, exacerbated the issue between Langdon and the fan. Tempers were heated. Voices were raised.

"Suddenly, I heard gunfire," Langdon recalled.

The fan pulled out a pistol and opened fire at Langdon. That's how you should dress for a softball tournament. Wear the pants with the big pockets to hide your .44 magnum.

The bullet missed Langdon, but hit a fan of the BYM Club from Pittsburgh, nicking him in the head and taking out a piece of his ear. There were not many places to hide at Rose Field. Langdon dove into foul territory. Others crawled under the benches in the dugouts. There were a couple policemen on security duty and they chased the shooter, who took off running. He lived in the neighborhood. The cops eventually found him and hauled him off to jail. He was drunk and he had his two young sons with him. The fan from Pittsburgh was treated and released. His wound was minor. When he refused to press charges, police had to release the shooter the next morning. The man from Pittsburgh just wanted to get out of town.

* * *

In Louisville, Kentucky, the umpires packed heat. It was standard equipment when Dave Neale came to town. Neale, who managed Ted Stepien's Competitors in a short-lived professional league, had barely started a fierce argument when the umpire pulled out a monster sidearm and placed it upon Neale's shoulder.

"That shows you how hard it was to win in Louisville," said Langdon. "Even the umpires were against us."

In the pro league, Louisville played doubleheaders on Saturday and Sunday nights. Near the end of one Saturday night twin bill the public address announcer reminded fans that the next night's doubleheader would start at seven o'clock, whereupon Hank Gibson of Stepien's Competitors jumped out of the dugout and shouted, "And the cheating will start at 7:05." Even the Louisville fans applauded him.

Neale never got along with umpires. Back home at Morgana Park in the 1972 citywide tournament, Hall of Fame umpire Don Schirmer working behind the plate called out Neale's son, John. He called him out on strikes, which was highly unusual at that level of softball, especially in such an important tournament game.

John lost his mind.

"I've never struck out in my life," screamed John.

"You just did," said Schirmer.

John may have been young, but he unleashed a veteran's vocabulary and Schirmer threw him out of the game.

"I bent over to brush off the plate but I peeked between my legs and I could see John's father heading toward me from behind," said Schirmer. "He called me every name in the book. 'You're gone, too,' is all I said to him."

Schirmer and his umpiring partner, Lou Barracato, went up to the press box after the game to collect their eight dollars for the night's work. From the press box they could look down and see the reception waiting for them. It was not umpire appreciation night. Ohio Sealants had just defeated Pyramid Cafe, 14-10, a loss that eliminated Pyramid from the city-wide tournament. It meant Pyramid would not qualify for the impending national tournament, which was Pyramid's goal every year.

"There were two guys waiting for us behind the backstop, two more at one gate, two more at another gate and two more in the parking lot," Schirmer said. "Lou Barracato was a Cleveland policeman so he made a call. Within a minute you could hear sirens. Four black and white squad cars and two unmarked detective cars pulled up."

The two umpires left Morgana Park with a police escort, but that was not the end of it. Schirmer wrote a letter of complaint to the Cleveland Baseball Federation protesting Dave Neale's language. The Cleveland Baseball Federation ruled that Neale must write a letter of apology to Schirmer and four other people whose ears were offended, which further infuriated Neale.

"When pigs fly! That's when I'll apologize," Neale declared, or words to that effect.

The Cleveland Umpires Association was equally angry. The umpires demanded that Neale be suspended. When he was neither suspended nor apologetic, the umpires boycotted the remaining league schedule and the players umpired their own games for the rest of the season.

Schirmer and Barracato lived to throw out Neale another night.

Preston Powell swings from the heels. The onetime Browns' running back gained fame on the softball diamonds. *(Greater Cleveland Softball Hall of Fame)*

Coincidentally, Barracato and Neale were inducted into the Softball Hall of Fame together in 1988. They were seen enjoying a beer together that night.

* * *

Langdon reminisced about his life in softball while sitting in the Slow Pitch Hall of Fame and Museum in Euclid, surrounded by his cherished treasures from the game's history. He was 75 years old and had spent more than half a century in the game. His career was almost equally divided between the drinking years and the non-drinking years. Like most people who quit drinking, Buddy needed a hobby so he started the Hall of Fame in 1985. With the help of his wife, Marge, and his children and some friends, he built fascinating displays on the second floor of Euclid's old city hall building. The Polka Hall of Fame is on the first floor. Buddy became softball's official historian. He spends several hours a week there waiting for visitors, but much of the time is spent alone.

Langdon actually was born to play baseball. The St. Louis Cardinals signed him to a contract when he was only 17 years old. He was already on the train to spring training in St. Petersburg, Florida, when baseball adopted a rule that outlawed signing players under the age of 18. Buddy was taken off the train and sent back home to Euclid. It had to be a crushing disappointment, but in all these years I never heard him complain.

"He had an arm," said the old sportswriter Chuck Webster. "He had the best arm I ever saw in softball. The first time I saw him play he made a catch against the left-field fence and he made a throw to the plate on the fly. It was on a line six feet off the ground all the way."

Langdon now engages in deep philosophical commentary. For example, he discussed the quirky difference between East Siders and West Siders.

"West Side guys bet on baseball. East Side guys never bet on baseball," he says.

"East Side guys go to bars and only talk about sports. West Side guys go to bars and talk about politics, girls, everything.

"East Side guys have one bar. When you're looking for a guy, you know he'll eventually show up. West Side guys have many bars."

Langdon was an East Sider and his watering hole was Lach's Bar on Superior Ave. and E. 79th St.

"I loved the guys at Lach's Bar. I played for Lach's Bar for only four years but I stayed for 30," he said.

Chuck Webster:
At the Beginning

The media didn't turn slow pitch softball into a monster all by ourselves, but we did our part. We're entitled to take a bow.

Slow pitch softball was the most popular recreation sport in Greater Cleveland in the 1960s and into the '70s. It was more popular than golf, tennis and bowling. For several years the number of softball players in uniform exceeded the Indians' nightly home attendance. Let's look at the early 1970s. From 1971 to '73, the Indians' home attendance averaged 7,500 per game. In 1972 the number of elite softball teams entered in the city-wide tournament numbered 290. In addition, there were hundreds of other teams in company leagues, church leagues, suburban rec leagues, Sunday morning leagues, co-ed leagues and women's leagues. *The Plain Dealer* even had a team in a media league. I played on the WHK radio team, which featured Gib Shanley at shortstop and Michael Stanley in left-center field. Channel 8 had a team featuring Dick Goddard, Big Chuck and Little John that barnstormed all over the viewing area. Everybody seemed to be on a softball team. Players, managers and coaches numbered about 20 per team. Conservatively, there must have been 10,000 people playing in organized softball leagues. Double that when you add wives, husbands, children, friends and actual spectators. The Indians couldn't compete with the energy of the softball craze.

Chuck Webster remembers the moment that triggered the explosion.

"Lou Mio and I were sitting around the News-Herald in 1963 and Gene Lapierre came in. He said we ought to have a softball tournament. The paper should sponsor it. Lou said, 'That's for

old guys.' Gene said, 'Oh, no. You should get in on it.' Gene said
if we got behind the tournament and promoted it, he could get
Sheffield Bronze to come in. I don't know if we really believed
he could get Sheffield Bronze, but we said, 'OK, we'll do it.' We
thought we might get eight teams. Within a couple of days we
had 64 teams, including Sheffield Bronze," said Webster.

Let me identify the key people in this historic scenario. Lou
Mio and Chuck Webster were sports writers at the *Willoughby
News-Herald*, the daily newspaper known today as the *Lake
County News-Herald*. Gene Lapierre was the commissioner of the
Freeway League in Lake County. Sheffield Bronze was the most
famous softball team in Ohio. Sanford Gross, otherwise known
as "Mr. Softball," owned the Sheffield Bronze paint company and
managed the softball team, which was the perennial Cleveland
city champion.

"The tournament lasted two weeks," said Webster. "We scrambled to find fields. That was a problem. Daniels Field in Willoughby was our main field, but we needed more, many more. A
lot of people helped. The City of Wickliffe called. They offered us
a field. It turned out to be a baseball field with a pitcher's mound.
For softball there was a hill between the pitcher's rubber and second base. We lived with it. It rained. We were up all night re-
scheduling games. The tournament was a huge success. We drew
big crowds. Sheffield Bronze won it, as they should have. People
came out and saw how good these guys were."

Riding the crest of a spectacular triumph, the *News-Herald*
sports department sizzled with enthusiasm. They began covering games. The Freeway League was the premier league in Lake
County. They wrote feature stories about the teams and players.
They picked all-star teams. Their readers ate it up. Their coverage
helped sell newspapers, which was, to use the cliché, the name of
the game. The coverage also promoted the game.

Mio and Webster moved on and spread the gospel. Webster
went to work covering sports for *The Plain Dealer*. Mio hired on
with the Associated Press and later he also settled into a desk in

The Plain Dealer city room. Tom Bruening, a teletype operator for the AP who also happened to be one of the best softball players in town, eventually became a copy editor in *The Plain Dealer* sports department. They were like missionaries. They spread the message.

On the last Thursday of summer in 1964, *The Plain Dealer* joined the game. I used an entire wide-open page to feature our softball teams that were headed for world tournaments out of town over Labor Day weekend. Within two years the sandlot page was a weekly feature every Thursday, covering premier adult softball and top-level sandlot baseball. We began writing about softball sluggers the way baseball scribes had written about Roger Maris only a few years earlier. We carried stats on a dozen leagues. We picked all-star teams. We ran ratings, just like high school football teams. Softball was a second chance at youth.

"It was baseball played in less than two hours," said Webster. "That was part of its appeal."

The rest of the allure was the long ball.

After Maris hit 61 home runs in 1961, the rest of the '60s became baseball's most boring decade. Pitchers dominated ruthlessly. By 1968 the sacrifice bunt was baseball's big weapon. Bob Gibson led the National League with an earned run average of 1.12 and Luis Tiant of the Indians led the American League with 1.60. The American League's earned run average was 2.98 and the National League's was 2.99. The San Francisco Giants pitching staff had 77 complete games; Juan Marichal had 30 of them. Dennis McLain won 31 games and completed 28 for Detroit.

In 1968 the softball sluggers were launching rocket shots over 270-foot fences at a record clip. By August 1, Steve Loya had hit 19 home runs in 70 at bats. A typical score in the *PD*-Major softball league at Morgana Park was 12-10. Four years later Non-Ferrous Metal averaged 20 runs a game and sometimes scored more than 30.

Webster and I loved covering softball games. For one thing, we could phone in a few highlights and then go drinking with the players. In a brilliant stroke of urban planning, the back door of an American Legion hall was located about 20 paces from the main gate of Morgana Park on Cleveland's southeast side at Broadway Ave. and East 65th Street. You didn't even have to cross a main thoroughfare. You crossed an alley.

"The American Legion paid no attention to any liquor laws," Webster observed.

Webster had a particular affinity for the Pyramid Cafe team and traveled with it to several out of town tournaments. Webster took his entire family to the 1974 national tournament in York, Pennsylvania, over the Labor Day Weekend.

"It was a wonderful time. Helen really enjoyed it," Webster said, somewhat exaggerating his wife's appreciation for the holiday getaway. He could have said, "She was a good sport," and left it at that.

"Guess whose autograph my daughter got," Webster said.

"Jim Galloway!" I said.

"Joe Yocabet," said Webster

Galloway was all-world from Long Island County Sports. Yocabet was all-Lakewood.

Webster was in the press box waiting for the first game to start and he was puzzled. Nobody was there. The stands were empty.

"I stepped outside the press box and looked down the street and there was a huge line of people. It must have been a quarter mile long. They were lined up at the ticket window but nothing was happening. They didn't seem to be buying tickets," said Webster.

He walked down to investigate.

Bobby Schmuck, a long-time player and coach from Eastlake, Ohio, was the first person in line to buy his ticket. As always, he was clutching his beer cooler.

"What do you have in the cooler?" the ticket taker asked him.

"Beer," said Schmuck.

"You can't bring that in. There's no beer allowed in the park," the man said. "We don't sell it and you can't bring it."

"Then I'm not going in," said Schmuck. He set down his cooler and sat on it. Everyone knew that Schmuck was a man of high principles.

The word was passed down the line and everybody refused to enter the park. They were outraged. The line did not move. Most people had beer coolers. A softball tournament with no beer was like a church with no preaching.

York mayor John D. Krout turned out to be one pragmatic politician. Several members of city council were inside the park involved in many volunteer jobs so mayor Krout called an emergency council meeting. He said they had a quorum, although no one recalls anyone counting heads. Mayor Krout called for a vote on beer. The result was unanimous. Prohibition inside the York Recreation Complex was repealed. Bobby Schmuck led the charge through the gate.

Schmuck died in May 2011, and I wasn't surprised that his children placed his cooler on the floor next to his casket at the funeral home in Willoughby. He never left home without it.

"Schmuck was very patriotic," Webster pointed out. "Sometimes we would stop at a Chinese restaurant on Superior Ave. late at night after games. Schmuck never liked going there. The only reason he did was that it was open until four o'clock in the morning. We were usually full of beer. Bobby would stand up on a table and hold up an egg roll like the Statue of Liberty holding the torch and he would sing, 'God Bless America.' He would get everybody in the restaurant singing. He could sing pretty good, too. The Chinese guy who ran the place never complained."

* * *

Several national championships were held at State Road Park in Parma in the 1960s and '70s and officials always claimed the total attendance for the five-day tournament was 50,000. In a sense, that's true, although the same people were counted about 10 times each because they had to buy another ticket every four hours. There were separate admissions for morning, afternoon and evening sessions. Nevertheless, we gleefully trumpeted the attendance figures because they reinforced our evangelism. Because of rain and extra-inning games, tournaments always fell behind schedule and games were played through the night. We had helped create this monster and always remained on duty until the bitter end.

During the 1967 national tournament in Parma, I was supposed to meet a girl for a beer after the last game on Saturday night. It ended at 1:30 in the morning.

"I don't think this is going to work out," she said.

How right she was. She disappeared into the night and missed out on a late-night snack at a Chinese restaurant on Superior Ave.

In 1977, Jay Friedman took softball to the next level. He turned pro. Friedman entered his team, the Jaybirds, in a pro league. He held tryouts and signed the best players. The first player to sign was Steve Loya, the greatest slugger of that generation. Ted Stepien took over the team in 1980. The players couldn't live on their softball salaries. They played on the weekends and worked real jobs during the week. Actually, it wasn't far removed from life in the *PD*-Major or any of the other top amateur leagues. Stepien's Competitors played their home games at Daniels Field in Willoughby, where the Freeway Major played during the week.

"He fixed it up real nice," said Jim Bizzell, a catcher and outfielder. "He put up new fences and moved them back to 330 feet. He put up new lights. Mudcat Grant and Gus Johnson broadcast our games on the radio. With Ted Stepien everything was first class. When we played in New Jersey he chartered a plane from Wright Airlines. For short trips he chartered a bus."

The Jaybirds and Competitors never captured the hearts of the fans and the pro league slowly faded away. There was not much difference between the pro game and the amateur game they had been watching, except the pros charged for tickets and the amateur game was free. Everybody became bored with piano movers who hit the ball 300 feet. Eventually rules were adopted that penalized teams that hit too many home runs. There's now a limit. After you reach your limit, any home run is an out. It

Andy Loya shows that the piano movers were complete athletes. *(Greater Cleveland Softball Hall of Fame)*

sounds incongruous and it is. There are no dominant teams and
no star players.

"The long ball ruined the game," said Chuck Webster.

Bernie Yun, the sporting goods dealer, once made a lot of
money selling softball uniforms.

"Every suburb had an adult men's softball league they all wore
complete uniforms," Yun recalled. "Now there are fewer leagues
and they wear tee shirts and caps. I bet we sell more uniforms for
senior baseball teams than for softball teams."

The game suffered in other ways. Webster became a lawyer
and quit drinking. I got married, had a bunch of kids, and didn't
have time for softball. The heroes we wrote about 40 years ago
got old. We get together every October at the Greater Cleveland
Slow Pitch Hall of Fame dinner in Euclid and each year there's
one or two fewer. Slow pitch softball had its day and we covered
the hell out of it.

The only thing that survived is the Chinese restaurant. We
shouldn't be surprised.

Looking back, I can say that softball was as addictive as cocaine. Softball got in the way of jobs and people were fired. The

game broke up marriages. In 1975 the wife of Bob Reid, the all-world softball star from Pyramid Cafe, hired a hit man to kill him. The hit man broke the assassin's cardinal rule, however. He left a witness. He only wounded Reid, who recovered to testify against both his wife and the hit man. Many old softball players spent their final years broke and alone. In my files I came across a piece I wrote about Ron Fleger that appeared in *The Plain Dealer* on January 16, 1973.

I hadn't seen Ron Fleger for several months when I encountered him last week. Because of his immense girth and sagging jowls, he's unmistakable even from a great distance, but this time he appeared different.

"I am different," he announced. "I'm finished. I'm through. I'll never have anything to do with another softball team."

Most people viewed the fat man merely as the sidekick of Gene Poldruhi, the manager of softball teams in Parma. Fleger was his coach. Actually, he was considerably more than that. Fleger was a softball addict. He never was a great player, although he says, "I had my moments." But he recognized talent. He was a recruiter of rare perception. He scouted players in various leagues around the city, often uncovering the proverbial diamonds in the rough. He helped bring many players under one roof to form the Parma Major team headed by Steve and Andy Loya and managed by Poldruhi. For several years it was one of the best teams in the city—and the world, as well.

Fleger went through life with dust on his shoes, dirt under his fingernails and suds in his stomach. He devoted his life to softball and his only reward was a uniform that he wore proudly on the sidelines. In fact, there were periods when he didn't remove his uniform for days. He became a softball bum and he's the first to admit it. After Tuesday night's games he could be found in taverns where softball is spoken and he'd be there until time to report for Thursday night's game.

He never married because he couldn't hold a job. He's 43 now and he lives with his mother, who has virtually supported him for years. Something always interfered with work, things like softball games, softball tournaments, softball meetings and a multitude of nefarious matters attendant to the monkey on his back. He'd taxi players to games. He'd taxi them home. When his car broke down, he'd borrow money to have it fixed. Somehow, he made softball a 12-month costly profession.

"I've been a fool," he said. "I'm in debt. I've lost my team. There are no thanks in this game. How many jobs did I lose because of softball? I'd write them down but you don't have enough paper. I can't remember them, anyway. For what?"

Fleger is still bitter because of the incident last summer when their players on the Gene's-Angelo's team in Parma abruptly voted him and Poldruhi out as coach and manager.

Ever optimistic, Poldruhi is assembling a new team and he harbors high hopes. It's easy to understand why he and Fleger are kindred spirits. Poldruhi once owned a huge service station and truck stop on Brookpark Road. The cost of supporting a high-level softball team brought it down, however, and Poldruhi now works for somebody else.

The scars on the sidekick haven't healed, however.

"I'm putting my life back together," Fleger said.

His life is no longer a one-way boulevard of softball dreams. He says he has a job as a manufacturer's rep. He's acquiring some lines. When I saw him, he was nattily dressed in a suit and tie. His gray hair was neatly combed. I told him I'd like to tell his story.

"Sure," he said. "It's about time I got some ink."

Ron had just turned 70 when he died a few years ago. When I stopped in Chambers Funeral Home to pay my respects at his wake, there were half a dozen people milling around. His only family was softball and there was hardly anybody there. There weren't enough mourners to form a softball team. He was buried at the Western Reserve National Cemetery for military veterans in Rittman.

Sluggers:
They Ruined the Game

They were the biggest heroes in softball. The sluggers. These physical giants with wooden cudgels changed the game in the 1960s. This was sandlot softball played in neighborhood parks, but their names were in the papers regularly in those summers and almost everybody who followed sports knew their names. Here are some of their stories.

Preston Powell was a rookie running back from Grambling who was drafted in the seventh round by the Browns in 1961 and it didn't take him long to catch everybody's attention. At six feet, two inches tall and 225 sinewy pounds, he backed down from nobody, not even the great Jim Brown.

It was an ordinary practice in summer training camp and Preston was in the huddle. It was his turn to carry the ball as the feature running back, which was Jim Brown's role. Nobody was going to take Brown's job. Everybody knew that, including Powell. Preston's job was to make the team. Oddly, for no apparent reason, Brown came up from behind and pushed him. It was needless bullyism by the great running back, who had led the league in rushing for four straight seasons, but in this case he picked on the wrong rookie. Brown was the only person I ever knew who provoked Preston Powell, the mild-mannered gentleman from Winnifield, Louisiana.

"I pushed back," said Powell. "I wasn't afraid of him."

The incident simmered for the rest of the afternoon. After practice as they were walking off the field, one word led to another and suddenly they squared off. This was a championship fight, a prelude to Ali-Frazier, which was 10 years away.

"I landed a couple on him. He landed a couple on me. Our teammates broke it up," said Preston.

Years later Brown admitted to Powell, "Of all the players who came here to take my spot, you were the one I was afraid of."

There never was a rematch. Powell made the team but he incurred two knee injuries during the course of the season and his pro football career was over after one season. He played in all 12 games, but he carried the ball only once for a five-yard gain and he returned 16 kickoffs. After that season the Browns traded him to the Dallas Cowboys, who traded him the following year to the Chicago Bears, but he never played in an official NFL game again. For his last two seasons he usually rode the bench, the injured list or the cab squad.

Preston actually was recruited to play basketball by Grambling coach Fred Hobdy, which triggered a tug of war among Hobdy, football coach Eddie Robinson and baseball coach Ralph Waldo Emerson Jones, who also was president of the college. With a name like that, he was born to be a college president. Robinson and Jones won. Powell never played college basketball. College rules at the time limited athletes to two sports. Preston played football and baseball. He was a two-time all-American in football, but he might have been a better baseball player.

"I could hit the ball. I hit line drives," he said. "I played center-field and second base. Could I have played in the major leagues? I'm not saying yes and I'm not saying no."

We'll never know because the baseball coach gave him bad advice. He changed his stance. Preston knew something was wrong. It didn't feel right. It didn't feel natural. But he couldn't defy the coach who also was the college president. Dr. Jones converted Powell from a line drive hitter to an upper cut long ball hitter, which was fine for slow pitch softball but it was deadly for baseball. The well-intentioned president ruined Preston's baseball career.

Look at Preston's football coaches—Eddie Robinson, Paul Brown, Tom Landry and George Halas. It is possible that in the history of the game no single player ever was coached by such a collection of gridiron legends.

But a man named Joe Nato changed Preston's life.

"After I was through with football, I walked around looking for something to do," said Powell, who remained in Cleveland after being cut by the Bears. He played some handball. He tried softball in a Sunday morning league at Woodland Hills Park on Cleveland's East Side, where he caught the eye of Otis Chapman, a softball veteran who later was inducted into the Softball Hall of Fame. Chapman tipped off Nato, the sponsor and manager of the Star Motel team in the *PD*-Major slow pitch league. Nato came out one Sunday morning to see for himself and what he saw was potential greatness. He had never witnessed such pure, raw talent. He thrust a contract in Powell's face and Preston signed it. Just like that, Preston had something to do and Nato had his first superstar.

However, as all former baseball players discovered, hitting the blooper ball tossed underhand is not as easy as it looks. All his life Preston had perfected the art of attacking 90-mile-an hour fastballs thrown overhand. In all of sports, there is no more difficult task. Hitting a ball tossed underhand is one of the easiest. Preston, however, had to start at the beginning. He and Nato spent hours together on empty diamonds.

"He would pitch to me," Preston said. "We had one outfielder— his wife. She would return the balls—with a smile on her face! She never complained. He told me, wait on the ball. Keep your hands back. Be patient. Don't give up. Shelly Hoffman started coming around. He would also pitch to me. Joe Nato would call and wake me up in the middle of the night. It was crazy. 'I'm in bed,' I would say. 'Get out of bed. Meet me at the Chinese restaurant at East 40th and Superior. There's something I've got to tell you.' Joe Nato helped develop me into somebody."

What Nato developed was one of the greatest home run hitters in the history of the game and, without a doubt, the greatest player Nato ever managed. The 270-foot fences at Morgana Park could not contain him.

In those days both Cleveland newspapers picked all-city all-star teams and Preston made all-city 10 straight years. Because of his football knee injuries, Preston could barely run, but he didn't have to. He once hit seven straight home runs in the city-wide tournament and, after making an out, hit three more in a row. Preston was a catcher, squatting behind the plate. His knees ached but he ignored the pain. At the age of 60, he had plastic knees installed. He truly played for the love of the game.

Preston spent a couple of years with Star Motel. Nobody stayed very long with Nato, who was volatile and quirky. Furthermore, Nato didn't pay his players. Many of the top stars were paid cash under the table. Preston moved on to Erie Sheet Steel, Non-Ferrous Metal and Ohio Sealants, all famous softball teams in the 1960s and '70s. He insists he never was paid except for gas money and other travel expenses.

"They didn't have to pay me. I wasn't looking for money," Powell said.

His favorite backer was George Opalich, owner of Non-Ferrous Metal.

"He picked up all the tabs. He never let you pay for anything," Powell said.

Preston played in 10 world tournaments. His teams won one world championship. Others finished third and fourth.

And he did all that while working two jobs. He always worked two jobs. For many years he was a Cuyahoga County deputy sheriff and at the same time he worked security at the Cleveland Clinic. Eighty hours a week on the clock was routine. For 10 years he owned an Open Pantry Food Market at E. 131st St. and Garfield Blvd. For the last 28 years he and his wife, Blanche, have worked security at Thistledown Racetrack. It is a good bet that Thistledown is a very secure place.

* * *

At the same time that Preston Powell was ripping the cover off the ball at Morgana Park on the East Side, the brothers Steve and Andy Loya were knocking down the fences on the West Side at State Road Park in Parma. The Loya boys moved to Cleveland in the late 1950s from the small coal-mining town of Thompson #2, Pennsylvania. The miners were not very creative with their names. It was the name of the mine and the name of the town, about 45 miles south of Pittsburgh. Their father worked in the mines all his life. There were five boys in the Loya family—all born at home; no hospital, no doctors, no nurses—and when they grew up they said defiantly, "We're not going down in the mines." All five boys moved to Cleveland to find work. At the time Cleveland was considered an upgrade from Thompson #2.

Steve was the first to find a job. He became an apprentice tool and die maker. Andy became an apprentice electrician. They made their livings at the plants, but they made their names on the softball diamonds and their fame extended far beyond State Road Park.

"As far as putting softball on the map, my brother and I did our part," Andy said. "We were in Mississippi for a tournament and a guy from Rochester came up to me and said, 'You're one of the Loya brothers.' Those were wonderful times. People were so nice."

"I can never forget those days," said Jan Loya, Steve's widow. "Wherever we went they treated Steve like a star."

Steve never behaved like a star. He was no prima donna. He never took shortcuts. For example, at out of town tournaments when his teams were fighting their way through the losers' brackets and were scheduled for eight o'clock games on Sunday mornings, most players skipped church. Not Steve. He got up early and went to the 6 a.m. Mass.

"He set such a good example for the younger players," said Jan.

Sadly, Steve died of cancer on Sept. 25, 1991. He was only 57 years old. He was in three halls of fame and was the first American softball player to turn pro. Many of them were paid under the table, but not Steve. He was never paid until he signed with Jay Friedman's Cleveland Jaybirds, the first American pro team. The signing ceremony took place in Pat Joyce's Tavern downtown on Feb. 10, 1977. Steve signed a ball for me but like the league itself the ink is almost completely faded. I should have put it in a plastic case.

Andy worked as a Local 1005 electrician at the Chevrolet plant in Parma until he retired in 2008 at the age of 72. Except for a touch of diabetes, he thought he was in good health. He continued to play in senior leagues, over-50, over-60 and over-65. Since retiring, however, he suffered a stroke, underwent a quadruple bypass, lost the sight in his right eye and does not see well out of his left eye and had his left leg amputated below the knee. All this within two years.

"If I had my leg and my eyesight, I'd be playing softball with my boy," said Andy.

The Loya brothers were inseparable. They always batted back-to-back in the order, Steve usually third and Andy usually fourth. Steve was the catcher; Andy played outfield and later moved to first base. They played most of their careers in the Parma Major with teams sponsored and managed by Gene Poldruhi, who owned gas stations in Parma. The teams were known as Gene's Sunoco and then Gene's Sohio and later he merged with Angelo's Pizza and became Gene's-Angelo's.

"One night they were late starting a game because of a dispute with league officials who didn't know if the merger was legal," recalled Chuck Webster, a *Plain Dealer* reporter at the time. "The lead on my story was, 'Ten guys standing around in the outfield proved that pizza and gasoline do mix.' Those days were a lot of fun."

Steve and Andy both batted around .700, but Steve's prodigious home run power set him apart. Back in Pennsylvania they called him Ozark Ike after the comic strip character. Steve and Preston Powell were inducted together into the Greater Cleveland Slow Pitch Hall of Fame in its first class of 1985. Steve also was inducted into the Greater Cleveland Sports Hall of Fame and the National Softball Hall of Fame in Oklahoma City.

"If I could take one player, I'd take my brother," said Andy.

"Me, too," said Jan Loya. "Steve and I met on a softball field.

Andy's wife, Liz, introduced us. Steve said, 'I'm gonna hit a home run for you tonight.' He did. It was magic."

Sometimes reality intruded on the magic. One cold spring night Jan huddled in the car with their three young children who acted the way kids do when they're stuck in a car with nothing to do. They drove their mother crazy. Steve, meanwhile, unaware of the mayhem in the car, was blissfully getting his three hits and four RBI.

The next night Steve poked around the laundry room looking for his uniform.

"Where's my uniform?" he called out to Jan.

"I burned it," Jan shouted.

Actually, she didn't burn it. She hid Steve's uniform in the attic and he played the rest of the season wearing a backup uniform.

"We knew what these guys were like when we married them," said Pat Poldruhi, whose husband, Gene Poldruhi, was Loya's manager and sponsor. "Even when somebody died or somebody had a baby, they never missed their game. I was lucky. At least Gene was there when we had our babies."

Pat Poldruhi recalls that their first daughter, Jill, was born on Wednesday, Aug. 30, 1967. Two days later she was at the National Tournament at State Road Park.

"I asked my doctor if I could go to a softball game on Friday," she said.

"I don't see why not," said the doctor.

She did not mention that the first game started at nine o'clock in the morning and the last game did not end until midnight.

Gene was not there, however, when their children held a surprise party for their 25th wedding anniversary.

"He had a tournament at Rose Field," said Pat Poldruhi. "He said he didn't know about the party because it was a surprise. But I know he did. He knew I would be angry, but he also knew that I'd be OK. Our children were much angrier than I was. 'How many 25th wedding anniversaries are you gonna have?' our son David asked him."

Pat Poldruhi says she is much more concerned about the thousands of dollars her husband spent on softball teams to compete against teams sponsored by business tycoons, bookmakers and other men of means. Poldruhi ran gas stations and worked on cars. Each summer his softball team cost him as much as some people earned in an entire year.

"It was such a passion. I'm glad I don't know how much he spent. I probably would kill him," she said.

Every year the Loya brothers were the most sought after free agents in softball. Andy recalled the night Skip Felice from the Teamsters flashed a wad of bills at them in the parking lot of State Road Park. The Teamsters were a perennial power at Morgana Park but often seemed to be one slugger short.

"He pulled a fistful of twenties, fifties and hundreds out of his pocket. He could barely get his hand around them. He offered us five thousand dollars each. I said, 'Steve, when you're up in a pressure situation and don't get a hit, they're gonna bring that up. They're gonna put the pressure on us.' We didn't take the money and we stayed with Gene's."

Betting on games added to the pressure. Andy said he and Steve were naive about the gambling until they played a weekend tournament in Pittsburgh.

"In the 10th inning I hit a home run with two on over a 280-foot fence. It was still climbing when it cleared the fence. It won the game. Fifteen thousand dollars was bet on that game," recalled Andy.

The next year the Pittsburgh team won back its money.

"I knew we were in trouble," Andy said. "They brought in umpires we never saw before from McKees Rocks. Before the game Art Rooney was sitting on our bench. I sat down next to him. 'How you doing?' I said. All he did was grunt at me. That's the kind of guys they had betting on them."

A doubleheader was arranged between Gene's Sohio and Pyramid Cafe purely for the betting, which was not unusual. Chet Oblock, owner of Pyramid Cafe and manager of his team, was always ready for action. He thrived on it. He drew strength from it. Gambling nourished him. Ron Perrotti, who owned RP's Lounge on Ridge Road, was a kindred spirit. Several of Gene's Sohio play-ers were known to visit Perrotti's bar when they weren't at the Last Stop Inn, so Perrotti, of course, put his money on Gene's. He supported his customers.

Perrotti proposed a parlay. He bet $1,500 on Gene's in the first game and he doubled the bet in the second game. Oblock snatched the bet before Perrotti could change his mind.

"In the first game I went five-for-five and Steve hit a couple of home runs. We won, 20-7," said Andy Loya. "In the second game I hit two home runs and we won, 20-3. I saw Chet Oblock hand over forty-five hundred dollars to Ron Perrotti like it was nothing."

Later, however, Oblock recruited the Loya brothers to his side. Buddy Langdon made the approach and persuaded Steve and Andy to join Pyramid Cafe and play in the *PD*-Major at Morgana Park. Andy insisted no money changed hands but they did get national championship rings.

For 14 straight years Steve and Andy played in national tour-naments over the Labor Day Weekend. If their team didn't qual-ify for the nationals, they were picked up by the team that did. Teams going to national tournaments were allowed to add two or three players from other teams. Steve was always an automatic addition. Andy's company team from the Chevrolet plant often qualified for the National Industrial tournament, as well.

"The kids thought that was our vacation time," Andy said.

Their most memorable vacation, however, was in their own backyard when Pyramid Cafe won the national tournament in 1975, the Loya boys' second year with Pyramid.

The tournament was played in Cleveland at Rose and Elder Fields adjacent to the zoo. Rain played havoc with the schedule. The tournament began on Thursday night of Labor Day weekend and it ended at three o'clock on the following Tuesday morning.

"We were tied, 7-7, in the top of the seventh inning against Poindexter, North Carolina, in the final game," said Andy. "We had the bases loaded. I hit one off the top of the fence. Three runs scored. Later I also scored and we led 11-7.

"In the last of the seventh they had a runner on first with one out. I prayed, don't hit it to Eddie DePompei at second base. Hit it to Bobby Hegedus at shortstop. Eddie is quicker on the pivot. I actually prayed, 'Hail Mary, full of grace, hit the ball to Bobby.' That's exactly how it happened, a one-bouncer to Hegedus. He flipped it to DePompei. Eddie made the pivot and threw it to me, knee high, double play. We won. 11-7."

The victors celebrated much of the day at the Pyramid Cafe, where local liquor laws were temporarily suspended. Even the police cruising the Second District stopped in to raise a glass.

* * *

Mike Macenko was a 16-year-old student at Midpark High School when Tom Coyne, the future mayor of Brook Park, Ohio, discovered him in 1973. The Brook Park Merchants were short a player and they asked Macenko if he wanted to play that night in the Brook Park Men's League. He was unskilled but he was a big kid, six-foot-three-inches tall and weighing 285 pounds. He batted four times that night and he hit four home runs.

"When I came around third base, Tom Coyne, who was coaching at third, said, 'You've got to sign this.' It was a contract," said Macenko.

Coyne could recognize talent. Macenko went on to lead the Brook Park Men's League with 16 home runs, playing only half the season.

The next year, at the age of 17, he won a home run derby in Lakewood sponsored by Hoty's Sporting Goods. In the final round he slammed nine home runs in 15 swings—using a borrowed bat. People were talking about him and the buzz reached the ears of Dave Neale, whose Hillcrest Tavern team was among a handful of elite teams in the Cleveland area. Neale told his son, John, to contact Macenko, which he did. John Neale asked Mike to travel with them to a weekend tournament in Pittsburgh.

"I've got to ask my mother," said Mike.

Mike had a good tournament and Dave Neale offered him a full time spot on the roster. But Mike was still under contract to Tom Coyne, his first softball mentor. Coyne knew he could never hold him back and willingly gave Mike his release. They remained life long friends. When Mike was inducted into the Greater Cleveland Sports Hall of Fame at a huge banquet at Landerhaven in 2010, Tom Coyne was there to lead the applause.

Mike also developed a life long friendship with Dave Neale. Mike played for Neale for most of the next quarter century. He quit high school. He had no driver's license. He wasn't old enough to vote. And he was playing with and against the best softball players in the world. Playing with Neale's Hillcrest Tavern team in the *PD*-Major, Mike was the league MVP four straight years. At the time he worked as a Local 310 construction laborer. One summer he poured 275 yards of concrete per day. That's a lot of concrete. It's ten truckloads per day. By the 1980s his concrete days were history. He was barnstorming coast-to-coast with Steele's Sports, another of Neale's teams, to promote the Steele sporting goods products, especially its aluminum bats. Their travel budget was $500,000 a year. They would start in February in California and work their way east, playing small town teams for $3,000 a night. In 1986 *Sports Illustrated* magazine ran a lengthy feature on the team that was headlined, "Men of Steel." Ron Fimritre, one of the magazine's stars, wrote it. Mike played for Steele Sports for 14 years.

When his competitive playing career ended in 1999, a statistician added up his home runs and they totaled more than 7,000. The only other slugger with more than 6,000 was Don Arndt who spent 26 seasons with Howard's Furniture of Denver, North Carolina. In 1987, Mike hit 844 home runs and the next year he hit 830. He was the greatest home run hitter in the history of the planet. He hit them in every state in the Union except Alaska, although it is said that some home runs he hit on the mainland came down in Alaska. Mike was named to 34 different all-world teams. He was national tournament MVP five times. He is a member of five halls of fame.

At the peak of his prowess, he was booked into baseball stadiums for home run exhibitions. He hit them out of Tiger Stadium in Detroit, the Seattle Kingdome, Mile High Stadium in Denver, the Oakland Coliseum and the old Cleveland Stadium. He was more than a big name. He had grown to well over 300 pounds.

There were consequences to Macenko's greatness. The game never recovered. It is said that Babe Ruth's popularity saved baseball in the wake of the Chicago Black Sox scandal in 1919. Macenko had just the opposite effect. Fans became bored with the long ball. Nobody hit home runs like Macenko, but aluminum bats and balls with poly core centers made everyone a slugger. Steele Sports was located in Grafton, Ohio, in Lorain County, but the "Men of Steele" were forced

Mike Macenko was the greatest slugger of all time. *(Greater Cleveland Softball Hall of Fame)*

to play a national schedule because they were too good for local leagues. In 1988, for instance, they piled up a record of 365 wins and only 19 losses. The mystique of the *PD*-Major and Parma Major belonged to antiquity. Macenko had set the bar too high. Steele's beat a team in El Paso, Texas, 109-7. They crushed another team, 89-22. They would unzip their bat bag and balls started flying over the fences.

One morning at breakfast Macenko asked Neale, "Do you think we created a monster by hitting all those home runs?"

"No," said Neale, who was selling a lot of Steele bats. "Maybe we made a mistake playing with poly core balls."

Steele's perfected the home run formula—aluminum bats and balls with poly core centers, such as the juiced up Dudley, instead of the old reliable Harwood with cork centers.

"We would use both Dudley and Harwood balls," Mike said. "We would usually start a game with two new balls and one used one. If a Harwood got fouled off early in the game, nobody would go after it. We would rather play with a used Dudley."

Macenko and Craig Elliott batted back-to-back in Steele's lineup from 1985 to 1989, possibly the most dangerous one-two punch of that era.

"I saw Craig Elliott hit nine screaming line drives in a row, all for base hits," Macenko recalled. "He was nine for nine and was really upset. He said, 'Hell, if I want to hit singles I should stay home. I came here to hit home runs.' Little did they know that with about 30 years of technology we would be able to produce the perfect softball bat—where everyone can hit home runs. Size doesn't matter like it did in the old days."

The perfect bat was the brainchild of Ray DeMarini of Portland, Oregon. It became known as the DeMarini double wall when it hit the market in 1987 and revolutionized the game. It was a two-piece bat with a composite handle and an aluminum alloy double wall barrel—one inside the other. Its "sweet" spot was much larger than that of more primitive aluminum bats. The key words in its official description were "indestructible, reflexes upon impact, recoils with a burst of ball-launching energy." It sounds like something that would interest the Pentagon. There was a time when softball sluggers were built like piano movers. DeMarini made sluggers out of piano teachers. DeMarini died of cancer in 2001. He was only 55. They named a softball field after him in Portland.

Since Macenko took off his uniform for the last time in 1999, he has worked full time as a sporting goods salesman. Besides all those years with Steele's, Mike represented Louisville Slugger, Worth, Anderson bats, Nike, Bombat, Combat and currently Anaconda Sports.

For almost 40 years his life has revolved around softball. He met his wife, Antoinette, at a softball diamond. Their daughter, Amanda, set all the major softball pitching records at Cleveland State University and Brunswick High School. Look at what Tom Coyne started.

Sunday Slow Pitch:
A Bad Team

In the summer of 1956, Jim Carey threw two fastballs past me and I almost screwed myself into the ground flailing at them. Carey was good. He went on to pitch at Notre Dame and later signed with Boston. He was smart. He was too smart. He figured I would be looking for another fastball so he tried to fool me with a changeup. When he laid that changeup across the plate my eyes got bigger than the hubcaps on a Buick. I lined it to left for a single. Throwing a changeup to a lousy hitter is a gift. It was the last hit I ever got in a legitimate league baseball game. The dumb guys just kept throwing fastballs past me and drove me out of the game at the age of 18.

That's why they invented slow pitch softball. In the 1960s and '70s all old athletes played slow pitch softball. It perpetuated a fantasy world in which everybody was equal and everybody could be a hero. Guys who dropped out of baseball because they could not get around on the fastball could smash a blooper pitch tossed underhand. Ordinary guys could compete with super stars and nobody knew the difference.

I liked writing about softball players and I enjoyed drinking with them in the bars after games. I enjoyed them so much that in 1974 I collected some media people and put together my own team in a loosely organized Sunday morning league. We were an exceptional team. By that, I mean we were the exception to the rule. We were not equal. We were not heroes.

My first lineup included Cavs' announcer Joe Tait at first base, *Plain Dealer* reporter George Condon Jr. pitching, *Plain Dealer* reporter Joe Wagner, WERE radio newsman George Yarborough,

David Haas from *Plain Dealer* sports, Carl Giaimo from the *Plain Dealer* city room and me behind the plate.

We won two games all summer, both by forfeit when the other team did not have enough players, but we had some magic moments. There was the time, for instance, when we loaded the bases with nobody out.

Condon, Haas and Yarborough hit consecutive singles. That had never happened before. Stepping to the plate was Joe Tait.

"Maybe you should pinch hit for Joe," said Giaimo.

I was shocked.

"This is Sunday morning softball. It's not the pros," I said. "I'm not telling Joe to sit down."

"Joe won't mind," said Wagner. "He only comes here because you asked him. He doesn't seem to be having any fun."

"Have you counted heads?" I said. "We only have 10 players. We don't have a pinch hitter."

And so, Joe threw a greedy glare at the pitcher and dug in at the plate. The first pitch floated temptingly through the strike zone and Joe swung mightily. His aluminum bat met the ball with a solid thunk and everybody started running. Chaos reigned. It looked like an FBI raid in a bookie joint on Super Bowl Sunday.

Joe ripped a slow roller down the third-base line. Condon raced home from third, deftly avoiding the rolling ball. The third baseman straddled the bag and waited agonizing seconds for the ball to reach him. He fielded it with his right foot on the bag for the first out and in one continuous motion rifled the ball to the second baseman, who forced out Yarborough. The second baseman pivoted cleanly and drilled a strike to first base, where Joe Tait was out by five steps to complete the triple play, the only triple play in the history of the Charlie Sheets Sunday Morning League at Impett Park in Cleveland.

Chester Meats:
Bull Held Hostage

I butchered my first job on television. I mean that literally. I played a butcher. It was my first big break. Lenny Axelband, a well-known advertising executive with the firm Axelband and Brown, had an epiphany. We were sitting together at an Indians baseball banquet when a lightning bolt came through the ceiling and drilled him right in the skull.

"You look like a butcher," Lenny said.

In baseball parlance, that's not a compliment. But Lenny explained.

"I have an idea for a commercial for one of our clients. You would be a perfect butcher," Lenny said.

The client was Chester Meats. Lenny envisioned a butcher dressed in white apron and white hat, measuring the fat content of Chester Meats' meat. Because I had grown a ridiculous mustache, Lenny saw me as that wacky butcher. They dressed me up in a white smock and white hat. I memorized my lines. The cameras rolled. And in 1972 I hit the air as the Chester Meats butcher. It wasn't my proudest moment, but the money was terrific, especially for a young sportswriter at *The Plain Dealer*. The spot ran for at least two years on late night television.

It all ended, however, one summer night in 1974 when the Chester Meats steer disappeared from the sidewalk in front of the old Cleveland Arena and I innocently became involved in a manhunt that stretched over two counties. The entire Cleveland Police Department and the police from almost every nearby suburb were on the lookout for the steer and for the criminals who stole it.

And me, I was only trying to keep my softball team out of jail.

As usual, I had to personally round up half of my Sunday morning softball team for our early games. Several of my infielders lived together in a big rental house on Lake Avenue at W. 116th Street, just across the border from Lakewood. They never locked their doors.

This was my Sunday morning ritual. My dog, Sandy, and I walked right through the front door and went directly upstairs, going from bedroom to bedroom, waking up the boys who usually were suffering from the effects of Saturday night revelry. My team had no curfew and no training rules. Sandy would leap on their beds, barking and nipping. Sometimes they were not alone. I had no sympathy for the femmes fatale who chose to bunk in with them and woke up face to face with a snarling German shepherd.

On this particular Sunday morning, however, everything was different. Sandy and I walked up the front steps and Sandy began barking because, to my horror, the Chester Meats steer was looking out at us through the big picture window.

I was terrified. My infielders had kidnapped the steer and displayed it like a trophy in their living room. It had been there already for 24 hours. If one lonely cop in a squad car had glanced through the front window, the SWAT team would have been on us like flies on a dung heap and I would have played a doubleheader shorthanded.

Frantically, I closed the drapes and rousted the boys. A few years ago, Mike Miller, one of my infielders, reflected on that weekend. It began, of course, with barley and hops. He and Jerry Grilli had been drinking Friday night on the East Side and on their way home they drove past the old Arena on Euclid Ave. where the crime of opportunity presented itself. It was after midnight, the steer was on the sidewalk unguarded and the boys happened to be driving Grilli's pickup truck.

"Grilli said, 'Let's kidnap the steer,' and that's no bull," Miller told me.

The steer was a majestic, full size fiberglass sculpture, the three-dimensional logo for Chester Meats, a large meat-packing plant on Mayfield Rd. in Chesterland. The steer was on loan to promote the rodeo, which was booked into the Arena at the time. It was the last event at the Arena before it closed.

Radio newscasters whimsically reported on Saturday that the bull had been stolen sometime Friday night. Later that day the story changed.

"I woke up Saturday morning and was still a little fuzzy," said Miller. "I saw that steer in the living room and I thought, 'Where did that come from?' Then it started to come back to me. After I woke up and had a couple of beers, I decided to take it up a notch. I called the Cleveland Police and said I was holding the bull for ransom. I demanded a bunch of food for a homeless shelter. That made it sound official. Then I said, 'And a case of Stroh's beer.' I don't know why I demanded the beer. I sure didn't give them our address."

The story that had been reported with a smile and a wink on the radio was now read with outright laughter when it became "bullnapping." It was the humorous "kicker" on all the TV news shows Saturday night and *The Plain Dealer* ran a light-hearted story in Sunday's paper.

At Chester Meats, however, the laughter was muted. They wanted their bull back. The Cleveland Police were on the hunt and suburban police were asked to join the lookout. Citizens throughout northeast Ohio were asked to report anything suspicious.

So here was my predicament. My softball family had pulled a prank, which they thought was funny, but my Chester Meats family was not smiling.

Being the guy caught in the middle, I hoped to return the steer without anybody getting arrested. Monday morning I called Chester Meats and asked them to cancel the all-points bulletin, which they did. I then called my famous cousin, Tom Coughlin, who owned a classic Lincoln four-door convertible. I don't know what happened to the pickup truck that was used for the original heist. It was no longer in the picture. The steer was too big for an ordinary convertible, but it fit nicely in the four-door Lincoln. We put the front hooves in the front seat and the rear hooves in the back seat. Tom drove and at the same time held onto a front leg. I clung tightly to a hind leg in the back seat.

With the top down, we were quite the spectacle driving out the East Shoreway, south down I-271 to Mayfield Rd. and then out into the country. Other drivers waved and pointed at us. My fear was that a suburban cop who hadn't gotten the word would flag us down and arrest us. But that didn't happen. Things were fine until it started to rain. There was no way to raise the top with that behemoth of a bull towering above us. The rain began as a sprinkle but within minutes it became torrential. Not only were we soaked, but the rain was running down the *inside* of the windshield. It also ran down my cousin's face and into his eyes. He was almost blinded. The water was rising around our feet. And we pushed on.

When we arrived at Chester Meats the rain had abated and two somber employees helped us lift the steer off the car and place it in the middle of the front lawn where it usually resided. I hoped that someone in charge would express gratitude by handing us each a package of steaks. But no one said anything. I never heard from them again. My career as a television pitchman was over. Furthermore, we lost a doubleheader that Sunday, as usual.

Gratitudes

Jane Leitch, for regaling me with stories about life with Harry

Dino Lucarelli, Doug Dieken and Bobby Franklin for insights into the strange world of Gene Hickerson

Mike Cleary for insights into George Steinbrenner

Dino Lucarelli for insights into Mike Cleary

The Plain Dealer for permission to use several columns retrieved from antiquity

Tim Hudak, author of *The Charity Game*

Kimberly Barth from the *Beacon Journal* for the photos

The Canton Repository for the image of Gene Hickerson

Jeff West and Jackie Sas from Great Lakes Brewing for the photo shoot

Robert Jackson for picking up all the tabs

Larry Zelina for keeping a promise

Brian Dowling for the 29-13 lead with a minute left

John Sheridan for Rowdy K

Bob Roberts for the topless beach of La Baule

Al McGuire for marriage counseling

Punxsutawney Phil for six more weeks of winter

Harry Caray for the clock radio

Buddy Langdon for the Softball Hall of Fame

LeBron James, thanks for nothing

Chuck Webster for sharing the stories

Willie Mays and Dusty Rhodes for completely screwing up the '54 Series

My Cousin Tommy Coughlin for showing Notre Dame how to recruit

For promoting and shamelessly hawking my first book:

Thanks to Andy Fishman (Fox 8), Tony Rizzo (WKNR 850), Tim Hyland, John Sheridan, Curt Brugh (Herb's Tavern), Jack Murphy (Tradewinds), Bob O'Connor (Cleats), Press Club president Ed Beyer, Ray Jeske (WTIG), Joe Smith, Mike Duda, Pro Football Hall of Fame Luncheon Club, Shelly Hoffman, Michael Heaton, Carmen Loparo, Maggie Murphy, Sharon the Younger, Patti Donnelly, East Side Irish American Club, West Side Irish American Club, Sheila Basch, Cathy Breninghouse, Larry Sheehe, Scott Dantio, Paul Tepley and the entire radio, television and print media of northeastern Ohio for unprecedented support for this humble neighborhood author.

Ah yes, Jane Lassar. It's up to Jane to promote this book. Every author I know who has worked with Jane says, "She's the best."

"Those New York publishing houses assign some marketing intern fresh out of college to work with an author and all they do is send out some press releases with misspelled words and they call that a promotional campaign," says Terry Pluto, one of her authors. "Jane treats you like a star."

"She makes you feel like Hemingway," said another.

She makes me feel like I'm her only client. She's my publicist. If I ever die, it won't be official until my she confirms it.

About the Author

Dan Coughlin has covered the Cleveland sports scene for 45 years as a newspaperman, magazine writer, television broadcaster and radio commentator. He was twice named Ohio sportswriter of the year and was honored with a television Emmy. He traveled with both the Cleveland Browns and Indians. He covered some of the biggest college football games of the 20th century, including five major bowl games. As a boxing writer he was at ringside for several world championship fights as well as the Muhammad Ali and Joe Frazier series. He covered 17 Indianapolis 500s and several auto races in Europe. While in college he broadcast Notre Dame basketball and baseball games on the student radio station.

Dan served his alma mater, St. Edward High School, as a member of its board of trustees for 20 years. Because of his generosity, several bartenders were able to send their sons to St. Edward. He is a member of the Greater Cleveland Softball Hall of Fame and the Press Club of Cleveland Hall of Fame, and he is a past president of the Press Club. He now lives in Rocky River, Ohio, with his wife, Maddy.

If you enjoyed **PASS THE NUTS** . . .
you'll love Dan Coughlin's first book:
CRAZY, WITH THE PAPERS TO PROVE IT

"I never met a wacko I didn't like," says Dan Cough-lin. Not only did he write about them, they became his best friends, including a degenerate gambler . . . a sportswriter who ripped open beer cans with his teeth . . . an Olympic champion who turned out to be a hermaphrodite . . . a football player who was a compulsive practical joker . . . and dozens of others.

**Available in Bookstores
and online from Amazon.com**

Read a sample at: www.grayco.com